DARK RAIN A New Orleans Story

MAT JOHNSON – Writer   SIMON GANE – Artist

LEE LOUGHRIDGE – Gray Tones & Color   PAT BROSSEAU – Letterer

Mat Johnson

For New Orleans, Home of the American soul.

Simon Gane

Simon wishes to thank the people he met in New Orleans for their help and generosity.

Karen Berger SVP Executive Editor Jonathan Vankin Editor Sarah Litt Asst. Editor
Robbin Brosterman Design Director, Books Louis Prandi Art Director

DC COMICS
Diane Nelson President Dan DiDio and Jim Lee Co-Publishers
Geoff Johns Chief Creative Officer John Rood Executive Vice President, Sales, Marketing and Business Development
Patrick Caldon Executive Vice President, Finance and Administration Amy Genkins Senior VP, Business and Legal Affairs
Steve Rotterdam Senior VP, Sales and Marketing John Cunningham VP, Marketing
Terri Cunningham VP, Managing Editor Alison Gill VP, Manufacturing David Hyde VP, Publicity
Sue Pohja VP-Book Trade Sales Alysse Soll VP-Advertising and Custom Publishing
Bob Wayne VP, Sales Mark Chiarello Art Director

Cover Design by Nessim Higson
Cover Photography by Daymon Gardner

DARK RAIN: A NEW ORLEANS STORY Published by DC Comics, 1700 Broadway, New York, NY 10019. Printed in the USA. First Printing. DC Comics, a Warner Bros. Entertainment Company. HC ISBN: 978-1-4012-2160-7 SC ISBN: 978-1-4012-2161-4

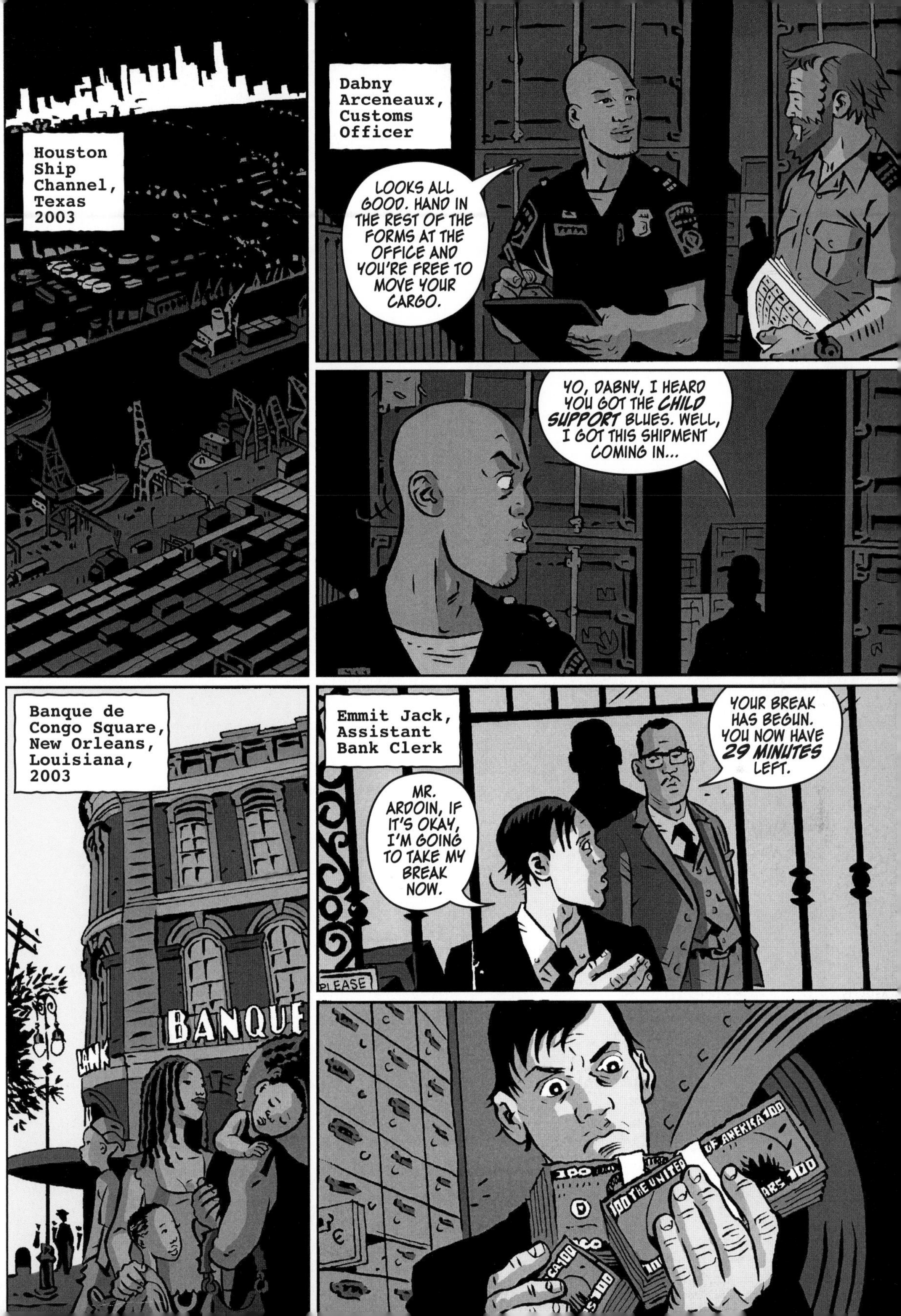
Houston Ship Channel, Texas 2003
Dabny Arceneaux, Customs Officer
LOOKS ALL GOOD. HAND IN THE REST OF THE FORMS AT THE OFFICE AND YOU'RE FREE TO MOVE YOUR CARGO.
YO, DABNY, I HEARD YOU GOT THE CHILD SUPPORT BLUES. WELL, I GOT THIS SHIPMENT COMING IN...
Banque de Congo Square, New Orleans, Louisiana, 2003
BANQUE
Emmit Jack, Assistant Bank Clerk
MR. ARDOIN, IF IT'S OKAY, I'M GOING TO TAKE MY BREAK NOW.
YOUR BREAK HAS BEGUN. YOU NOW HAVE 29 MINUTES LEFT.
PLEASE

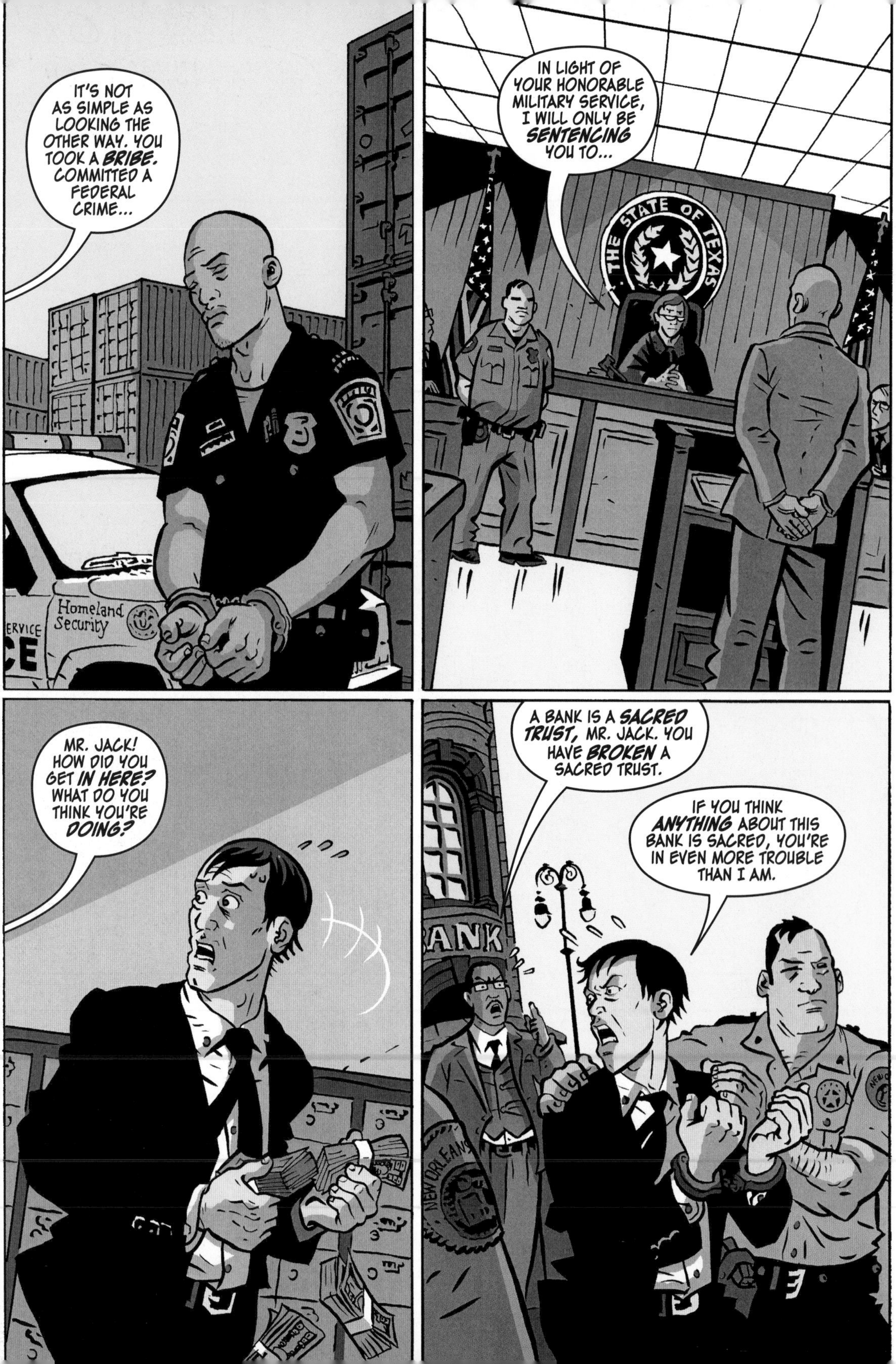
IT'S NOT AS SIMPLE AS LOOKING THE OTHER WAY. YOU TOOK A BRIBE. COMMITTED A FEDERAL CRIME...
Homeland Security
ERVICE
CE
IN LIGHT OF YOUR HONORABLE MILITARY SERVICE, I WILL ONLY BE SENTENCING YOU TO...
THE STATE OF TEXAS
MR. JACK! HOW DID YOU GET IN HERE? WHAT DO YOU THINK YOU'RE DOING?
A BANK IS A SACRED TRUST, MR. JACK. YOU HAVE BROKEN A SACRED TRUST.
IF YOU THINK ANYTHING ABOUT THIS BANK IS SACRED, YOU'RE IN EVEN MORE TROUBLE THAN I AM.
BANK
NEW ORLEANS

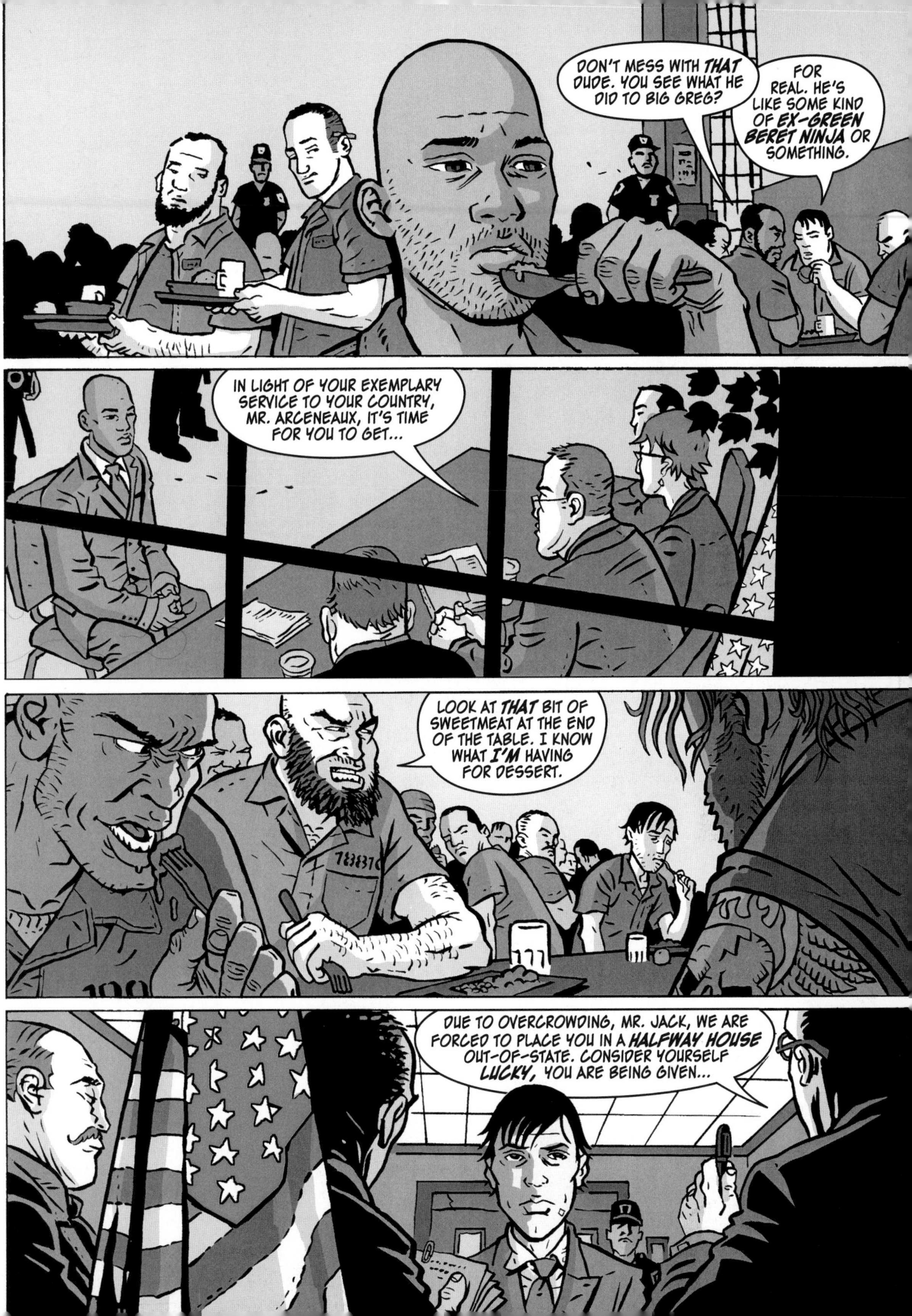
DON'T MESS WITH THAT DUDE. YOU SEE WHAT HE DID TO BIG GREG?
FOR REAL. HE'S LIKE SOME KIND OF EX-GREEN BERET NINJA OR SOMETHING.
IN LIGHT OF YOUR EXEMPLARY SERVICE TO YOUR COUNTRY, MR. ARCENEAUX, IT'S TIME FOR YOU TO GET...
LOOK AT THAT BIT OF SWEETMEAT AT THE END OF THE TABLE. I KNOW WHAT I'M HAVING FOR DESSERT.
DUE TO OVERCROWDING, MR. JACK, WE ARE FORCED TO PLACE YOU IN A HALFWAY HOUSE OUT-OF-STATE. CONSIDER YOURSELF LUCKY, YOU ARE BEING GIVEN...

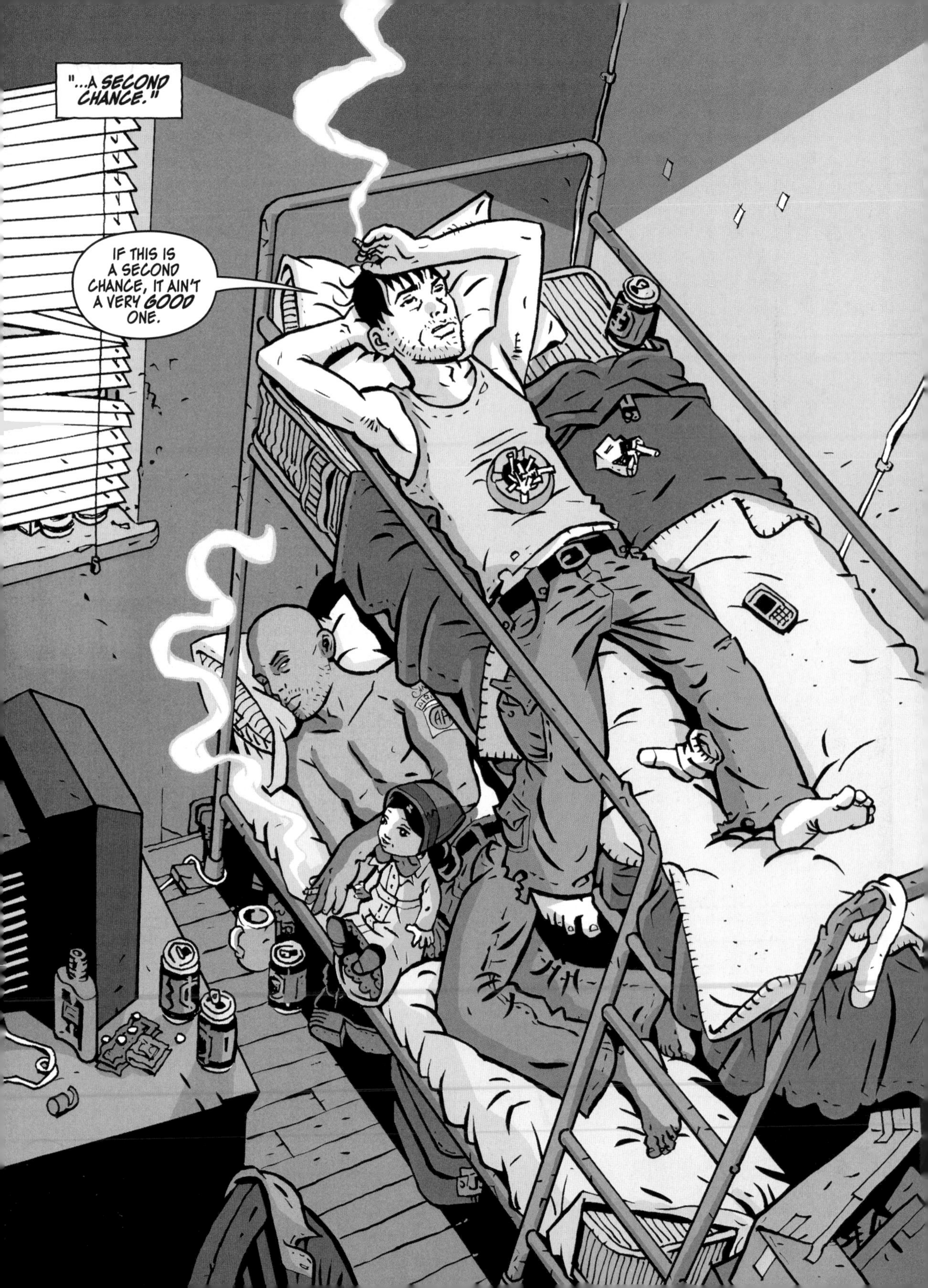

"...A SECOND CHANCE."
IF THIS IS A SECOND CHANCE, IT AIN'T A VERY GOOD ONE.

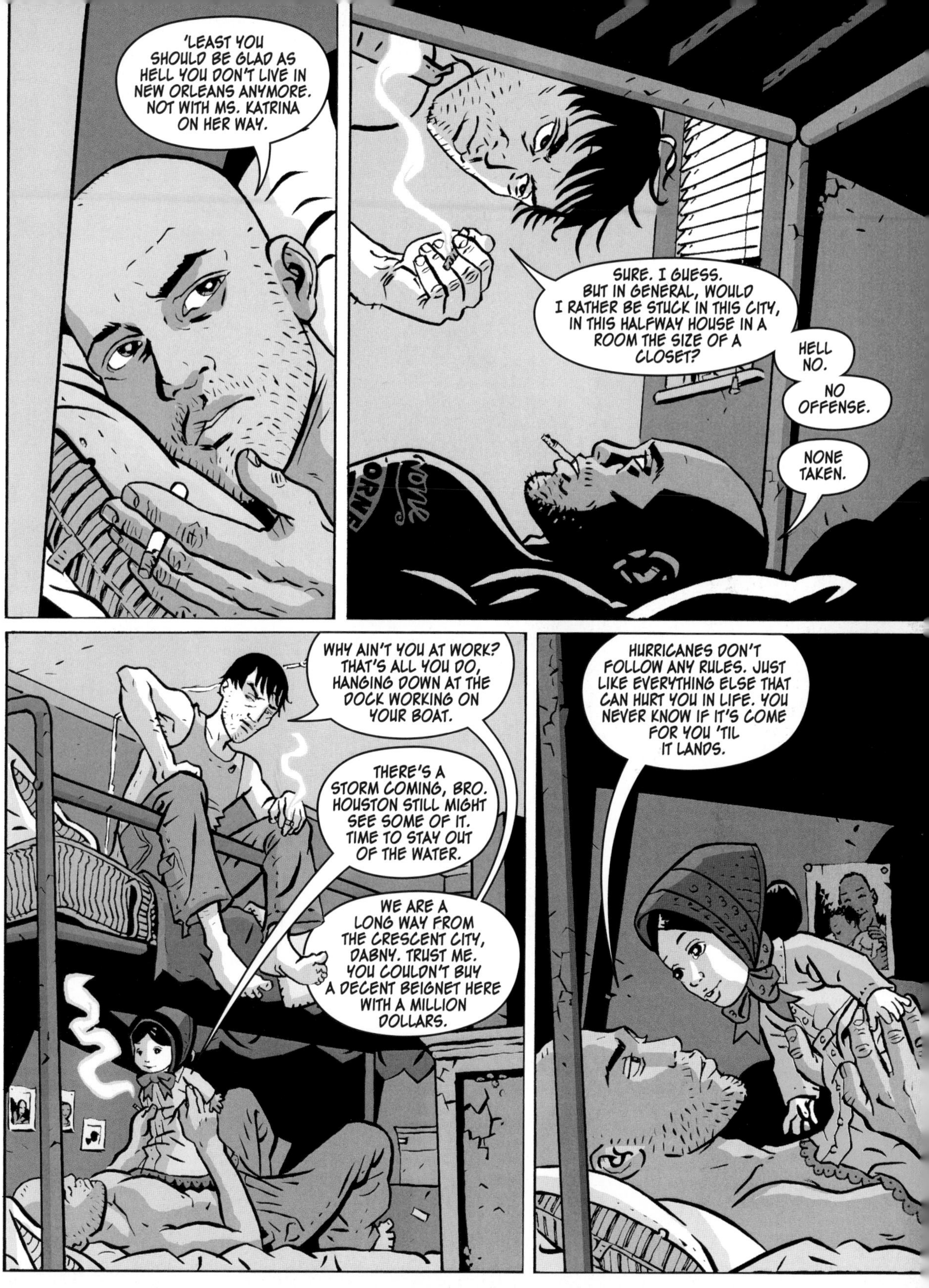
'LEAST YOU SHOULD BE GLAD AS HELL YOU DON'T LIVE IN NEW ORLEANS ANYMORE. NOT WITH MS. KATRINA ON HER WAY.
SURE. I GUESS. BUT IN GENERAL, WOULD I RATHER BE STUCK IN THIS CITY, IN THIS HALFWAY HOUSE IN A ROOM THE SIZE OF A CLOSET?
HELL NO.
NO OFFENSE.
NONE TAKEN.
WHY AIN'T YOU AT WORK? THAT'S ALL YOU DO, HANGING DOWN AT THE DOCK WORKING ON YOUR BOAT.
THERE'S A STORM COMING, BRO. HOUSTON STILL MIGHT SEE SOME OF IT. TIME TO STAY OUT OF THE WATER.
WE ARE A LONG WAY FROM THE CRESCENT CITY, DABNY. TRUST ME. YOU COULDN'T BUY A DECENT BEIGNET HERE WITH A MILLION DOLLARS.
HURRICANES DON'T FOLLOW ANY RULES. JUST LIKE EVERYTHING ELSE THAT CAN HURT YOU IN LIFE. YOU NEVER KNOW IF IT'S COME FOR YOU 'TIL IT LANDS.

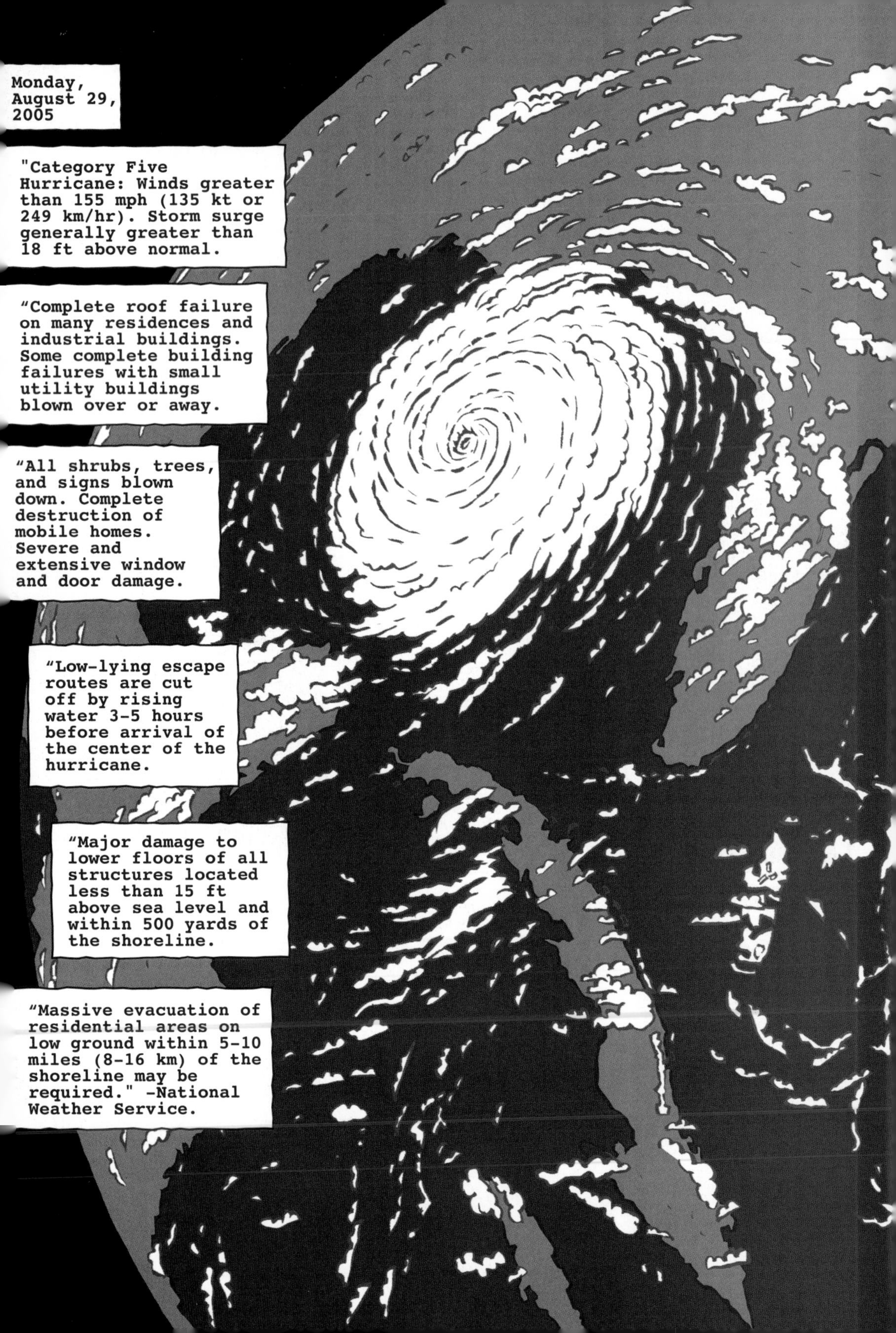
Monday, August 29, 2005
"Category Five Hurricane: Winds greater than 155 mph (135 kt or 249 km/hr). Storm surge generally greater than 18 ft above normal.
"Complete roof failure on many residences and industrial buildings. Some complete building failures with small utility buildings blown over or away.
"All shrubs, trees, and signs blown down. Complete destruction of mobile homes. Severe and extensive window and door damage.
"Low-lying escape routes are cut off by rising water 3-5 hours before arrival of the center of the hurricane.
"Major damage to lower floors of all structures located less than 15 ft above sea level and within 500 yards of the shoreline.
"Massive evacuation of residential areas on low ground within 5-10 miles (8-16 km) of the shoreline may be required." -National Weather Service.

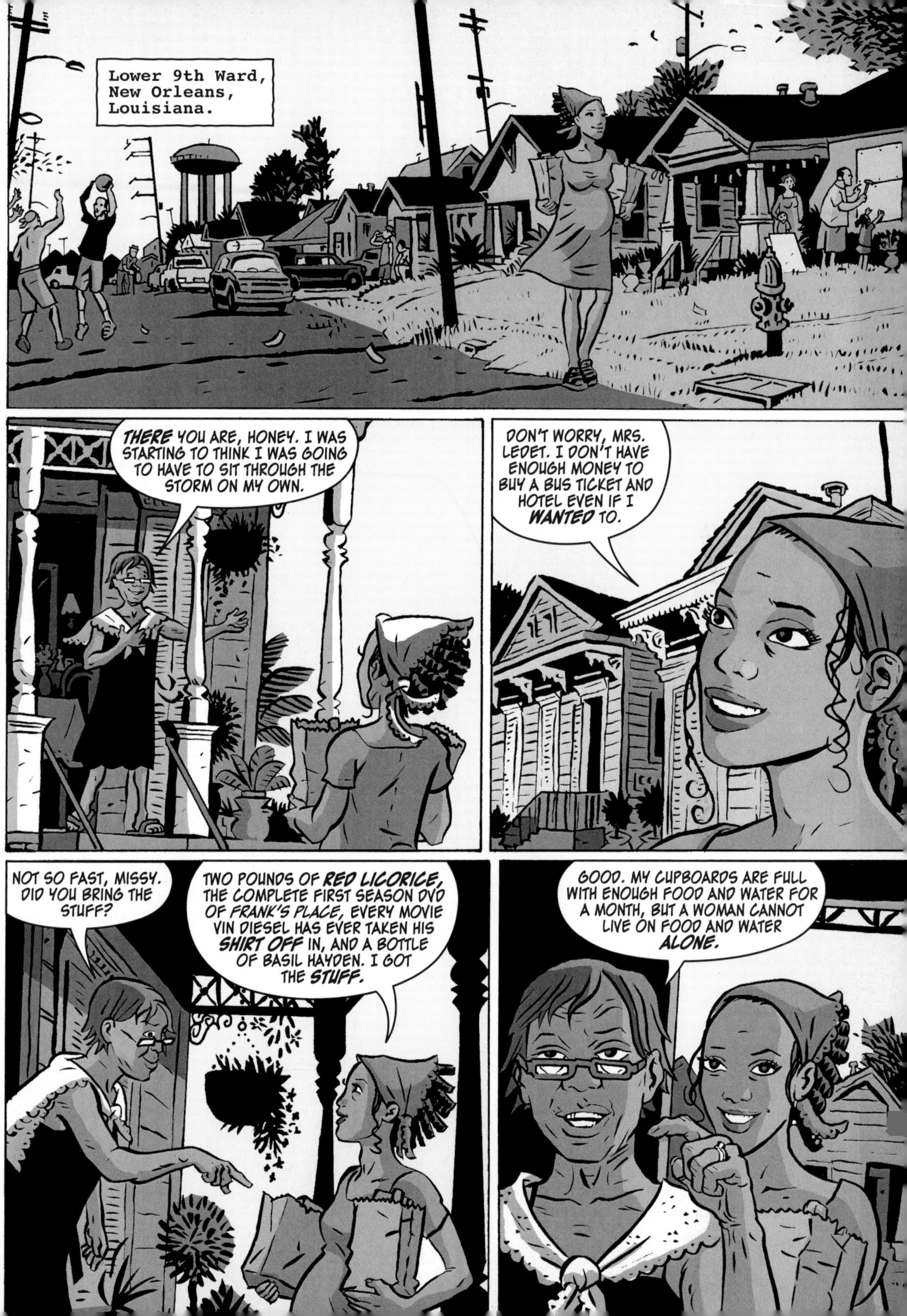
Lower 9th Ward, New Orleans, Louisiana.
THERE YOU ARE, HONEY. I WAS STARTING TO THINK I WAS GOING TO HAVE TO SIT THROUGH THE STORM ON MY OWN.
DON'T WORRY, MRS. LEDET. I DON'T HAVE ENOUGH MONEY TO BUY A BUS TICKET AND HOTEL EVEN IF I WANTED TO.
NOT SO FAST, MISSY. DID YOU BRING THE STUFF?
TWO POUNDS OF RED LICORICE, THE COMPLETE FIRST SEASON DVD OF FRANK'S PLACE, EVERY MOVIE VIN DIESEL HAS EVER TAKEN HIS SHIRT OFF IN, AND A BOTTLE OF BASIL HAYDEN. I GOT THE STUFF.
GOOD. MY CUPBOARDS ARE FULL WITH ENOUGH FOOD AND WATER FOR A MONTH, BUT A WOMAN CANNOT LIVE ON FOOD AND WATER ALONE.

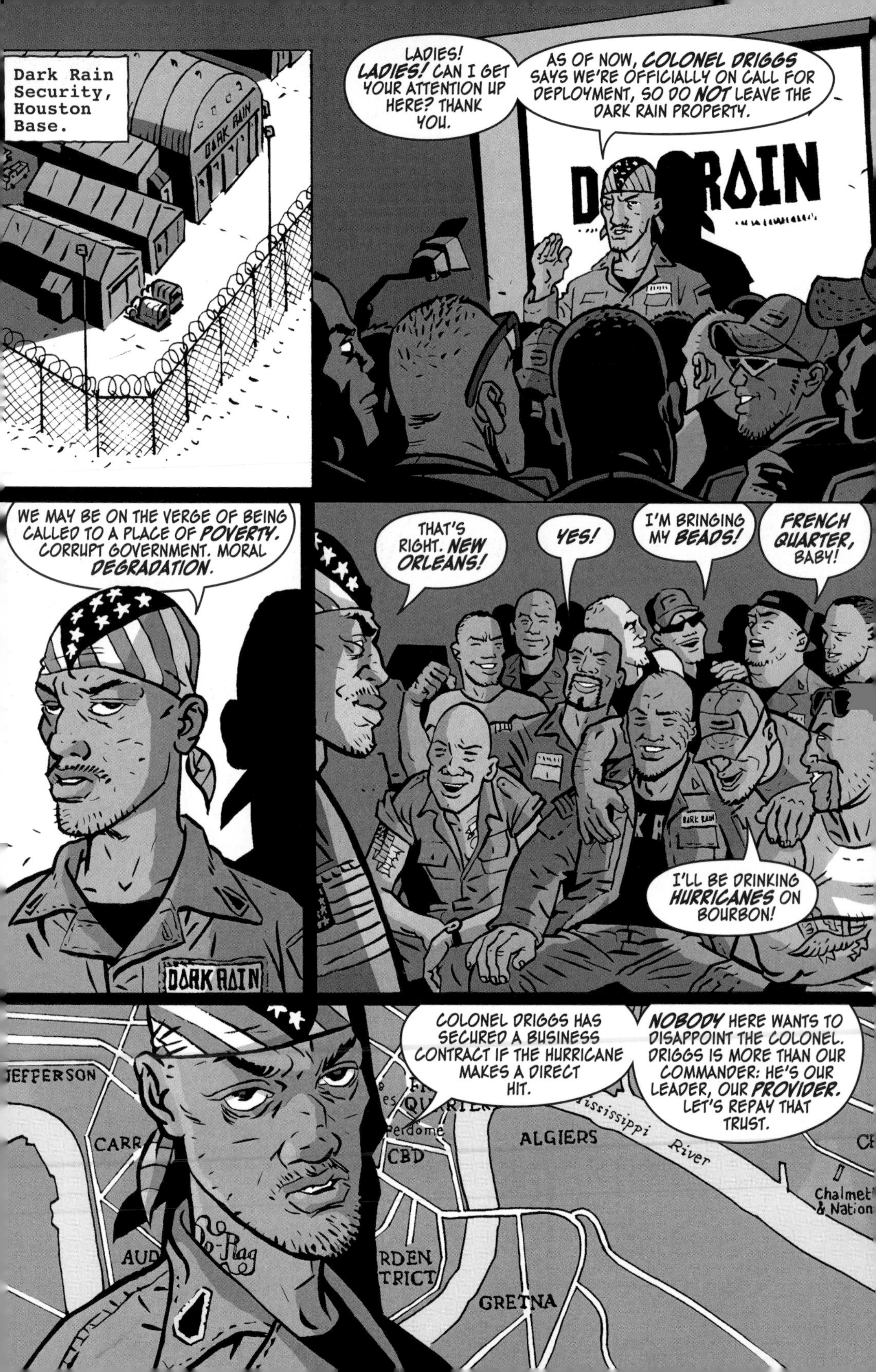

Dark Rain Security, Houston Base.
DARK RAIN
LADIES! LADIES! CAN I GET YOUR ATTENTION UP HERE? THANK YOU.
AS OF NOW, COLONEL DRIGGS SAYS WE'RE OFFICIALLY ON CALL FOR DEPLOYMENT, SO DO NOT LEAVE THE DARK RAIN PROPERTY.
WE MAY BE ON THE VERGE OF BEING CALLED TO A PLACE OF POVERTY. CORRUPT GOVERNMENT. MORAL DEGRADATION.
DARK RAIN
THAT'S RIGHT. NEW ORLEANS!
YES!
I'M BRINGING MY BEADS!
FRENCH QUARTER, BABY!
DARK RAIN
I'LL BE DRINKING HURRICANES ON BOURBON!
COLONEL DRIGGS HAS SECURED A BUSINESS CONTRACT IF THE HURRICANE MAKES A DIRECT HIT.
NOBODY HERE WANTS TO DISAPPOINT THE COLONEL. DRIGGS IS MORE THAN OUR COMMANDER: HE'S OUR LEADER, OUR PROVIDER. LET'S REPAY THAT TRUST.
JEFFERSON
CBD
ALGIERS
River
GRETNA
Do-Rag

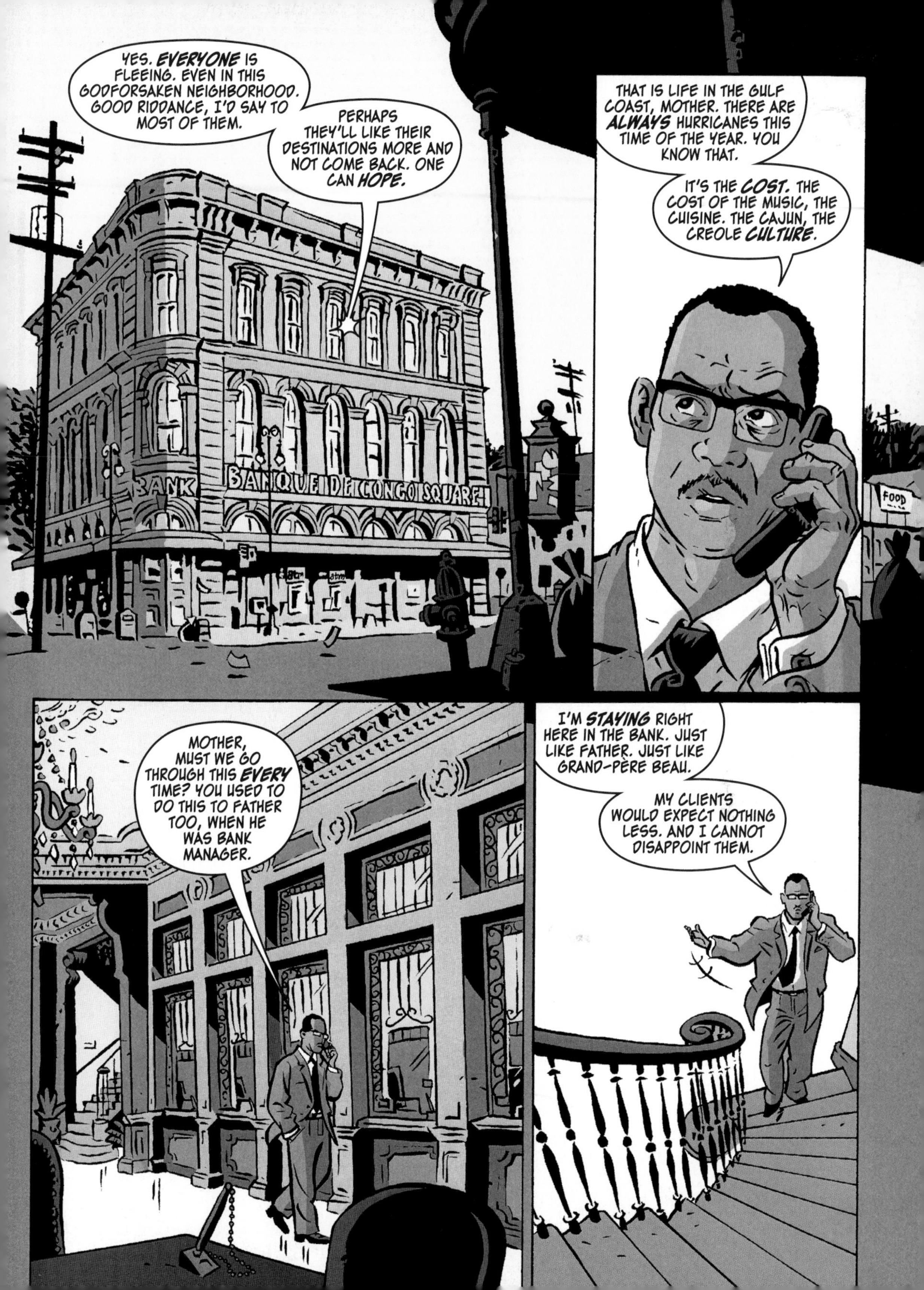
YES. EVERYONE IS FLEEING. EVEN IN THIS GODFORSAKEN NEIGHBORHOOD. GOOD RIDDANCE, I'D SAY TO MOST OF THEM.
PERHAPS THEY'LL LIKE THEIR DESTINATIONS MORE AND NOT COME BACK. ONE CAN HOPE.
BANK
BANQUE DE CONGO SQUARE
THAT IS LIFE IN THE GULF COAST, MOTHER. THERE ARE ALWAYS HURRICANES THIS TIME OF THE YEAR. YOU KNOW THAT.
IT'S THE COST. THE COST OF THE MUSIC, THE CUISINE. THE CAJUN, THE CREOLE CULTURE.
FOOD
MOTHER, MUST WE GO THROUGH THIS EVERY TIME? YOU USED TO DO THIS TO FATHER TOO, WHEN HE WAS BANK MANAGER.
I'M STAYING RIGHT HERE IN THE BANK. JUST LIKE FATHER. JUST LIKE GRAND-PÈRE BEAU.
MY CLIENTS WOULD EXPECT NOTHING LESS. AND I CANNOT DISAPPOINT THEM.

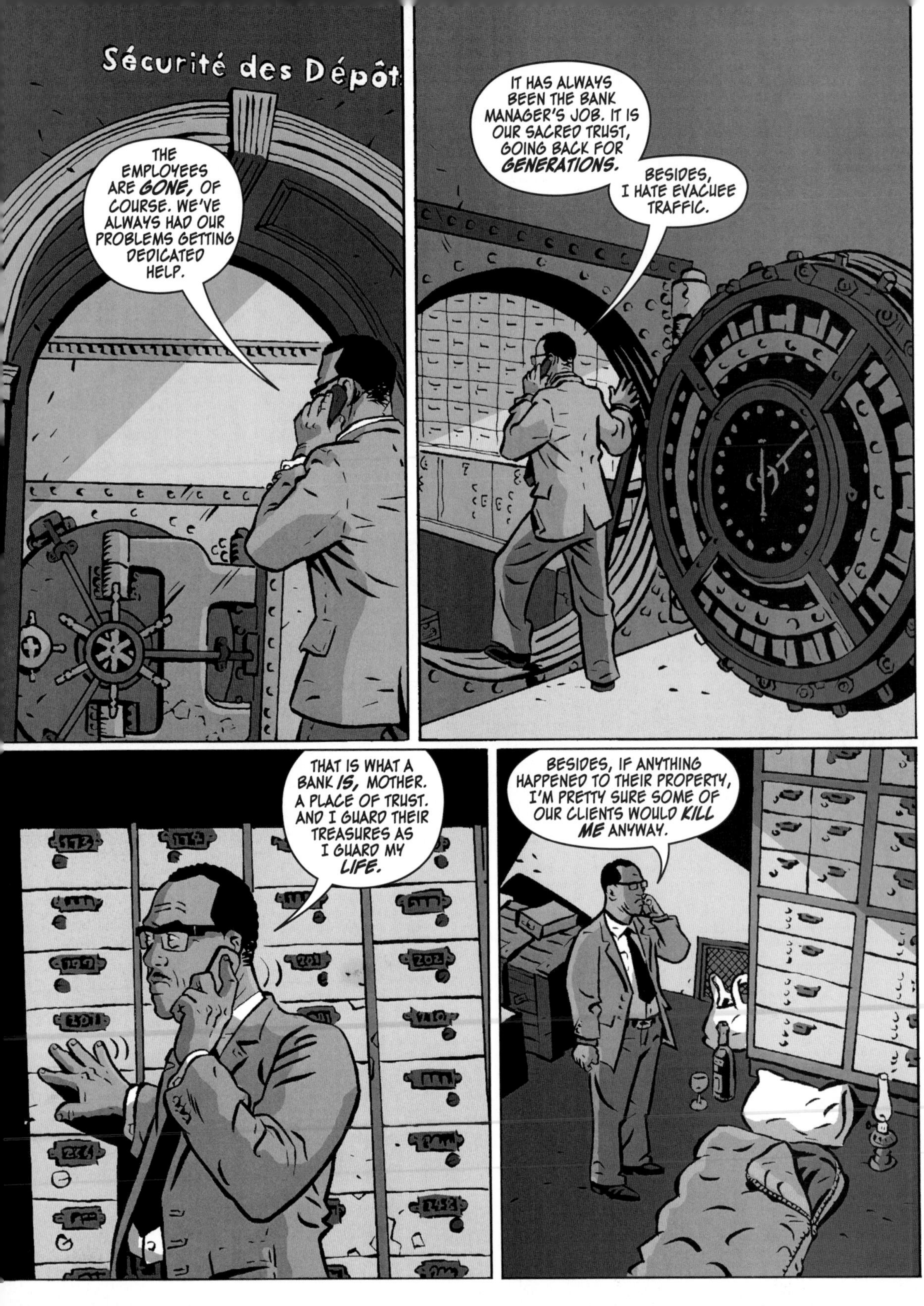
Sécurité des Dépôt
THE EMPLOYEES ARE GONE, OF COURSE. WE'VE ALWAYS HAD OUR PROBLEMS GETTING DEDICATED HELP.
IT HAS ALWAYS BEEN THE BANK MANAGER'S JOB. IT IS OUR SACRED TRUST, GOING BACK FOR GENERATIONS.
BESIDES, I HATE EVACUEE TRAFFIC.
THAT IS WHAT A BANK IS, MOTHER. A PLACE OF TRUST. AND I GUARD THEIR TREASURES AS I GUARD MY LIFE.
BESIDES, IF ANYTHING HAPPENED TO THEIR PROPERTY, I'M PRETTY SURE SOME OF OUR CLIENTS WOULD KILL ME ANYWAY.

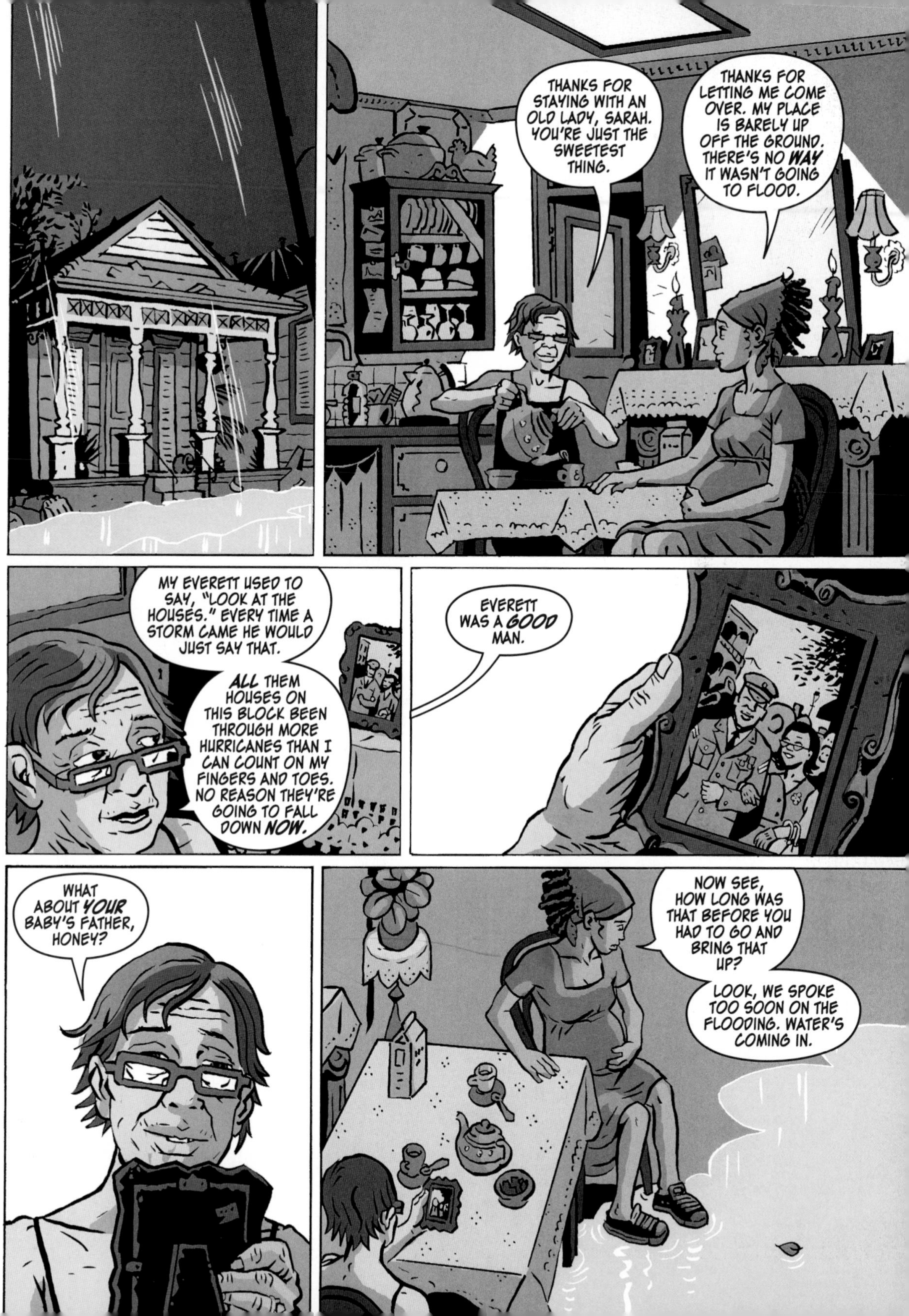
THANKS FOR STAYING WITH AN OLD LADY, SARAH. YOU'RE JUST THE SWEETEST THING.
THANKS FOR LETTING ME COME OVER. MY PLACE IS BARELY UP OFF THE GROUND. THERE'S NO WAY IT WASN'T GOING TO FLOOD.
MY EVERETT USED TO SAY, "LOOK AT THE HOUSES." EVERY TIME A STORM CAME HE WOULD JUST SAY THAT.
ALL THEM HOUSES ON THIS BLOCK BEEN THROUGH MORE HURRICANES THAN I CAN COUNT ON MY FINGERS AND TOES. NO REASON THEY'RE GOING TO FALL DOWN NOW.
EVERETT WAS A GOOD MAN.
WHAT ABOUT YOUR BABY'S FATHER, HONEY?
NOW SEE, HOW LONG WAS THAT BEFORE YOU HAD TO GO AND BRING THAT UP?
LOOK, WE SPOKE TOO SOON ON THE FLOODING. WATER'S COMING IN.

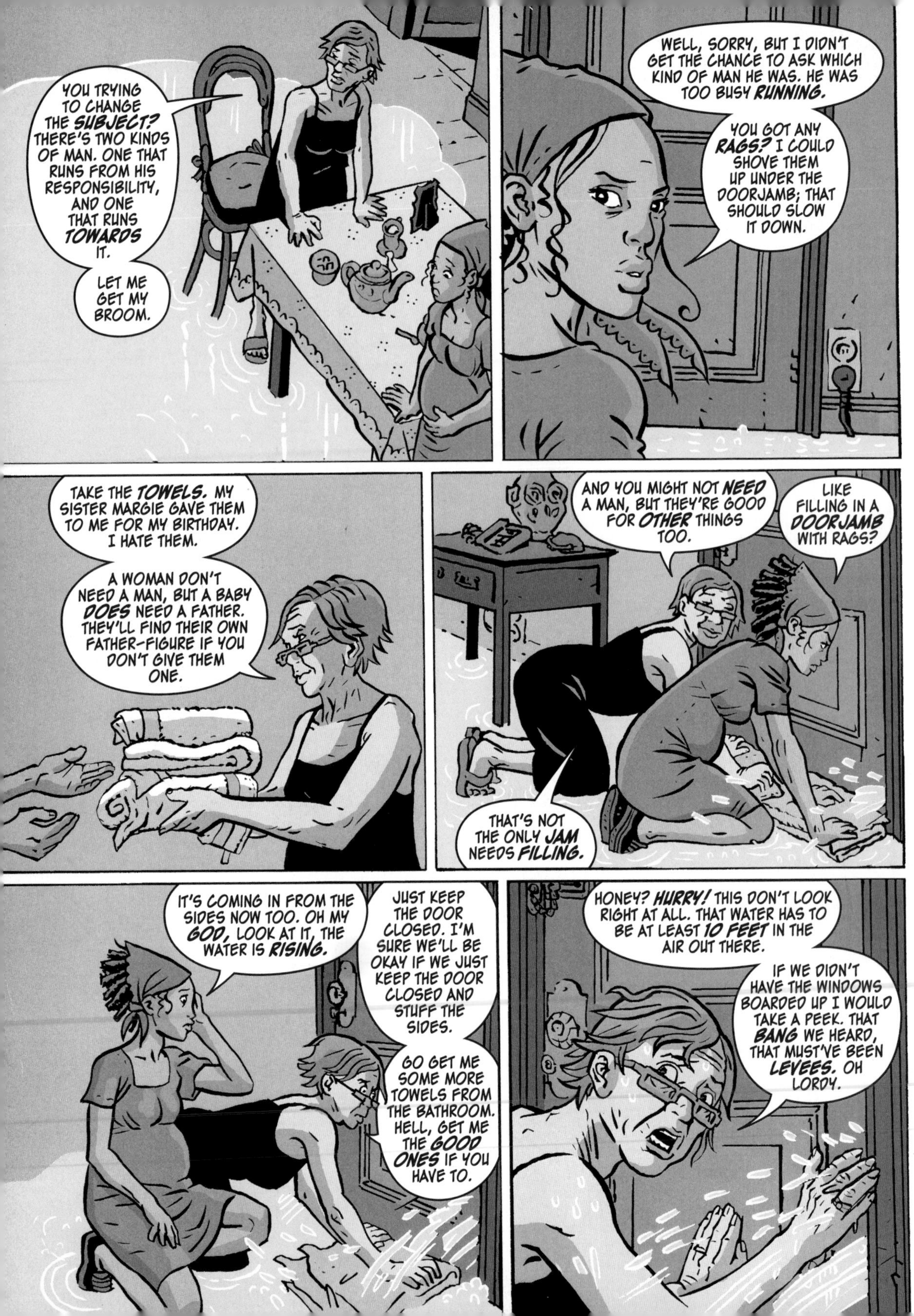
YOU TRYING TO CHANGE THE SUBJECT? THERE'S TWO KINDS OF MAN. ONE THAT RUNS FROM HIS RESPONSIBILITY, AND ONE THAT RUNS TOWARDS IT.
LET ME GET MY BROOM.
WELL, SORRY, BUT I DIDN'T GET THE CHANCE TO ASK WHICH KIND OF MAN HE WAS. HE WAS TOO BUSY RUNNING.
YOU GOT ANY RAGS? I COULD SHOVE THEM UP UNDER THE DOORJAMB; THAT SHOULD SLOW IT DOWN.
TAKE THE TOWELS. MY SISTER MARGIE GAVE THEM TO ME FOR MY BIRTHDAY. I HATE THEM.
A WOMAN DON'T NEED A MAN, BUT A BABY DOES NEED A FATHER. THEY'LL FIND THEIR OWN FATHER-FIGURE IF YOU DON'T GIVE THEM ONE.
AND YOU MIGHT NOT NEED A MAN, BUT THEY'RE GOOD FOR OTHER THINGS TOO.
LIKE FILLING IN A DOORJAMB WITH RAGS?
THAT'S NOT THE ONLY JAM NEEDS FILLING.
IT'S COMING IN FROM THE SIDES NOW TOO. OH MY GOD, LOOK AT IT, THE WATER IS RISING.
JUST KEEP THE DOOR CLOSED. I'M SURE WE'LL BE OKAY IF WE JUST KEEP THE DOOR CLOSED AND STUFF THE SIDES.
GO GET ME SOME MORE TOWELS FROM THE BATHROOM. HELL, GET ME THE GOOD ONES IF YOU HAVE TO.
HONEY? HURRY! THIS DON'T LOOK RIGHT AT ALL. THAT WATER HAS TO BE AT LEAST 10 FEET IN THE AIR OUT THERE.
IF WE DIDN'T HAVE THE WINDOWS BOARDED UP I WOULD TAKE A PEEK. THAT BANG WE HEARD, THAT MUST'VE BEEN LEVEES. OH LORDY.

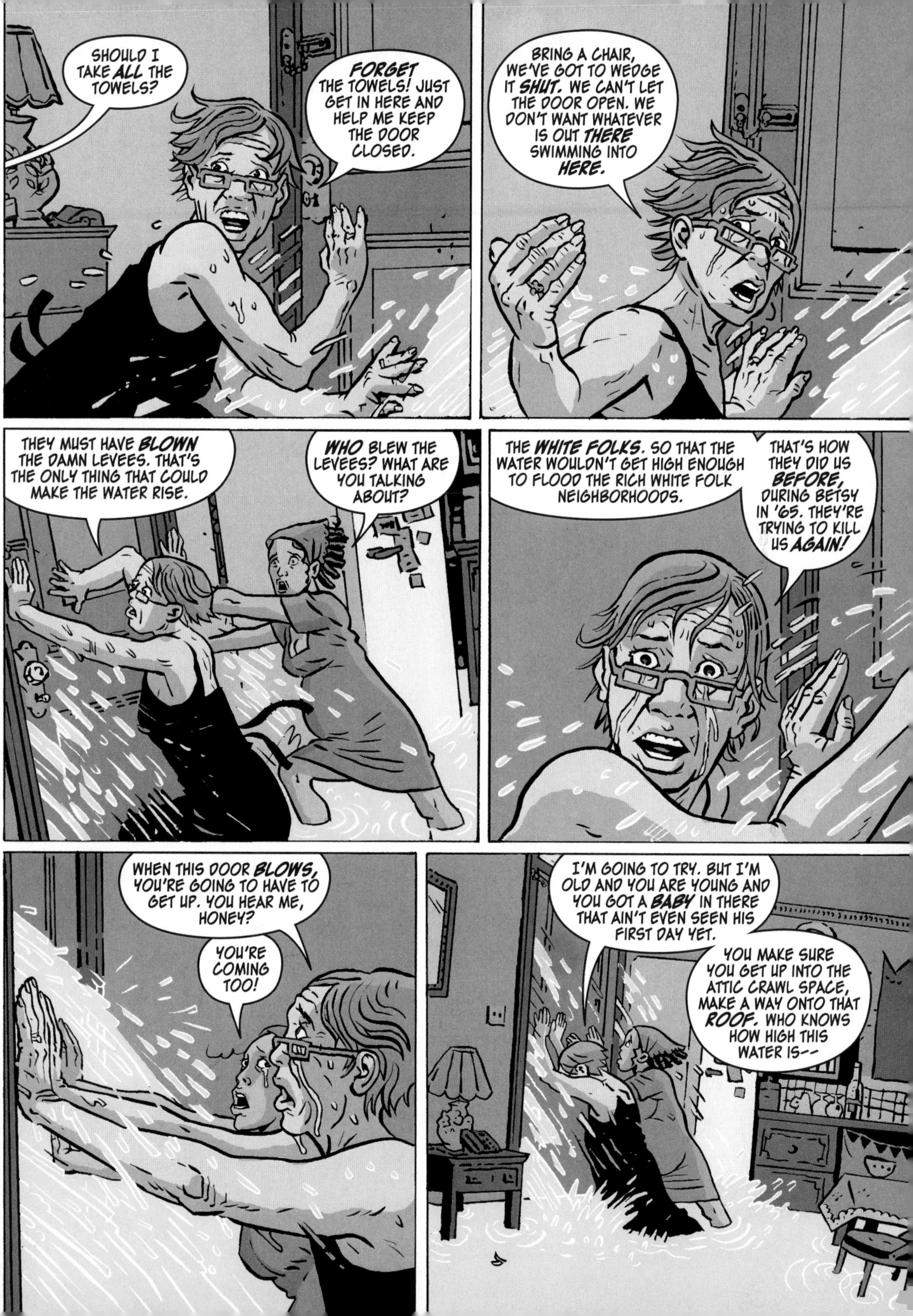
SHOULD I TAKE ALL THE TOWELS?
FORGET THE TOWELS! JUST GET IN HERE AND HELP ME KEEP THE DOOR CLOSED.
BRING A CHAIR, WE'VE GOT TO WEDGE IT SHUT. WE CAN'T LET THE DOOR OPEN. WE DON'T WANT WHATEVER IS OUT THERE SWIMMING INTO HERE.
THEY MUST HAVE BLOWN THE DAMN LEVEES. THAT'S THE ONLY THING THAT COULD MAKE THE WATER RISE.
WHO BLEW THE LEVEES? WHAT ARE YOU TALKING ABOUT?
THE WHITE FOLKS. SO THAT THE WATER WOULDN'T GET HIGH ENOUGH TO FLOOD THE RICH WHITE FOLK NEIGHBORHOODS.
THAT'S HOW THEY DID US BEFORE, DURING BETSY IN '65. THEY'RE TRYING TO KILL US AGAIN!
WHEN THIS DOOR BLOWS, YOU'RE GOING TO HAVE TO GET UP. YOU HEAR ME, HONEY?
YOU'RE COMING TOO!
I'M GOING TO TRY. BUT I'M OLD AND YOU ARE YOUNG AND YOU GOT A BABY IN THERE THAT AIN'T EVEN SEEN HIS FIRST DAY YET.
YOU MAKE SURE YOU GET UP INTO THE ATTIC CRAWL SPACE, MAKE A WAY ONTO THAT ROOF. WHO KNOWS HOW HIGH THIS WATER IS--

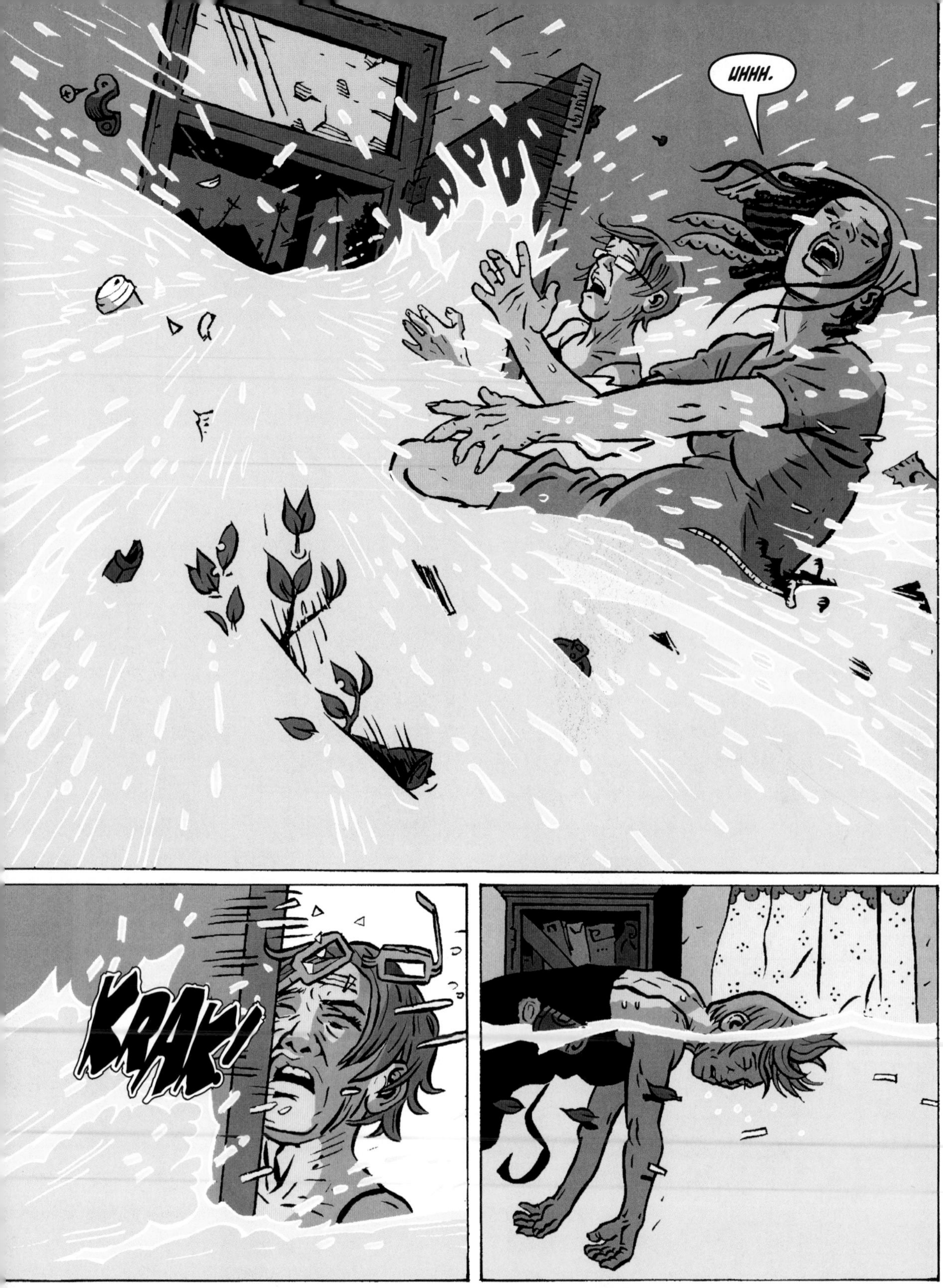
UHHH.
KRAK!

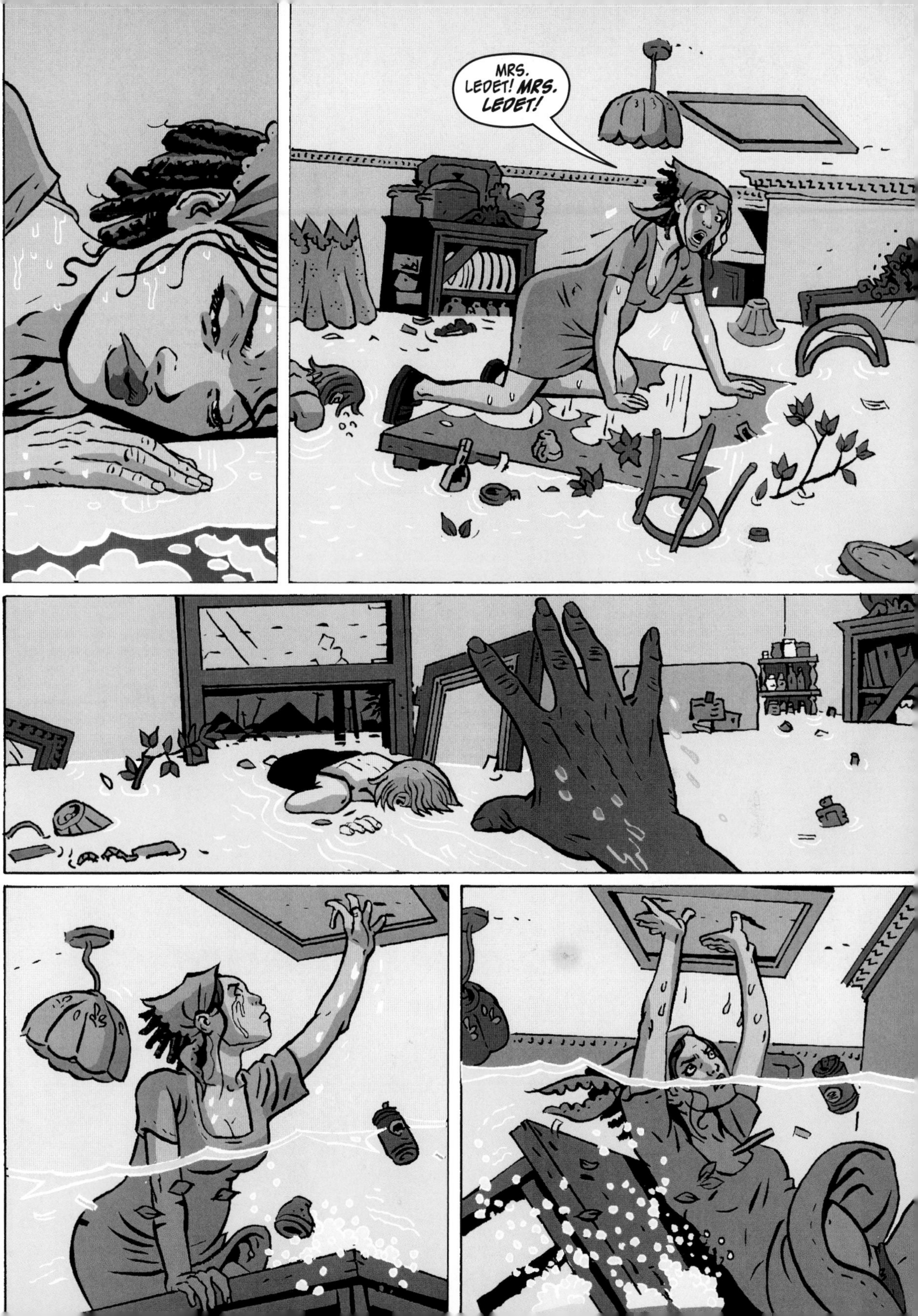
MRS. LEDET! MRS. LEDET!

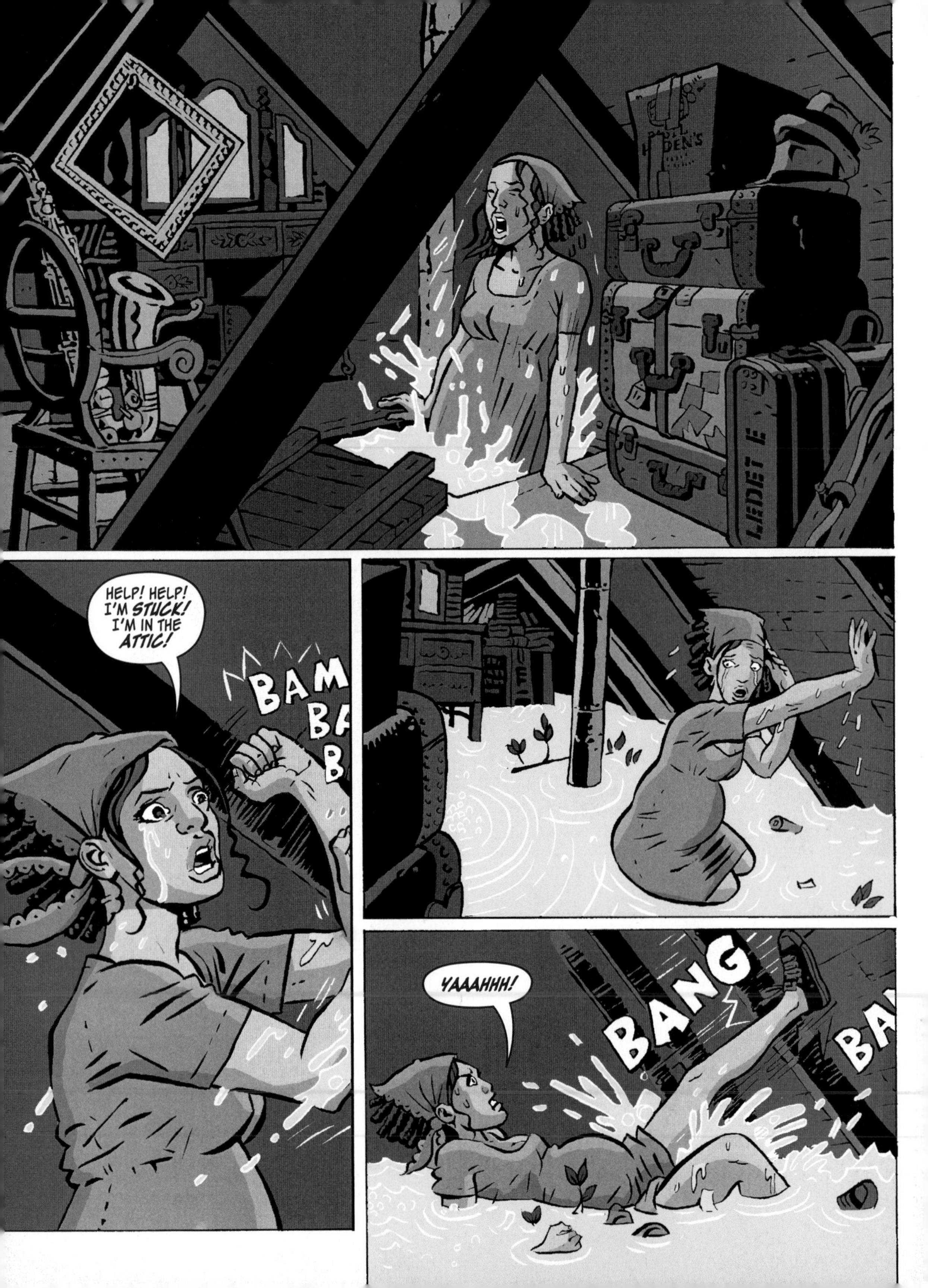
HELP! HELP! I'M STUCK! I'M IN THE ATTIC!
BAM
YAAAHHH!
BANG

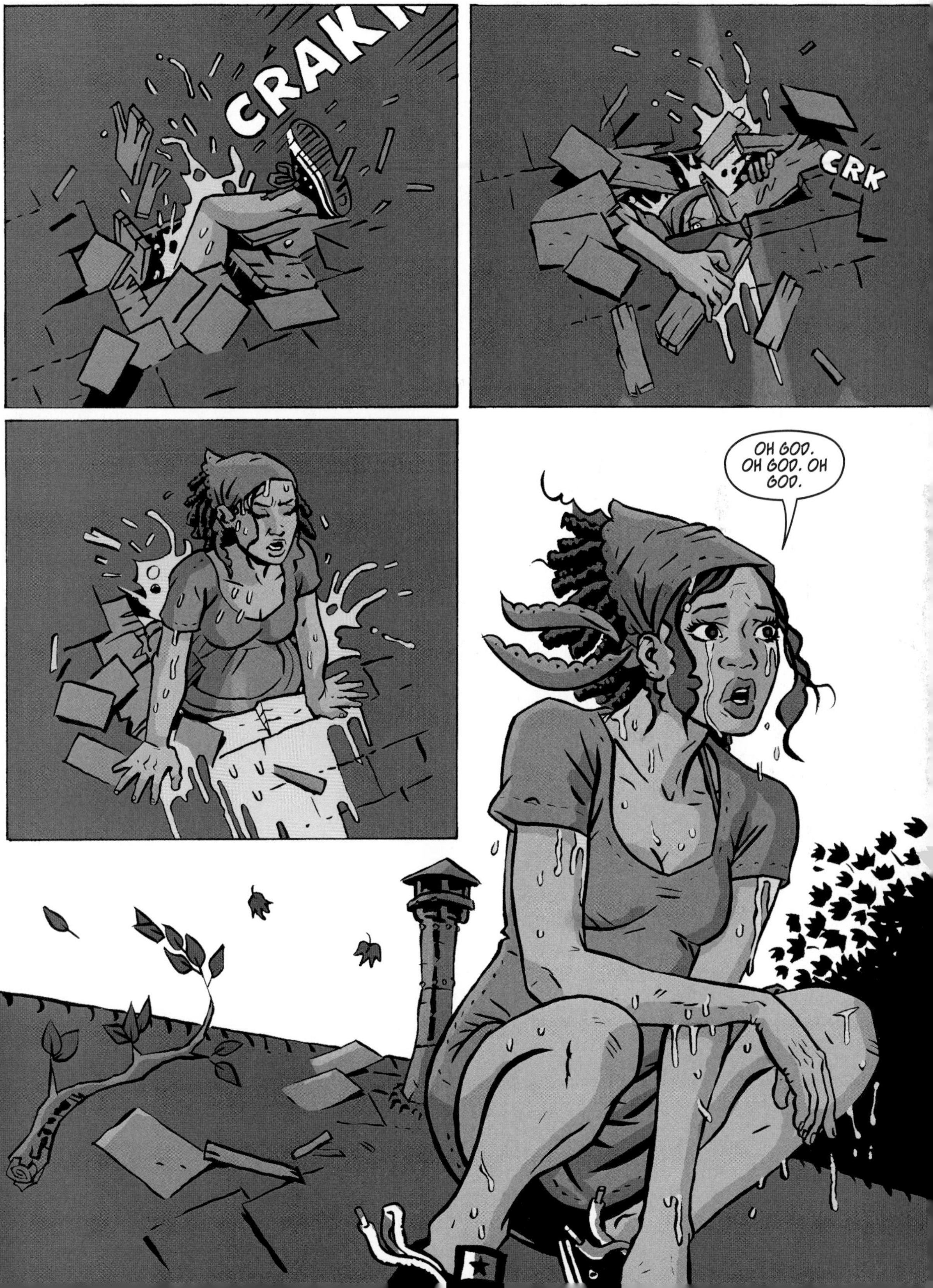
CRAK
CRK
OH GOD. OH GOD. OH GOD.

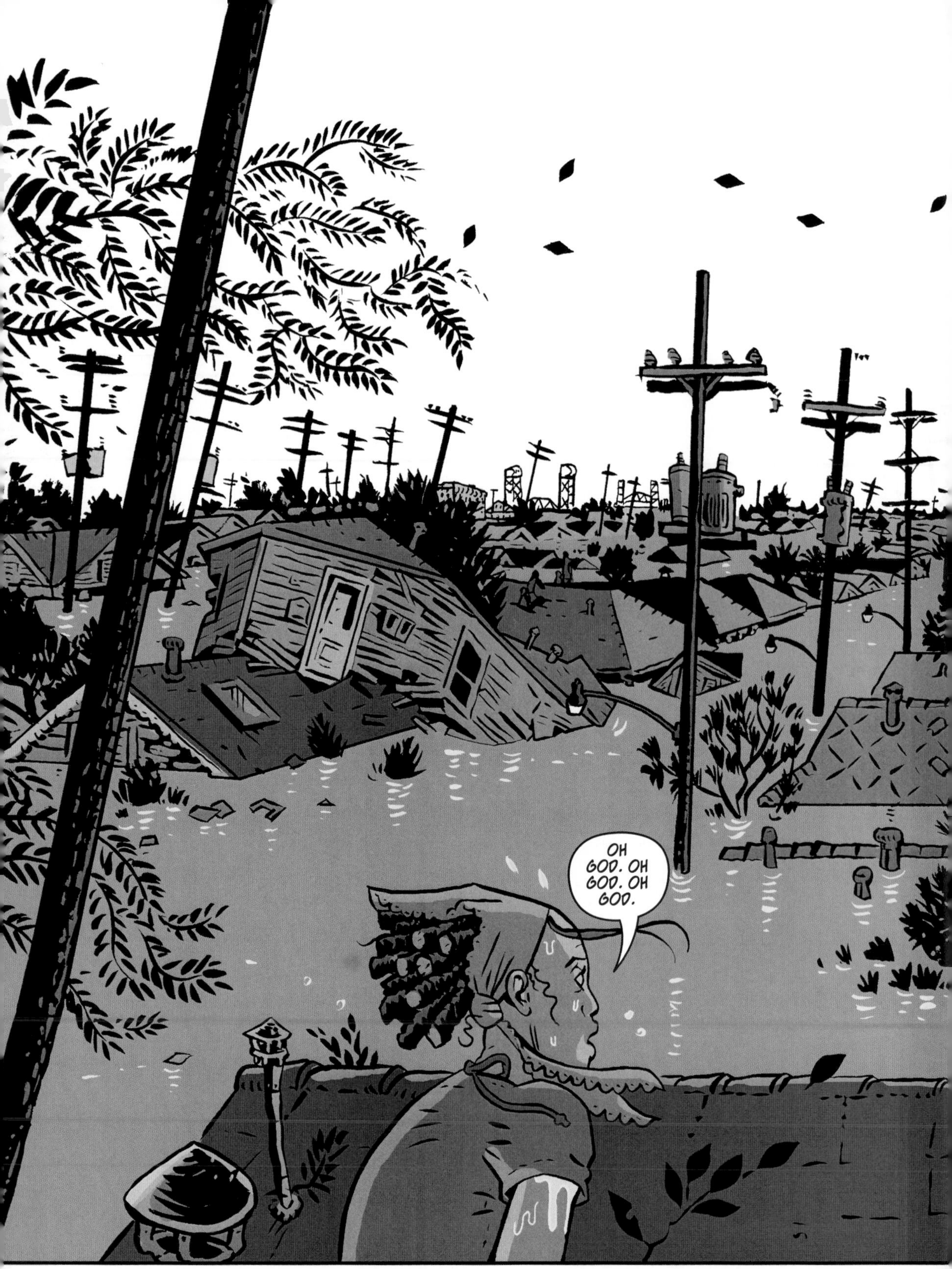
OH GOD. OH GOD. OH GOD.

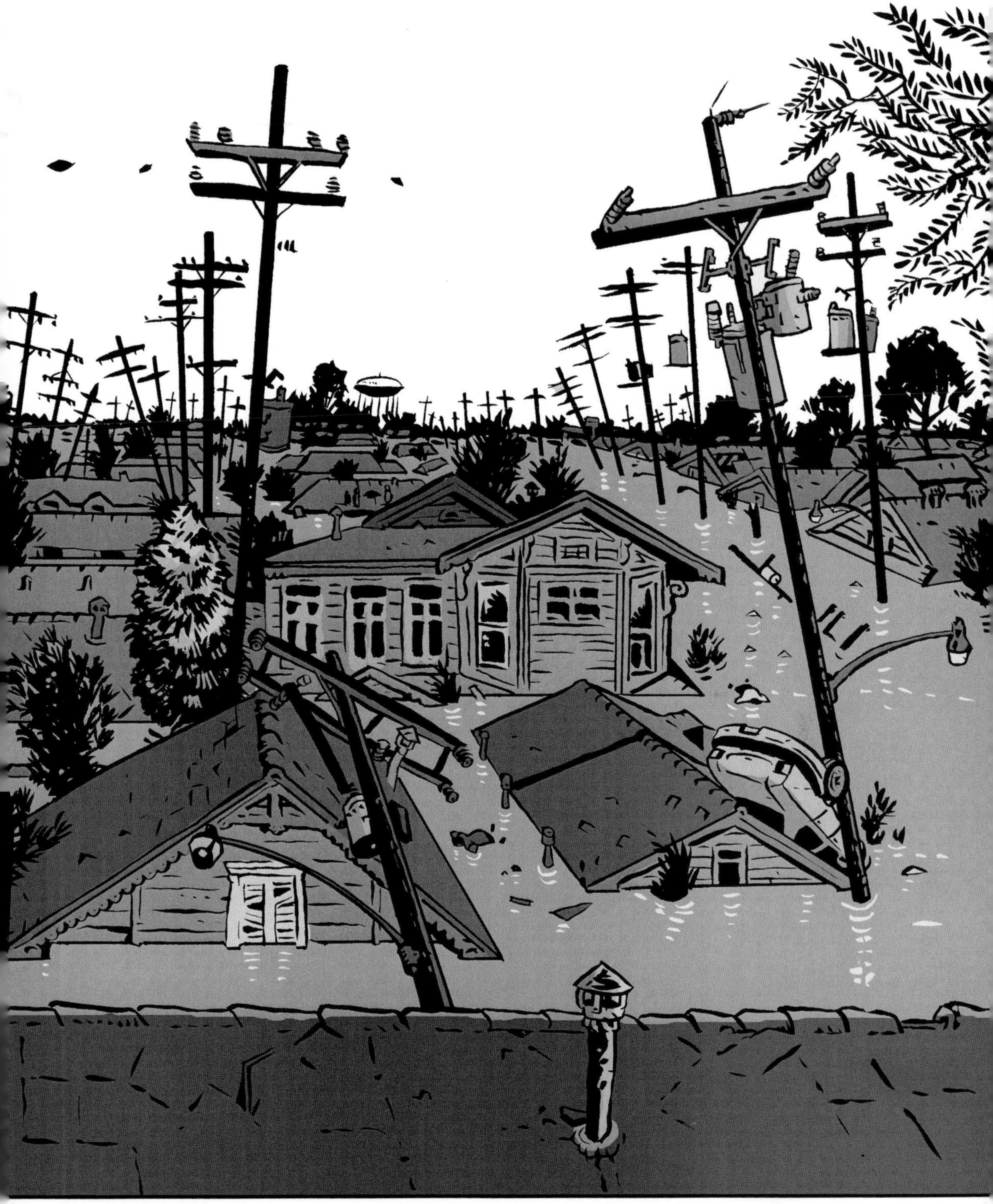

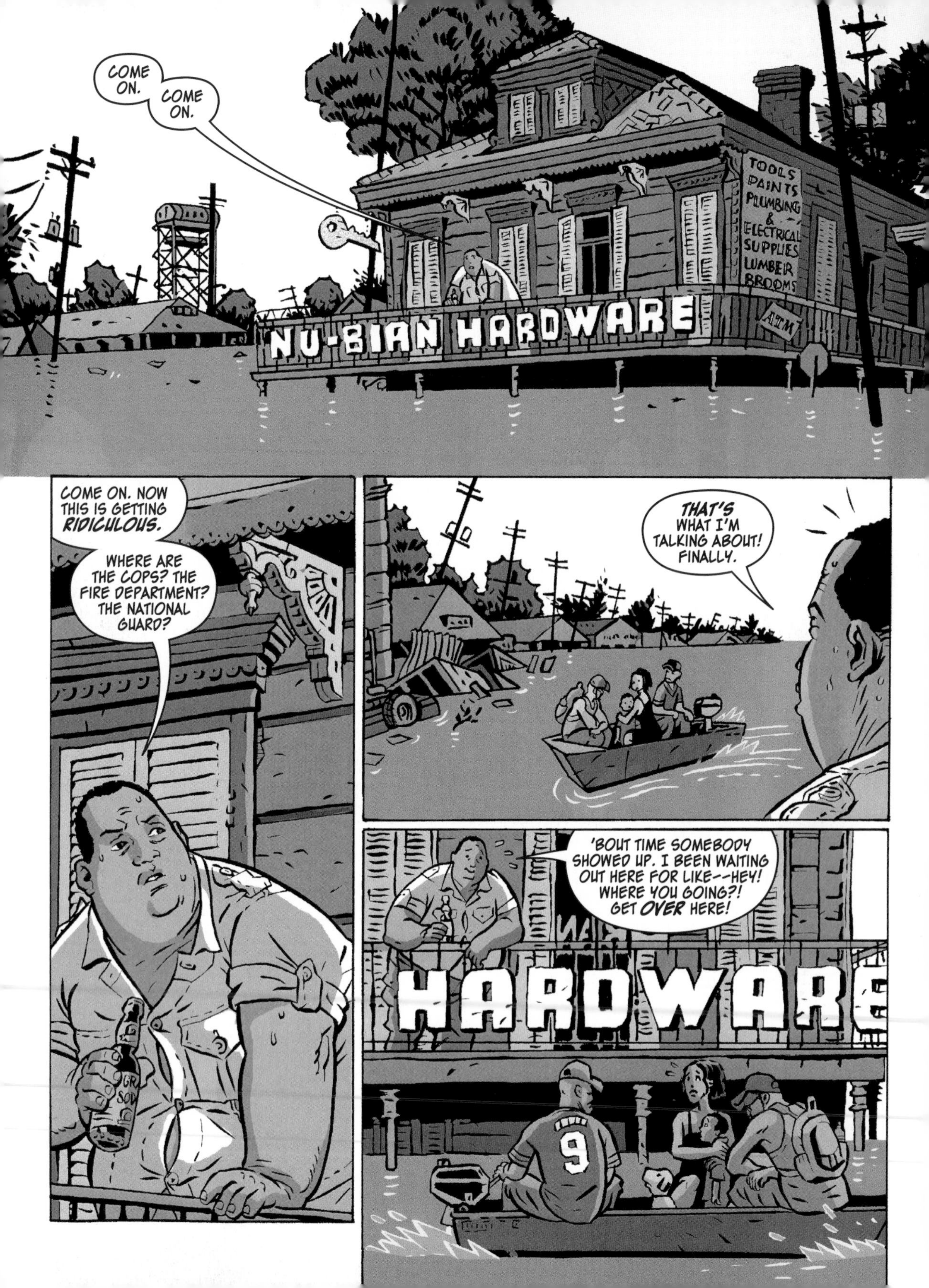
COME ON.
COME ON.
TOOLS PAINTS PLUMBING & ELECTRICAL SUPPLIES LUMBER BROOMS
NU-BIAN HARDWARE
ATM
COME ON. NOW THIS IS GETTING RIDICULOUS.
WHERE ARE THE COPS? THE FIRE DEPARTMENT? THE NATIONAL GUARD?
THAT'S WHAT I'M TALKING ABOUT! FINALLY.
'BOUT TIME SOMEBODY SHOWED UP. I BEEN WAITING OUT HERE FOR LIKE--HEY! WHERE YOU GOING?! GET OVER HERE!
HARDWARE
9

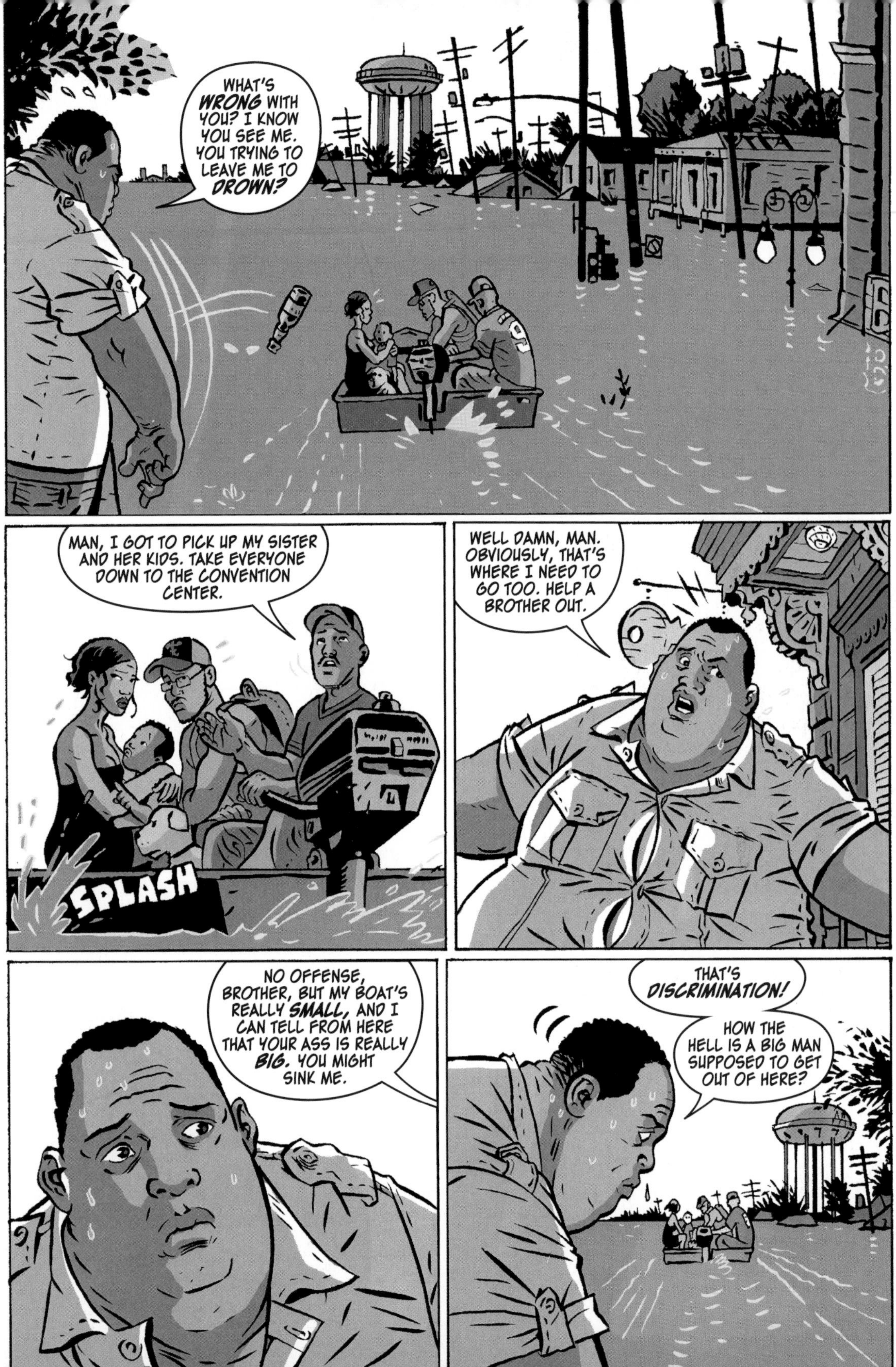
WHAT'S WRONG WITH YOU? I KNOW YOU SEE ME. YOU TRYING TO LEAVE ME TO DROWN?
MAN, I GOT TO PICK UP MY SISTER AND HER KIDS. TAKE EVERYONE DOWN TO THE CONVENTION CENTER.
SPLASH
WELL DAMN, MAN. OBVIOUSLY, THAT'S WHERE I NEED TO GO TOO. HELP A BROTHER OUT.
NO OFFENSE, BROTHER, BUT MY BOAT'S REALLY SMALL, AND I CAN TELL FROM HERE THAT YOUR ASS IS REALLY BIG. YOU MIGHT SINK ME.
THAT'S DISCRIMINATION!
HOW THE HELL IS A BIG MAN SUPPOSED TO GET OUT OF HERE?

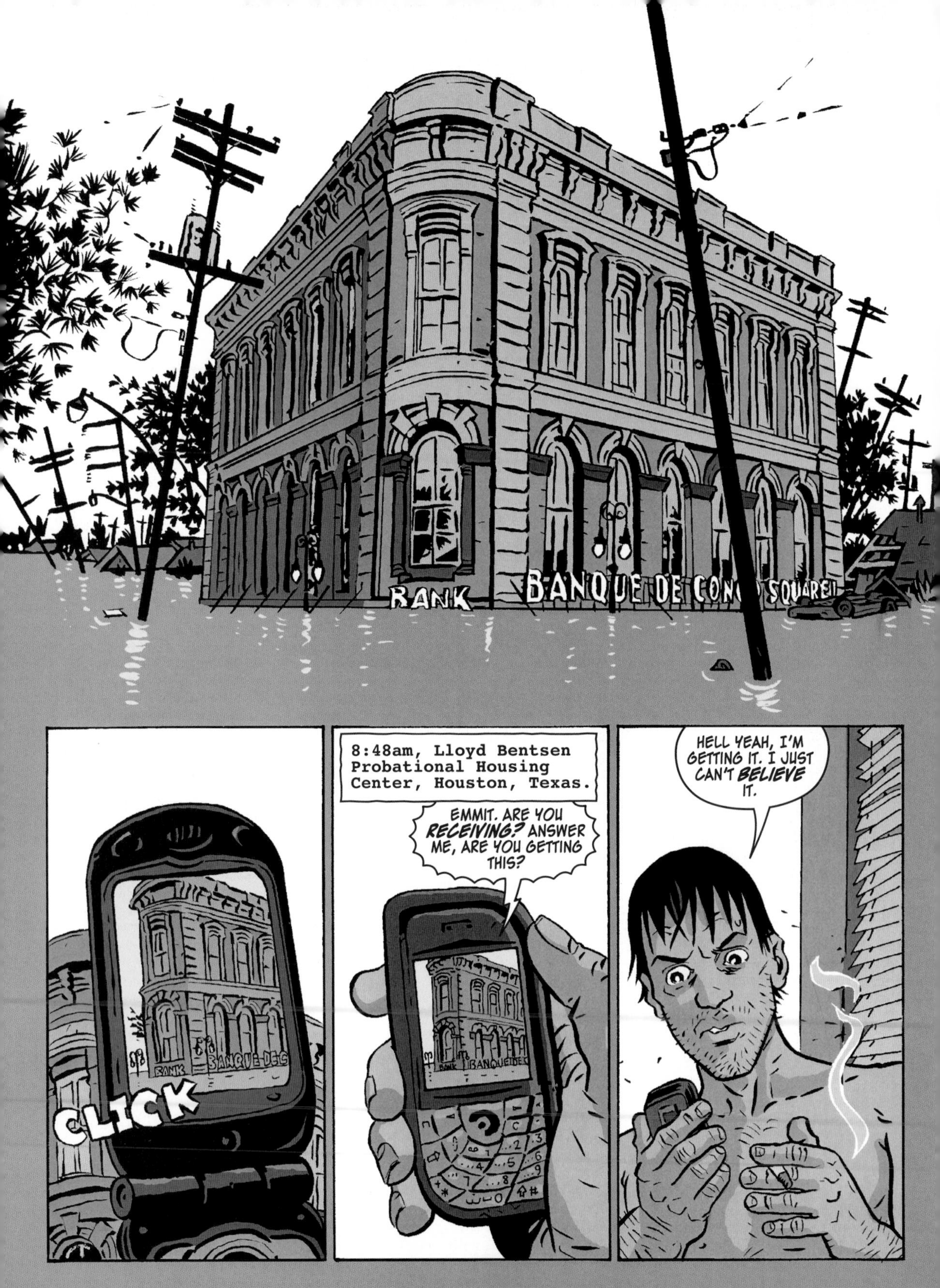
BANK
BANQUE DE CON
SQUARE
CLICK
8:48am, Lloyd Bentsen Probational Housing Center, Houston, Texas.
EMMIT. ARE YOU *RECEIVING?* ANSWER ME, ARE YOU GETTING THIS?
HELL YEAH, I'M GETTING IT. I JUST CAN'T *BELIEVE* IT.

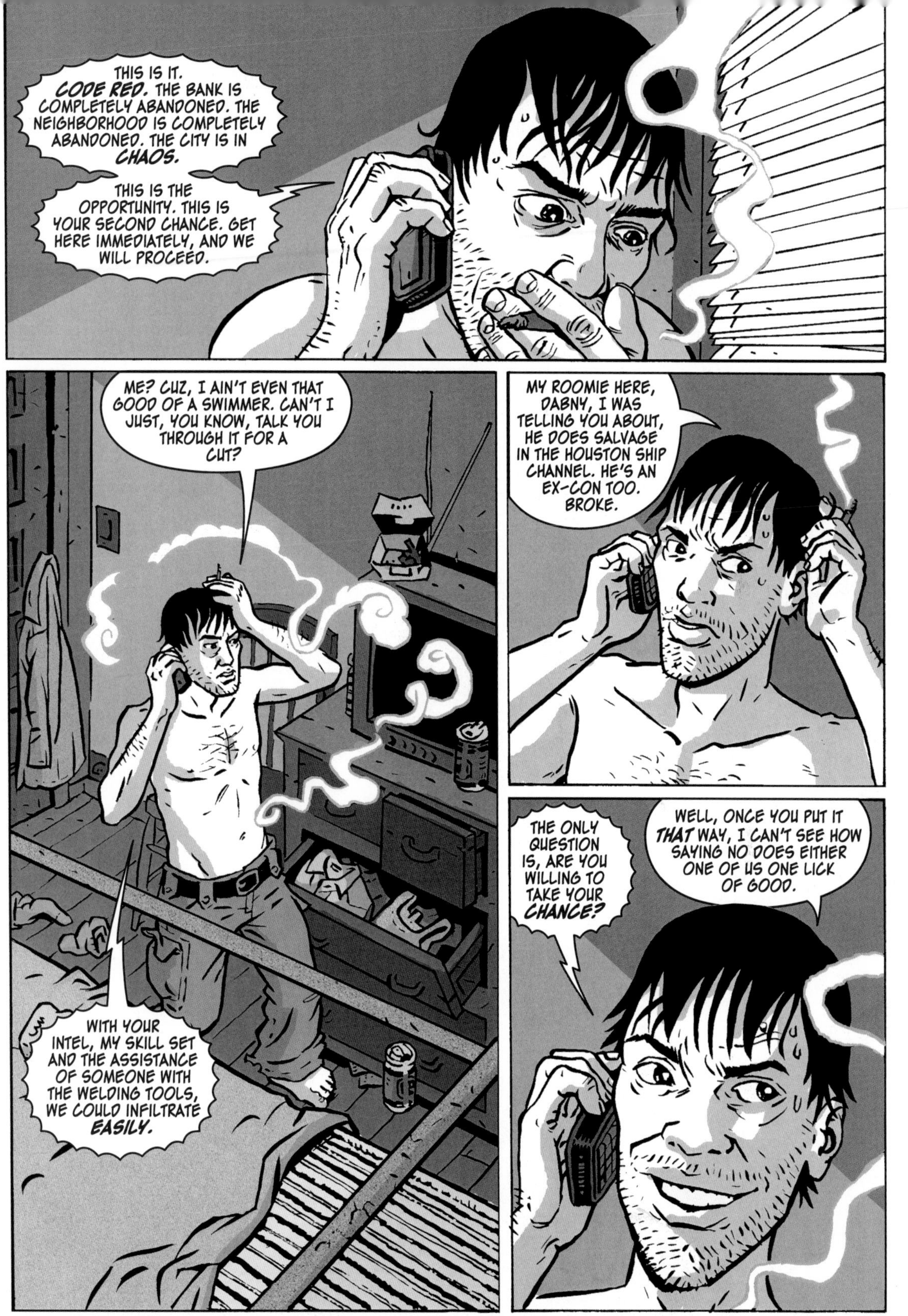
THIS IS IT. CODE RED. THE BANK IS COMPLETELY ABANDONED. THE NEIGHBORHOOD IS COMPLETELY ABANDONED. THE CITY IS IN CHAOS.
THIS IS THE OPPORTUNITY. THIS IS YOUR SECOND CHANCE. GET HERE IMMEDIATELY, AND WE WILL PROCEED.
ME? CUZ, I AIN'T EVEN THAT GOOD OF A SWIMMER. CAN'T I JUST, YOU KNOW, TALK YOU THROUGH IT FOR A CUT?
WITH YOUR INTEL, MY SKILL SET AND THE ASSISTANCE OF SOMEONE WITH THE WELDING TOOLS, WE COULD INFILTRATE EASILY.
MY ROOMIE HERE, DABNY, I WAS TELLING YOU ABOUT, HE DOES SALVAGE IN THE HOUSTON SHIP CHANNEL. HE'S AN EX-CON TOO. BROKE.
THE ONLY QUESTION IS, ARE YOU WILLING TO TAKE YOUR CHANCE?
WELL, ONCE YOU PUT IT THAT WAY, I CAN'T SEE HOW SAYING NO DOES EITHER ONE OF US ONE LICK OF GOOD.

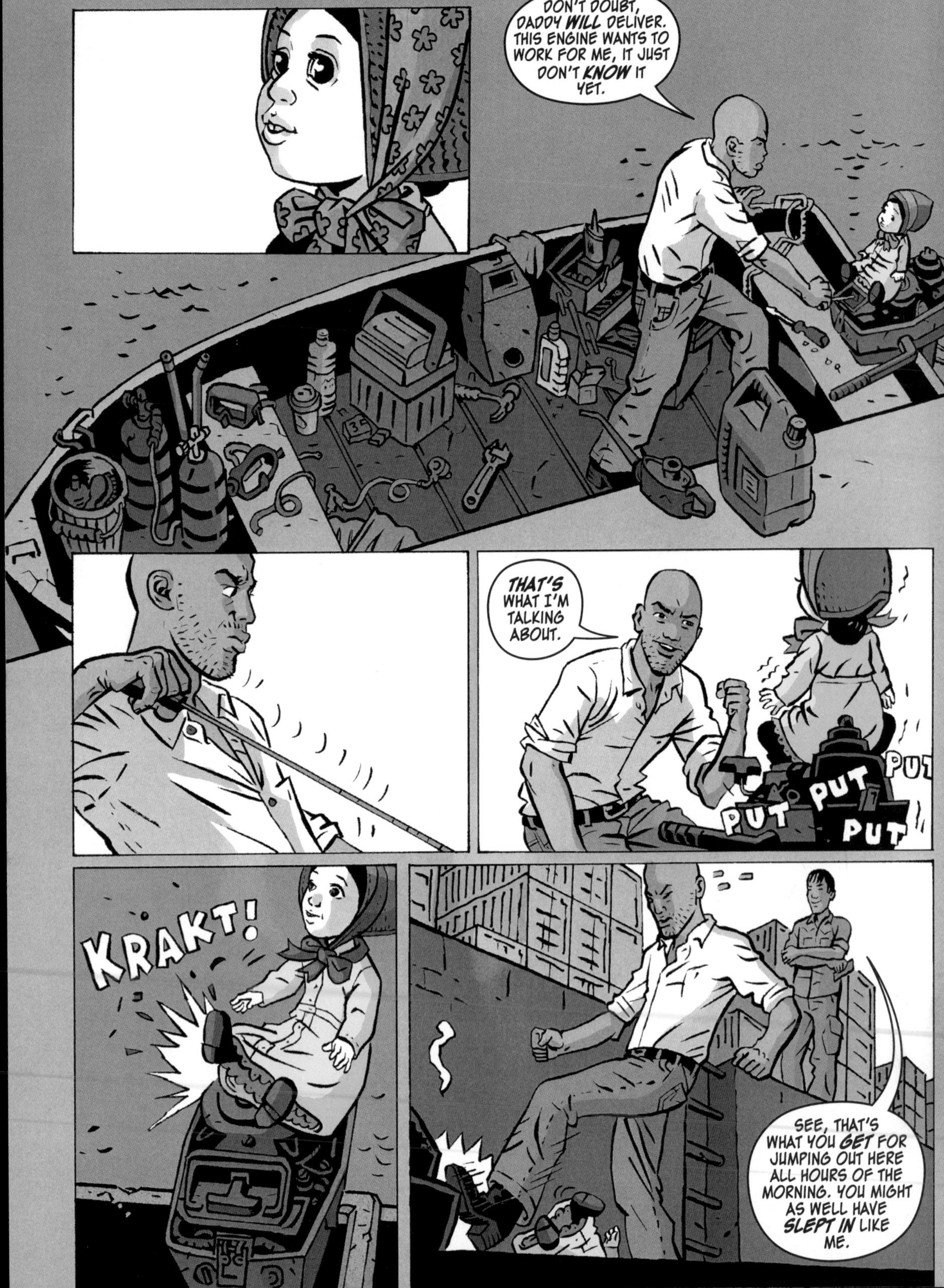
DON'T DOUBT, DADDY WILL DELIVER. THIS ENGINE WANTS TO WORK FOR ME, IT JUST DON'T KNOW IT YET.
THAT'S WHAT I'M TALKING ABOUT.
PUT PUT PUT PUT
KRAKT!
SEE, THAT'S WHAT YOU GET FOR JUMPING OUT HERE ALL HOURS OF THE MORNING. YOU MIGHT AS WELL HAVE SLEPT IN LIKE ME.

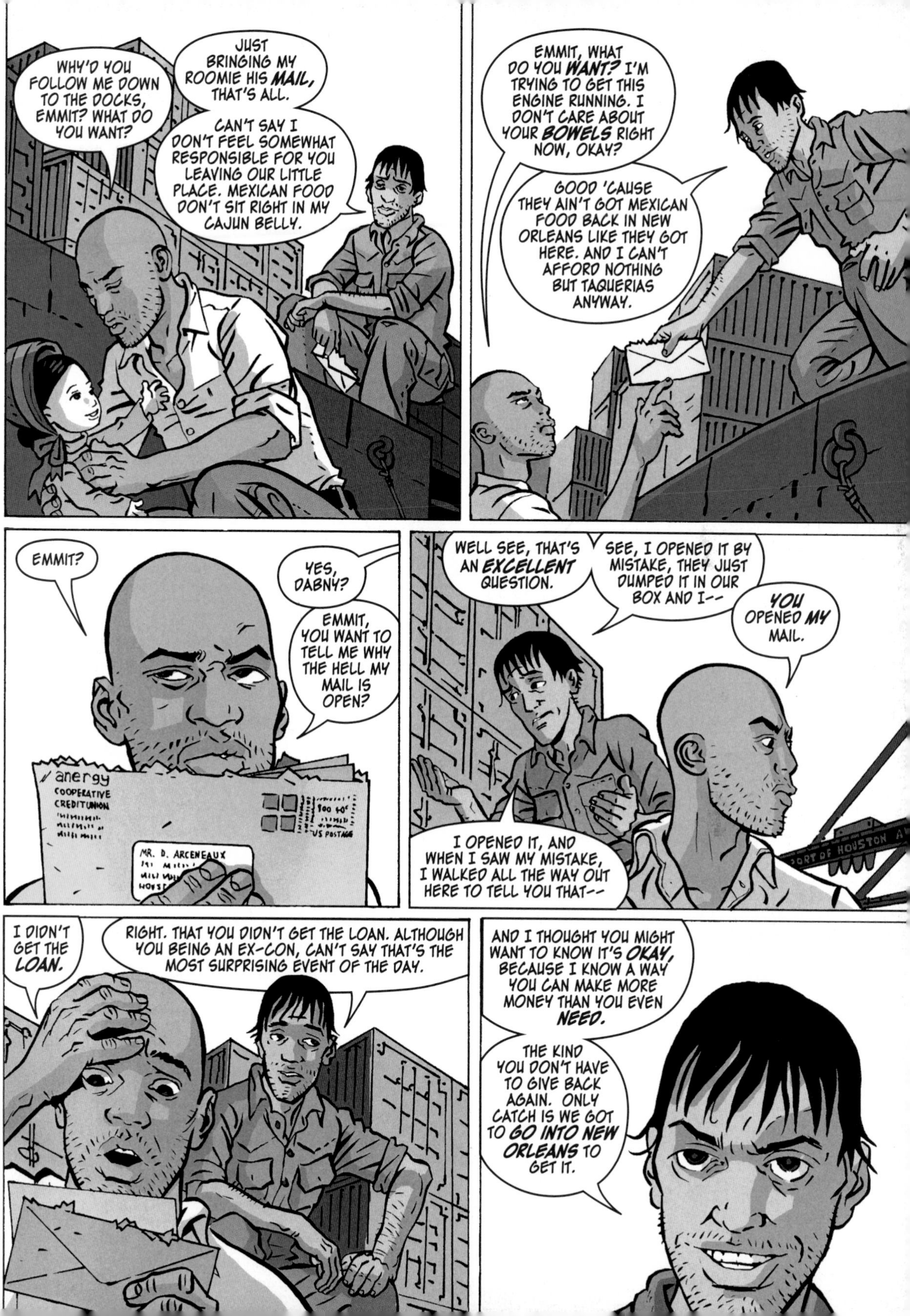
WHY'D YOU FOLLOW ME DOWN TO THE DOCKS, EMMIT? WHAT DO YOU WANT?
JUST BRINGING MY ROOMIE HIS MAIL, THAT'S ALL.
CAN'T SAY I DON'T FEEL SOMEWHAT RESPONSIBLE FOR YOU LEAVING OUR LITTLE PLACE. MEXICAN FOOD DON'T SIT RIGHT IN MY CAJUN BELLY.
EMMIT, WHAT DO YOU WANT? I'M TRYING TO GET THIS ENGINE RUNNING. I DON'T CARE ABOUT YOUR BOWELS RIGHT NOW, OKAY?
GOOD 'CAUSE THEY AIN'T GOT MEXICAN FOOD BACK IN NEW ORLEANS LIKE THEY GOT HERE. AND I CAN'T AFFORD NOTHING BUT TAQUERIAS ANYWAY.
EMMIT?
YES, DABNY?
EMMIT, YOU WANT TO TELL ME WHY THE HELL MY MAIL IS OPEN?
anergy
COOPERATIVE
CREDITUNION
US POSTAGE
MR. D. ARCENEAUX
WELL SEE, THAT'S AN EXCELLENT QUESTION.
SEE, I OPENED IT BY MISTAKE, THEY JUST DUMPED IT IN OUR BOX AND I--
YOU OPENED MY MAIL.
I OPENED IT, AND WHEN I SAW MY MISTAKE, I WALKED ALL THE WAY OUT HERE TO TELL YOU THAT--
PORT OF HOUSTON
I DIDN'T GET THE LOAN.
RIGHT. THAT YOU DIDN'T GET THE LOAN. ALTHOUGH YOU BEING AN EX-CON, CAN'T SAY THAT'S THE MOST SURPRISING EVENT OF THE DAY.
AND I THOUGHT YOU MIGHT WANT TO KNOW IT'S OKAY, BECAUSE I KNOW A WAY YOU CAN MAKE MORE MONEY THAN YOU EVEN NEED.
THE KIND YOU DON'T HAVE TO GIVE BACK AGAIN. ONLY CATCH IS WE GOT TO GO INTO NEW ORLEANS TO GET IT.

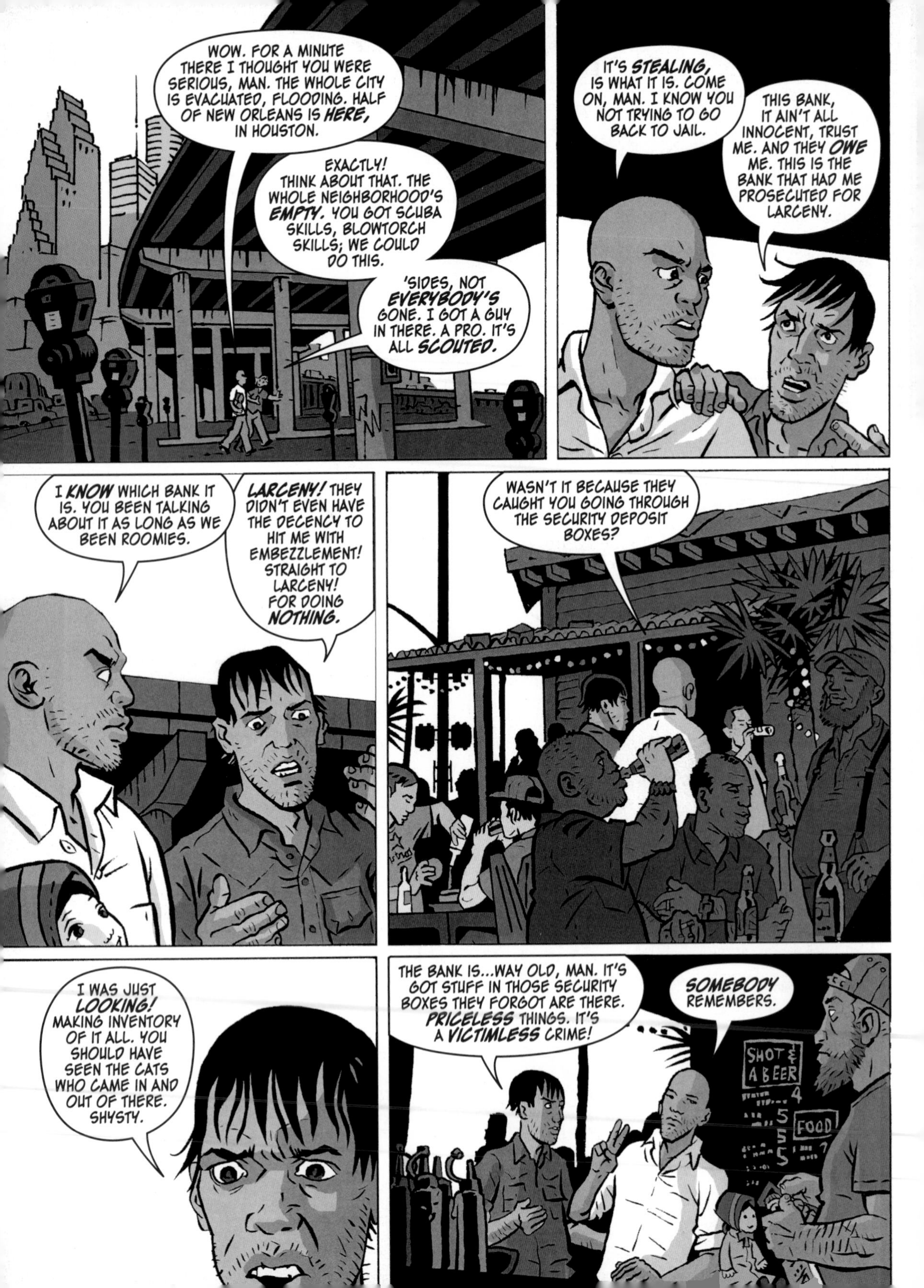
WOW. FOR A MINUTE THERE I THOUGHT YOU WERE SERIOUS, MAN. THE WHOLE CITY IS EVACUATED, FLOODING. HALF OF NEW ORLEANS IS HERE, IN HOUSTON.
EXACTLY! THINK ABOUT THAT. THE WHOLE NEIGHBORHOOD'S EMPTY. YOU GOT SCUBA SKILLS, BLOWTORCH SKILLS; WE COULD DO THIS.
'SIDES, NOT EVERYBODY'S GONE. I GOT A GUY IN THERE. A PRO. IT'S ALL SCOUTED.
IT'S STEALING, IS WHAT IT IS. COME ON, MAN. I KNOW YOU NOT TRYING TO GO BACK TO JAIL.
THIS BANK, IT AIN'T ALL INNOCENT, TRUST ME. AND THEY OWE ME. THIS IS THE BANK THAT HAD ME PROSECUTED FOR LARCENY.
I KNOW WHICH BANK IT IS. YOU BEEN TALKING ABOUT IT AS LONG AS WE BEEN ROOMIES.
LARCENY! THEY DIDN'T EVEN HAVE THE DECENCY TO HIT ME WITH EMBEZZLEMENT! STRAIGHT TO LARCENY! FOR DOING NOTHING.
WASN'T IT BECAUSE THEY CAUGHT YOU GOING THROUGH THE SECURITY DEPOSIT BOXES?
I WAS JUST LOOKING! MAKING INVENTORY OF IT ALL. YOU SHOULD HAVE SEEN THE CATS WHO CAME IN AND OUT OF THERE. SHYSTY.
THE BANK IS...WAY OLD, MAN. IT'S GOT STUFF IN THOSE SECURITY BOXES THEY FORGOT ARE THERE. PRICELESS THINGS. IT'S A VICTIMLESS CRIME!
SOMEBODY REMEMBERS.
SHOT & A BEER
FOOD

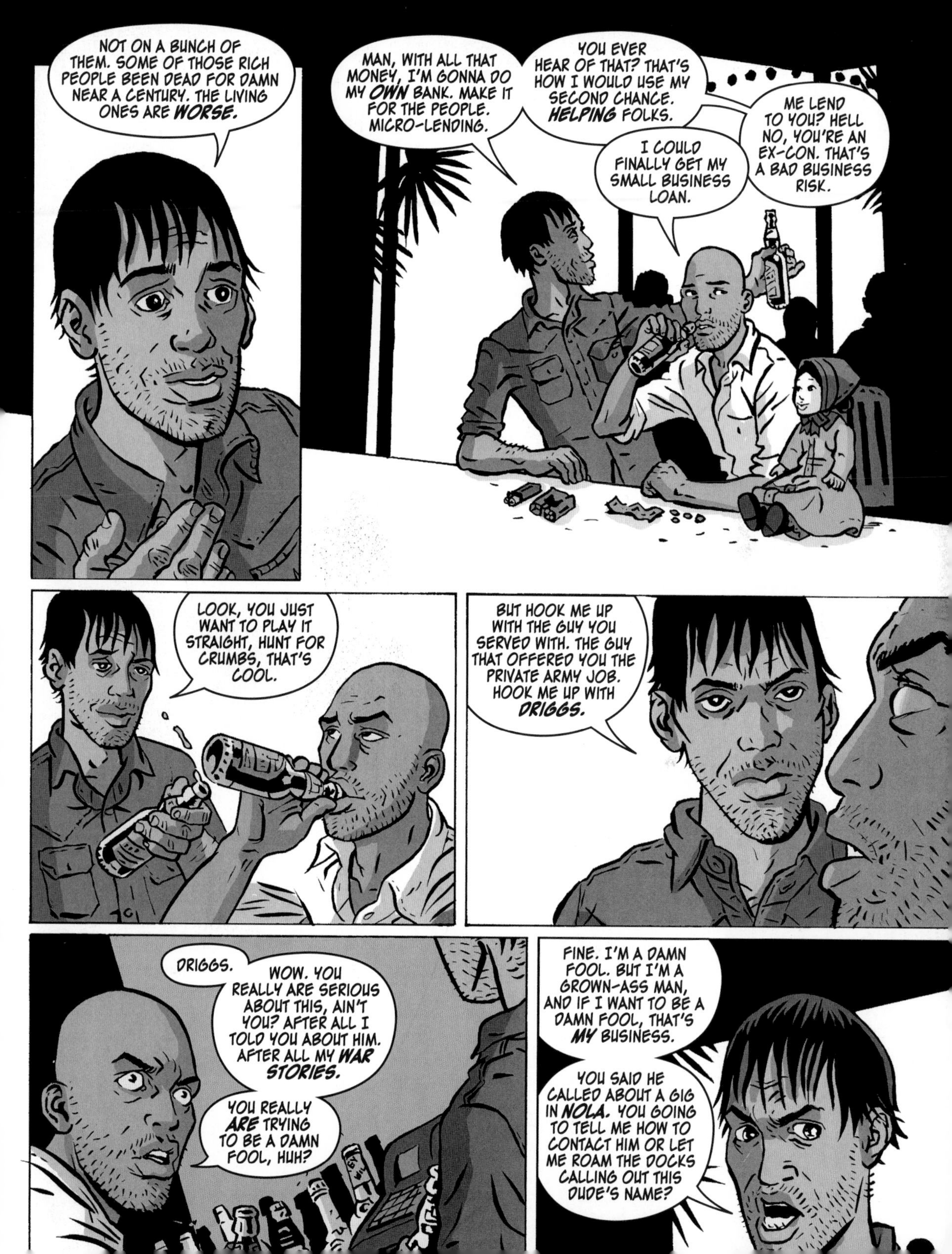
NOT ON A BUNCH OF THEM. SOME OF THOSE RICH PEOPLE BEEN DEAD FOR DAMN NEAR A CENTURY. THE LIVING ONES ARE *WORSE.*
MAN, WITH ALL THAT MONEY, I'M GONNA DO MY *OWN* BANK. MAKE IT FOR THE PEOPLE. MICRO-LENDING.
YOU EVER HEAR OF THAT? THAT'S HOW I WOULD USE MY SECOND CHANCE. *HELPING* FOLKS.
I COULD FINALLY GET MY SMALL BUSINESS LOAN.
ME LEND TO YOU? HELL NO, YOU'RE AN EX-CON. THAT'S A BAD BUSINESS RISK.
LOOK, YOU JUST WANT TO PLAY IT STRAIGHT, HUNT FOR CRUMBS, THAT'S COOL.
BUT HOOK ME UP WITH THE GUY YOU SERVED WITH. THE GUY THAT OFFERED YOU THE PRIVATE ARMY JOB. HOOK ME UP WITH *DRIGGS.*
DRIGGS.
WOW. YOU REALLY ARE SERIOUS ABOUT THIS, AIN'T YOU? AFTER ALL I TOLD YOU ABOUT HIM. AFTER ALL MY *WAR STORIES.*
YOU REALLY *ARE* TRYING TO BE A DAMN FOOL, HUH?
FINE. I'M A DAMN FOOL. BUT I'M A GROWN-ASS MAN, AND IF I WANT TO BE A DAMN FOOL, THAT'S *MY* BUSINESS.
YOU SAID HE CALLED ABOUT A GIG IN *NOLA.* YOU GOING TO TELL ME HOW TO CONTACT HIM OR LET ME ROAM THE DOCKS CALLING OUT THIS DUDE'S NAME?

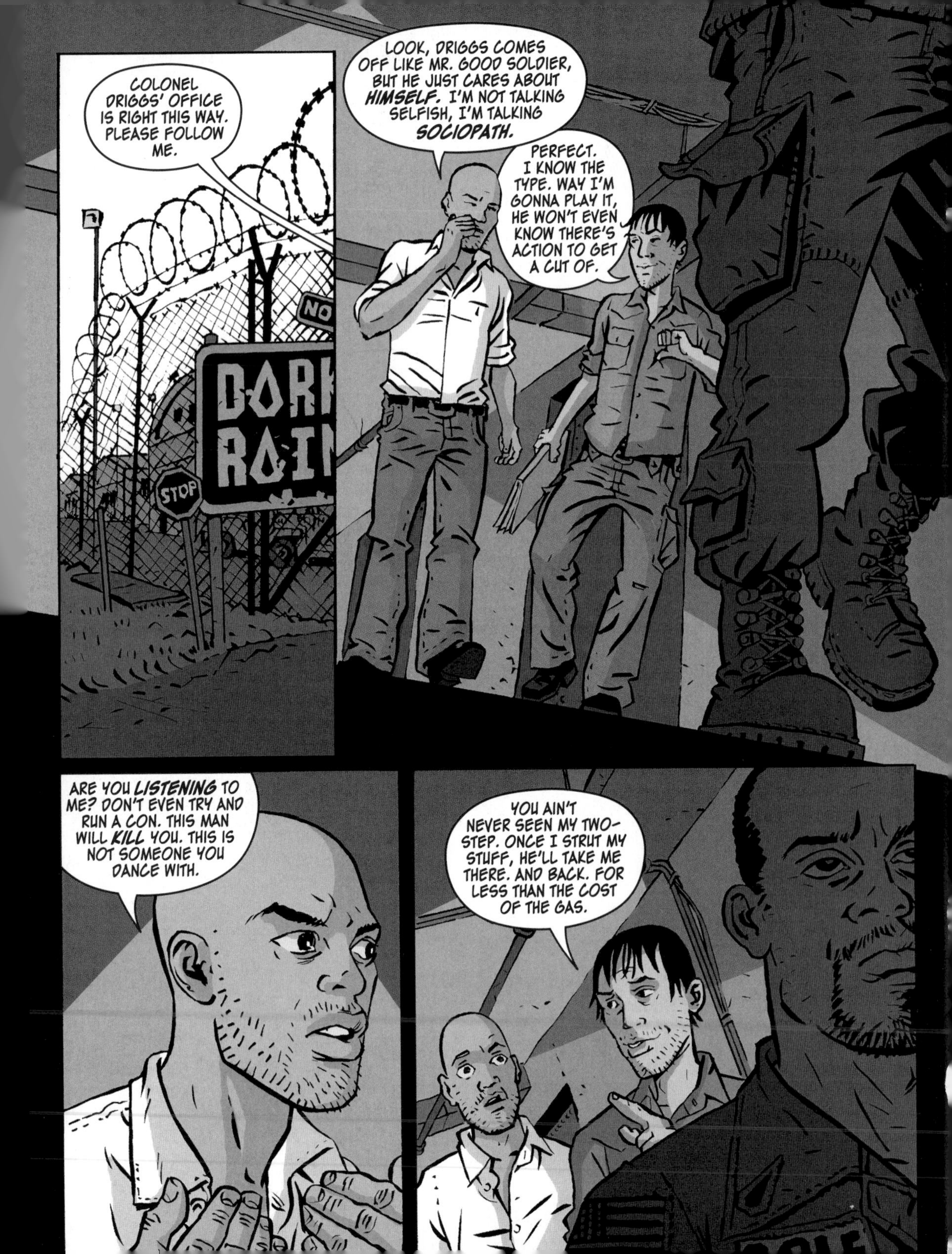
COLONEL DRIGGS' OFFICE IS RIGHT THIS WAY. PLEASE FOLLOW ME.
NO
DARK RAIN
STOP
LOOK, DRIGGS COMES OFF LIKE MR. GOOD SOLDIER, BUT HE JUST CARES ABOUT HIMSELF. I'M NOT TALKING SELFISH, I'M TALKING SOCIOPATH.
PERFECT. I KNOW THE TYPE. WAY I'M GONNA PLAY IT, HE WON'T EVEN KNOW THERE'S ACTION TO GET A CUT OF.
ARE YOU LISTENING TO ME? DON'T EVEN TRY AND RUN A CON. THIS MAN WILL KILL YOU. THIS IS NOT SOMEONE YOU DANCE WITH.
YOU AIN'T NEVER SEEN MY TWO-STEP. ONCE I STRUT MY STUFF, HE'LL TAKE ME THERE. AND BACK. FOR LESS THAN THE COST OF THE GAS.

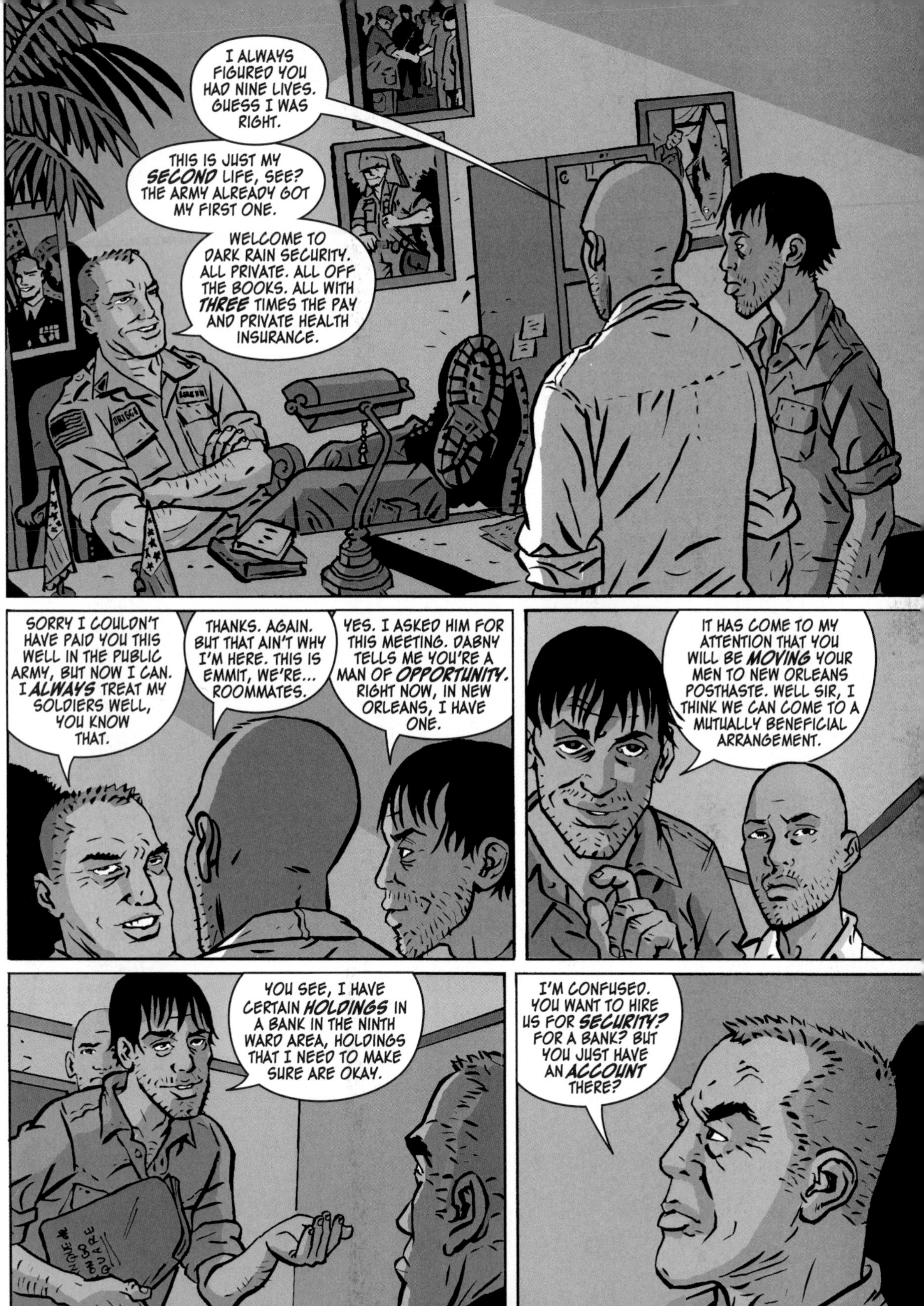
I ALWAYS FIGURED YOU HAD NINE LIVES. GUESS I WAS RIGHT.
THIS IS JUST MY SECOND LIFE, SEE? THE ARMY ALREADY GOT MY FIRST ONE.
WELCOME TO DARK RAIN SECURITY. ALL PRIVATE. ALL OFF THE BOOKS. ALL WITH THREE TIMES THE PAY AND PRIVATE HEALTH INSURANCE.
SORRY I COULDN'T HAVE PAID YOU THIS WELL IN THE PUBLIC ARMY, BUT NOW I CAN. I ALWAYS TREAT MY SOLDIERS WELL, YOU KNOW THAT.
THANKS. AGAIN. BUT THAT AIN'T WHY I'M HERE. THIS IS EMMIT, WE'RE... ROOMMATES.
YES. I ASKED HIM FOR THIS MEETING. DABNY TELLS ME YOU'RE A MAN OF OPPORTUNITY. RIGHT NOW, IN NEW ORLEANS, I HAVE ONE.
IT HAS COME TO MY ATTENTION THAT YOU WILL BE MOVING YOUR MEN TO NEW ORLEANS POSTHASTE. WELL SIR, I THINK WE CAN COME TO A MUTUALLY BENEFICIAL ARRANGEMENT.
YOU SEE, I HAVE CERTAIN HOLDINGS IN A BANK IN THE NINTH WARD AREA, HOLDINGS THAT I NEED TO MAKE SURE ARE OKAY.
I'M CONFUSED. YOU WANT TO HIRE US FOR SECURITY? FOR A BANK? BUT YOU JUST HAVE AN ACCOUNT THERE?

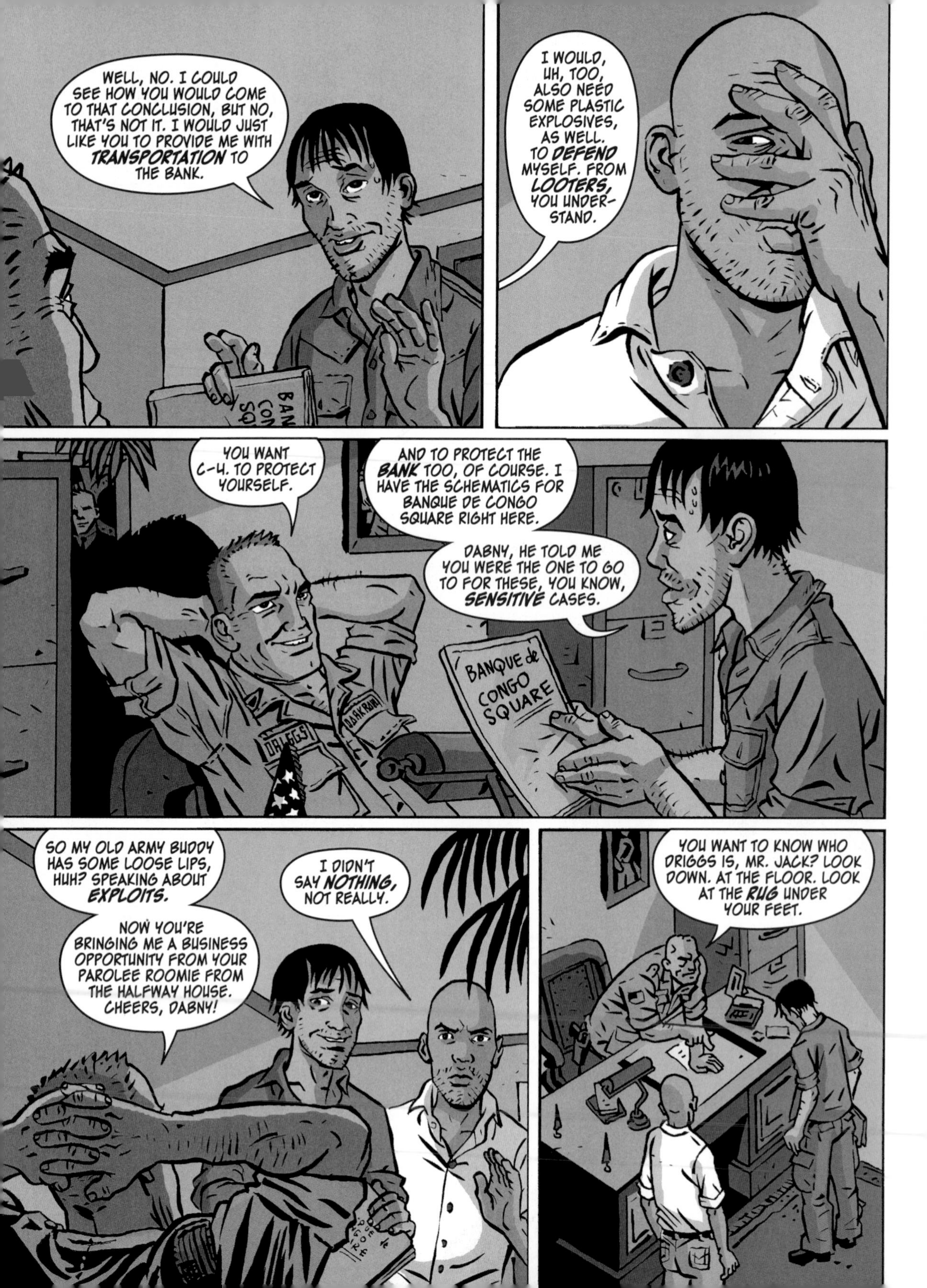
WELL, NO. I COULD SEE HOW YOU WOULD COME TO THAT CONCLUSION, BUT NO, THAT'S NOT IT. I WOULD JUST LIKE YOU TO PROVIDE ME WITH TRANSPORTATION TO THE BANK.
I WOULD, UH, TOO, ALSO NEED SOME PLASTIC EXPLOSIVES, AS WELL. TO DEFEND MYSELF. FROM LOOTERS, YOU UNDER-STAND.
YOU WANT C-4. TO PROTECT YOURSELF.
AND TO PROTECT THE BANK TOO, OF COURSE. I HAVE THE SCHEMATICS FOR BANQUE DE CONGO SQUARE RIGHT HERE.
DABNY, HE TOLD ME YOU WERE THE ONE TO GO TO FOR THESE, YOU KNOW, SENSITIVE CASES.
BANQUE de CONGO SQUARE
DRIGGS
SO MY OLD ARMY BUDDY HAS SOME LOOSE LIPS, HUH? SPEAKING ABOUT EXPLOITS.
NOW YOU'RE BRINGING ME A BUSINESS OPPORTUNITY FROM YOUR PAROLEE ROOMIE FROM THE HALFWAY HOUSE. CHEERS, DABNY!
I DIDN'T SAY NOTHING, NOT REALLY.
YOU WANT TO KNOW WHO DRIGGS IS, MR. JACK? LOOK DOWN. AT THE FLOOR. LOOK AT THE RUG UNDER YOUR FEET.

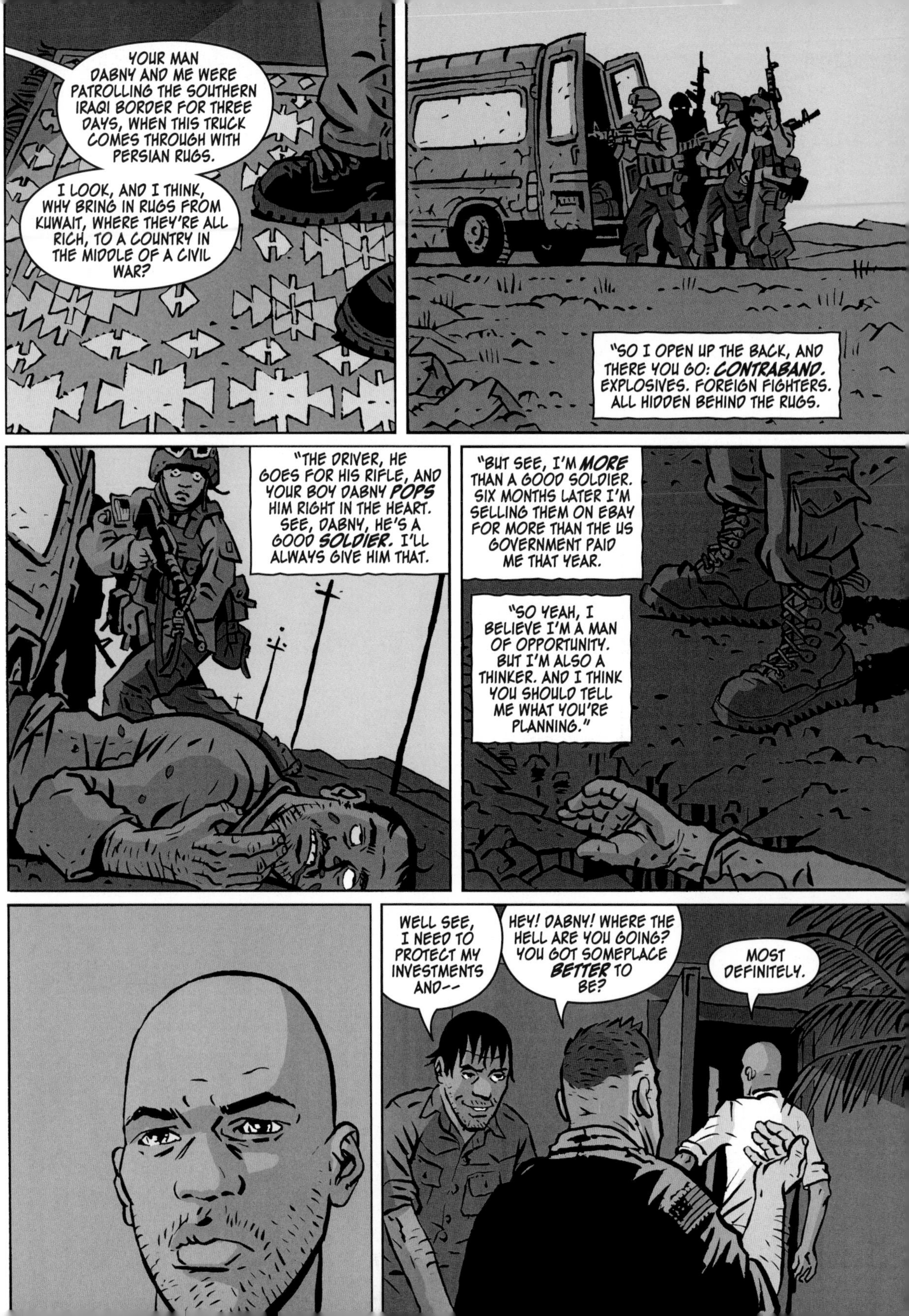
YOUR MAN DABNY AND ME WERE PATROLLING THE SOUTHERN IRAQI BORDER FOR THREE DAYS, WHEN THIS TRUCK COMES THROUGH WITH PERSIAN RUGS.
I LOOK, AND I THINK, WHY BRING IN RUGS FROM KUWAIT, WHERE THEY'RE ALL RICH, TO A COUNTRY IN THE MIDDLE OF A CIVIL WAR?
"SO I OPEN UP THE BACK, AND THERE YOU GO: CONTRABAND. EXPLOSIVES. FOREIGN FIGHTERS. ALL HIDDEN BEHIND THE RUGS.
"THE DRIVER, HE GOES FOR HIS RIFLE, AND YOUR BOY DABNY POPS HIM RIGHT IN THE HEART. SEE, DABNY, HE'S A GOOD SOLDIER. I'LL ALWAYS GIVE HIM THAT.
"BUT SEE, I'M MORE THAN A GOOD SOLDIER. SIX MONTHS LATER I'M SELLING THEM ON EBAY FOR MORE THAN THE US GOVERNMENT PAID ME THAT YEAR.
"SO YEAH, I BELIEVE I'M A MAN OF OPPORTUNITY. BUT I'M ALSO A THINKER. AND I THINK YOU SHOULD TELL ME WHAT YOU'RE PLANNING."
WELL SEE, I NEED TO PROTECT MY INVESTMENTS AND--
HEY! DABNY! WHERE THE HELL ARE YOU GOING? YOU GOT SOMEPLACE BETTER TO BE?
MOST DEFINITELY.

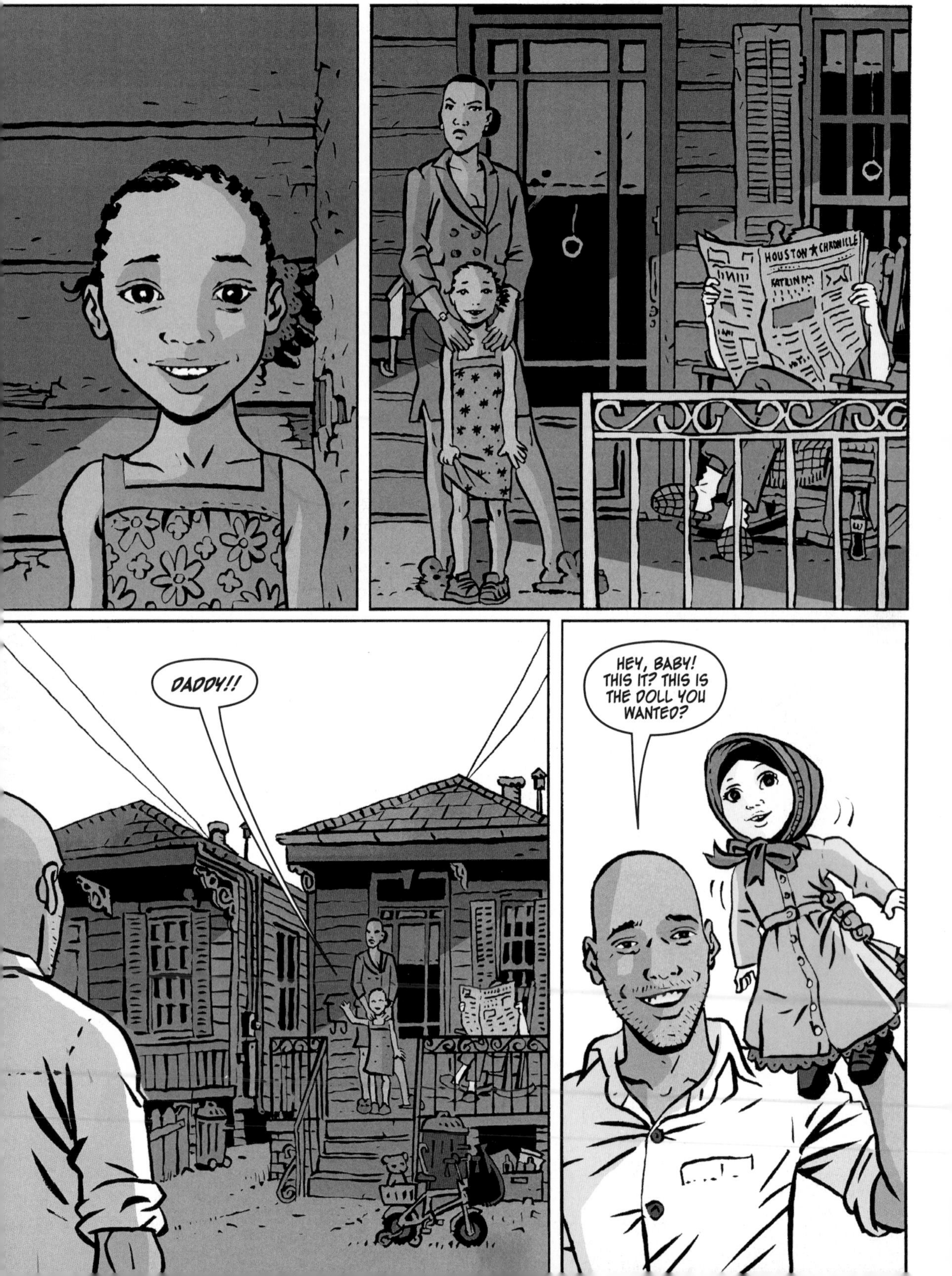
HOUSTON ★ CHRONICLE
DADDY!!
HEY, BABY! THIS IT? THIS IS THE DOLL YOU WANTED?

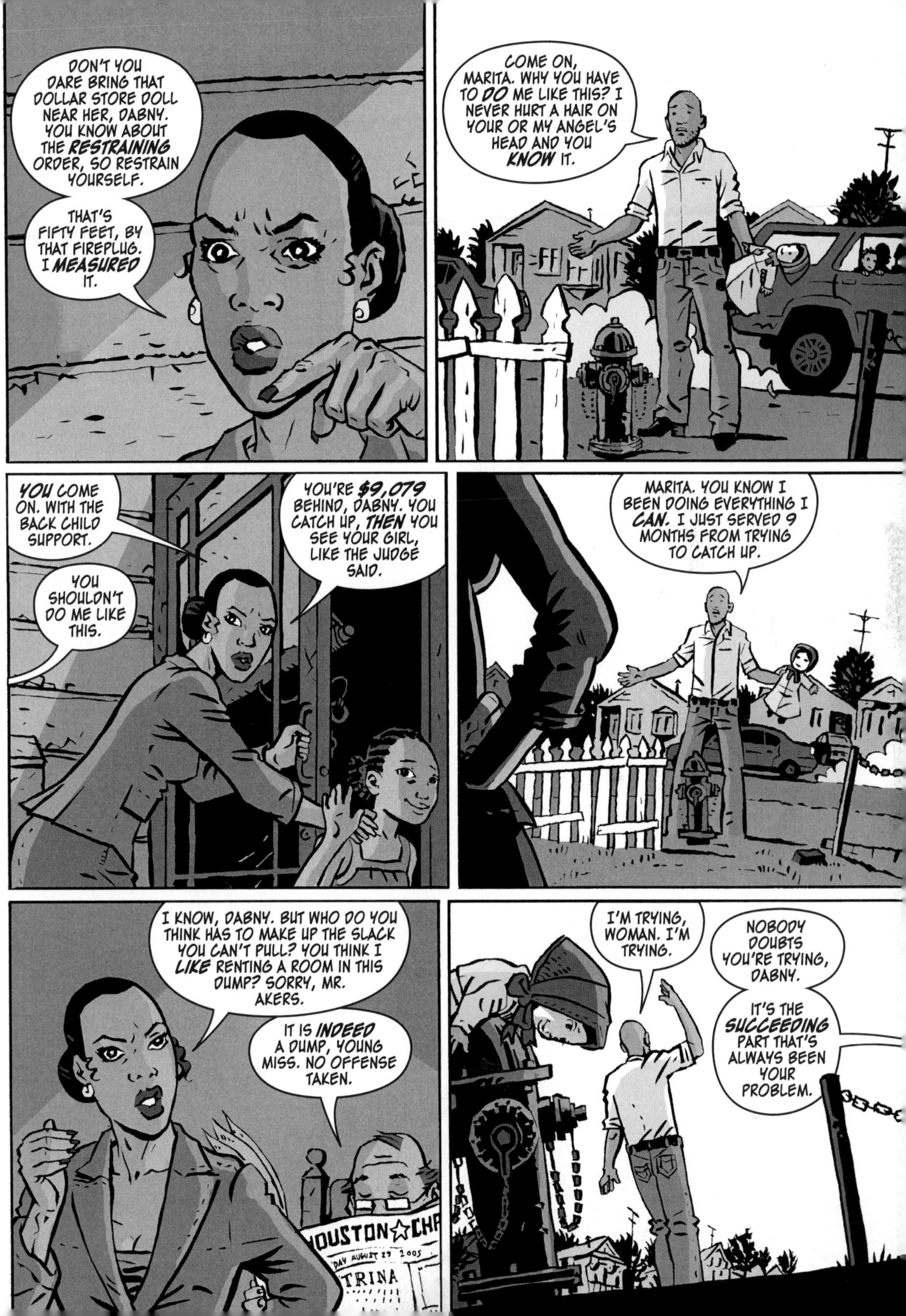
DON'T YOU DARE BRING THAT DOLLAR STORE DOLL NEAR HER, DABNY. YOU KNOW ABOUT THE RESTRAINING ORDER, SO RESTRAIN YOURSELF.
THAT'S FIFTY FEET, BY THAT FIREPLUG. I MEASURED IT.
COME ON, MARITA. WHY YOU HAVE TO DO ME LIKE THIS? I NEVER HURT A HAIR ON YOUR OR MY ANGEL'S HEAD AND YOU KNOW IT.
YOU COME ON. WITH THE BACK CHILD SUPPORT.
YOU SHOULDN'T DO ME LIKE THIS.
YOU'RE $9,079 BEHIND, DABNY. YOU CATCH UP, THEN YOU SEE YOUR GIRL, LIKE THE JUDGE SAID.
MARITA. YOU KNOW I BEEN DOING EVERYTHING I CAN. I JUST SERVED 9 MONTHS FROM TRYING TO CATCH UP.
I KNOW, DABNY. BUT WHO DO YOU THINK HAS TO MAKE UP THE SLACK YOU CAN'T PULL? YOU THINK I LIKE RENTING A ROOM IN THIS DUMP? SORRY, MR. AKERS.
IT IS INDEED A DUMP, YOUNG MISS. NO OFFENSE TAKEN.
HOUSTON CH
DAY AUGUST 29 2005
TRINA
I'M TRYING, WOMAN. I'M TRYING.
NOBODY DOUBTS YOU'RE TRYING, DABNY.
IT'S THE SUCCEEDING PART THAT'S ALWAYS BEEN YOUR PROBLEM.

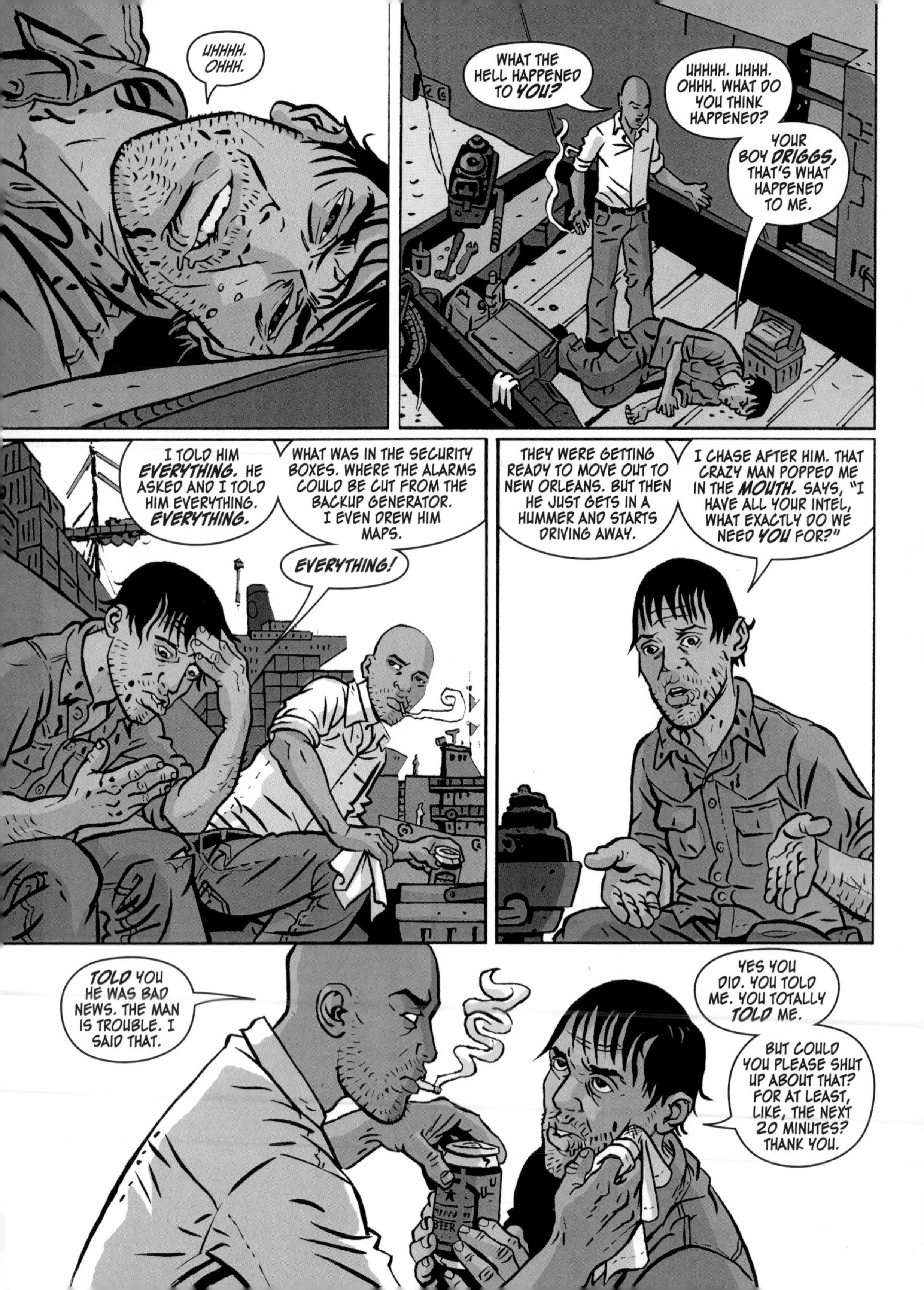
UHHHH. OHHH.
WHAT THE HELL HAPPENED TO YOU?
UHHHH. UHHH. OHHH. WHAT DO YOU THINK HAPPENED?
YOUR BOY DRIGGS, THAT'S WHAT HAPPENED TO ME.
I TOLD HIM EVERYTHING. HE ASKED AND I TOLD HIM EVERYTHING. EVERYTHING.
WHAT WAS IN THE SECURITY BOXES. WHERE THE ALARMS COULD BE CUT FROM THE BACKUP GENERATOR. I EVEN DREW HIM MAPS.
EVERYTHING!
THEY WERE GETTING READY TO MOVE OUT TO NEW ORLEANS. BUT THEN HE JUST GETS IN A HUMMER AND STARTS DRIVING AWAY.
I CHASE AFTER HIM. THAT CRAZY MAN POPPED ME IN THE MOUTH. SAYS, "I HAVE ALL YOUR INTEL, WHAT EXACTLY DO WE NEED YOU FOR?"
TOLD YOU HE WAS BAD NEWS. THE MAN IS TROUBLE. I SAID THAT.
YES YOU DID. YOU TOLD ME. YOU TOTALLY TOLD ME.
BUT COULD YOU PLEASE SHUT UP ABOUT THAT? FOR AT LEAST, LIKE, THE NEXT 20 MINUTES? THANK YOU.
BEER

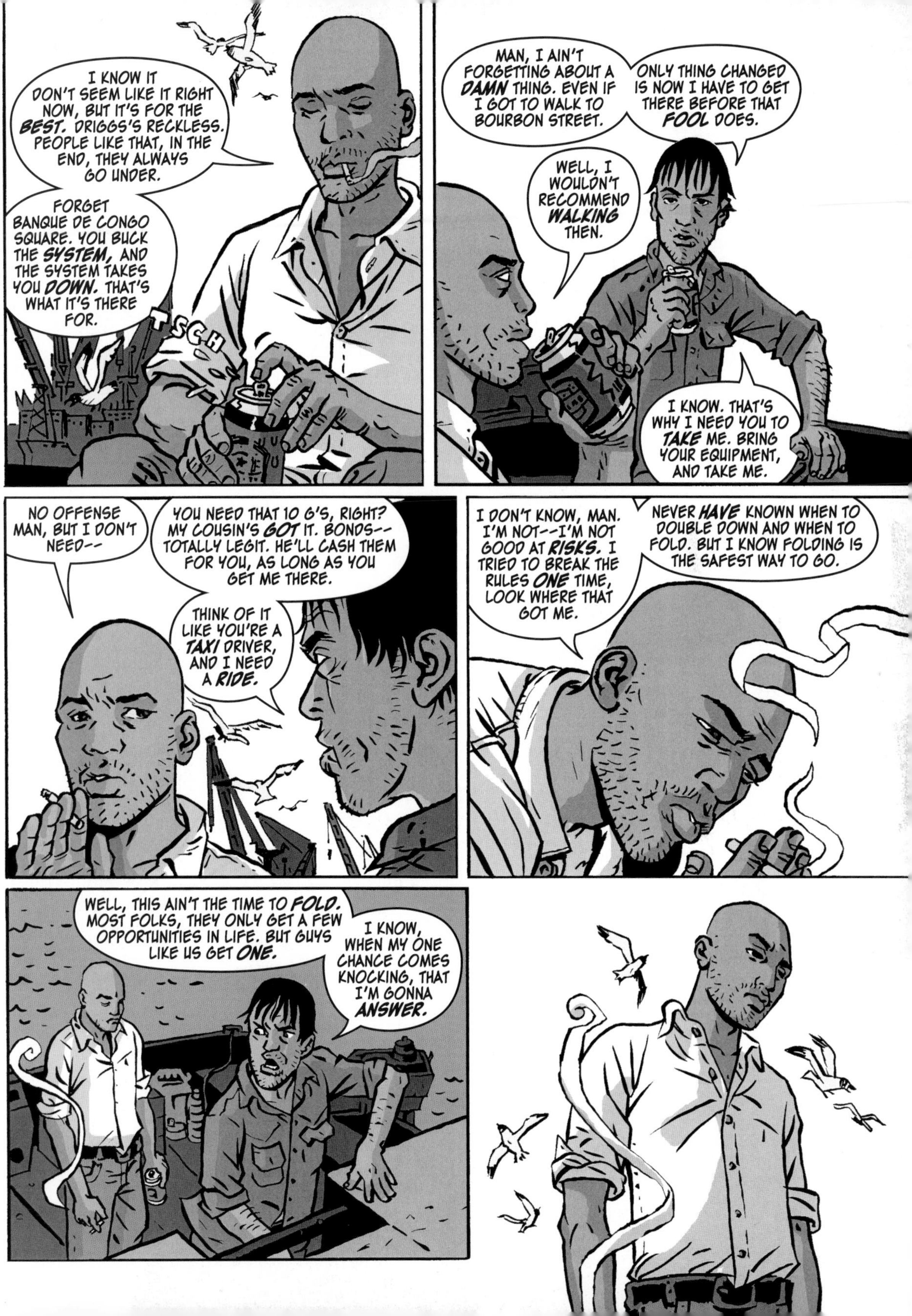
I KNOW IT DON'T SEEM LIKE IT RIGHT NOW, BUT IT'S FOR THE BEST. DRIGGS'S RECKLESS. PEOPLE LIKE THAT, IN THE END, THEY ALWAYS GO UNDER.
FORGET BANQUE DE CONGO SQUARE. YOU BUCK THE SYSTEM, AND THE SYSTEM TAKES YOU DOWN. THAT'S WHAT IT'S THERE FOR.
TSCH
MAN, I AIN'T FORGETTING ABOUT A DAMN THING. EVEN IF I GOT TO WALK TO BOURBON STREET.
ONLY THING CHANGED IS NOW I HAVE TO GET THERE BEFORE THAT FOOL DOES.
WELL, I WOULDN'T RECOMMEND WALKING THEN.
I KNOW. THAT'S WHY I NEED YOU TO TAKE ME. BRING YOUR EQUIPMENT, AND TAKE ME.
NO OFFENSE MAN, BUT I DON'T NEED--
YOU NEED THAT 10 G'S, RIGHT? MY COUSIN'S GOT IT. BONDS--TOTALLY LEGIT. HE'LL CASH THEM FOR YOU, AS LONG AS YOU GET ME THERE.
THINK OF IT LIKE YOU'RE A TAXI DRIVER, AND I NEED A RIDE.
I DON'T KNOW, MAN. I'M NOT--I'M NOT GOOD AT RISKS. I TRIED TO BREAK THE RULES ONE TIME, LOOK WHERE THAT GOT ME.
NEVER HAVE KNOWN WHEN TO DOUBLE DOWN AND WHEN TO FOLD. BUT I KNOW FOLDING IS THE SAFEST WAY TO GO.
WELL, THIS AIN'T THE TIME TO FOLD. MOST FOLKS, THEY ONLY GET A FEW OPPORTUNITIES IN LIFE. BUT GUYS LIKE US GET ONE.
I KNOW, WHEN MY ONE CHANCE COMES KNOCKING, THAT I'M GONNA ANSWER.

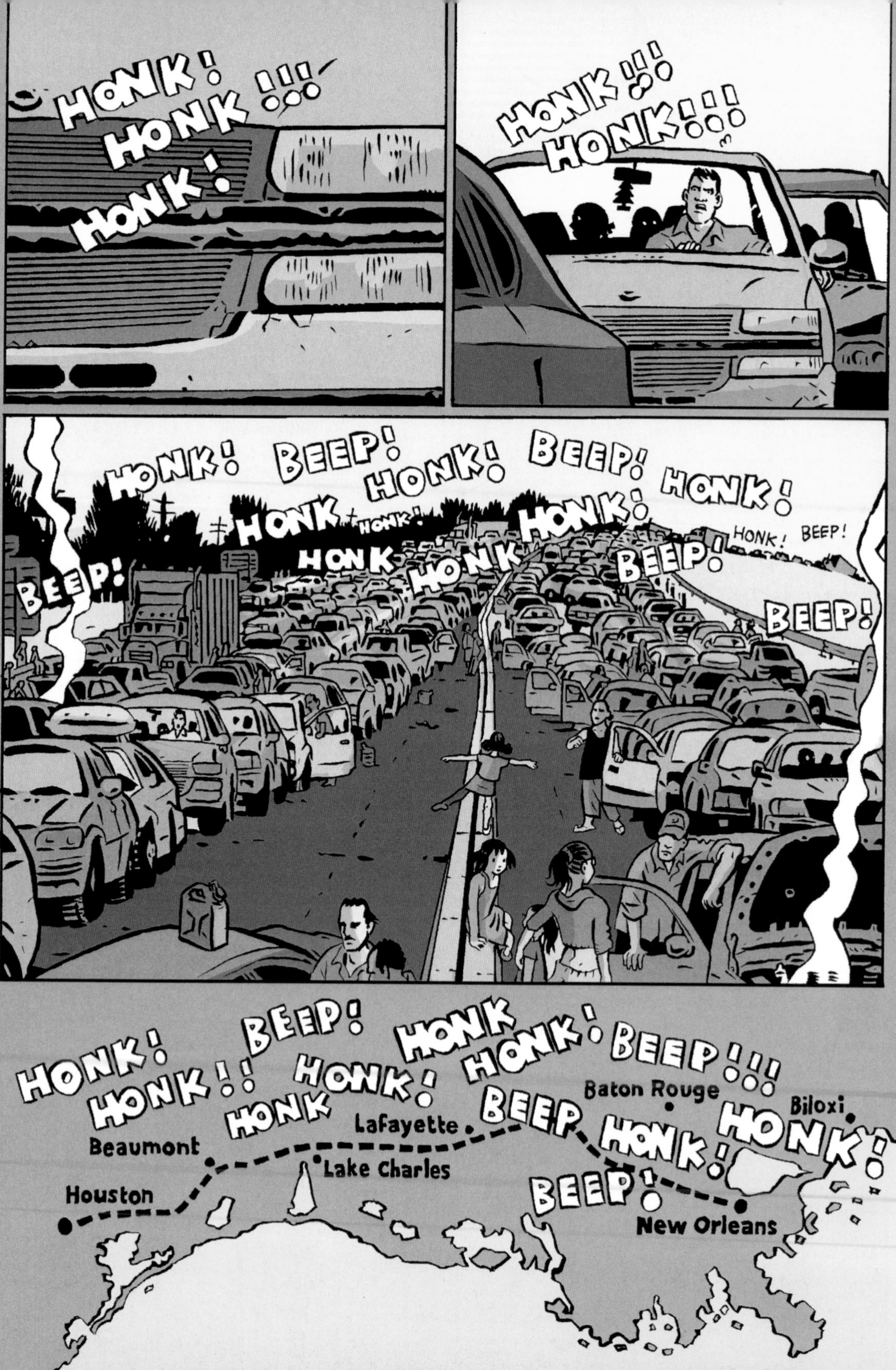
HONK!
HONK!!!
HONK!
HONK!!!
HONK!!!
HONK! BEEP! HONK! BEEP! HONK!
HONK HONK! HONK! HONK HONK
BEEP! BEEP! HONK! BEEP! BEEP!
HONK! BEEP! HONK HONK! BEEP!!!
HONK!! HONK! HONK! HONK
BEEP HONK! HONK! BEEP!
Houston
Beaumont
Lake Charles
Lafayette
Baton Rouge
Biloxi
New Orleans

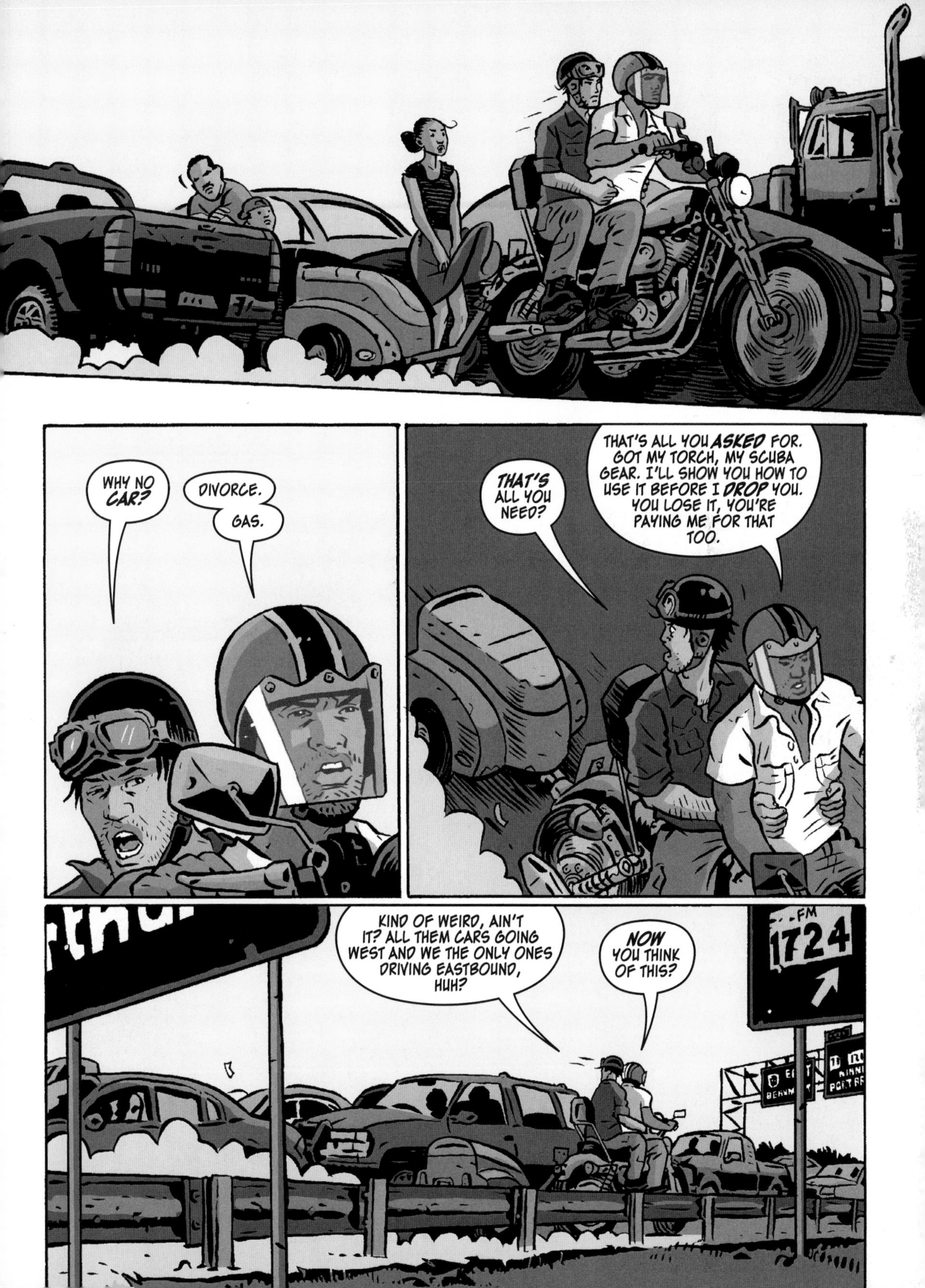
WHY NO CAR?
DIVORCE.
GAS.
THAT'S ALL YOU NEED?
THAT'S ALL YOU ASKED FOR. GOT MY TORCH, MY SCUBA GEAR. I'LL SHOW YOU HOW TO USE IT BEFORE I DROP YOU. YOU LOSE IT, YOU'RE PAYING ME FOR THAT TOO.
KIND OF WEIRD, AIN'T IT? ALL THEM CARS GOING WEST AND WE THE ONLY ONES DRIVING EASTBOUND, HUH?
NOW YOU THINK OF THIS?
FM
1724

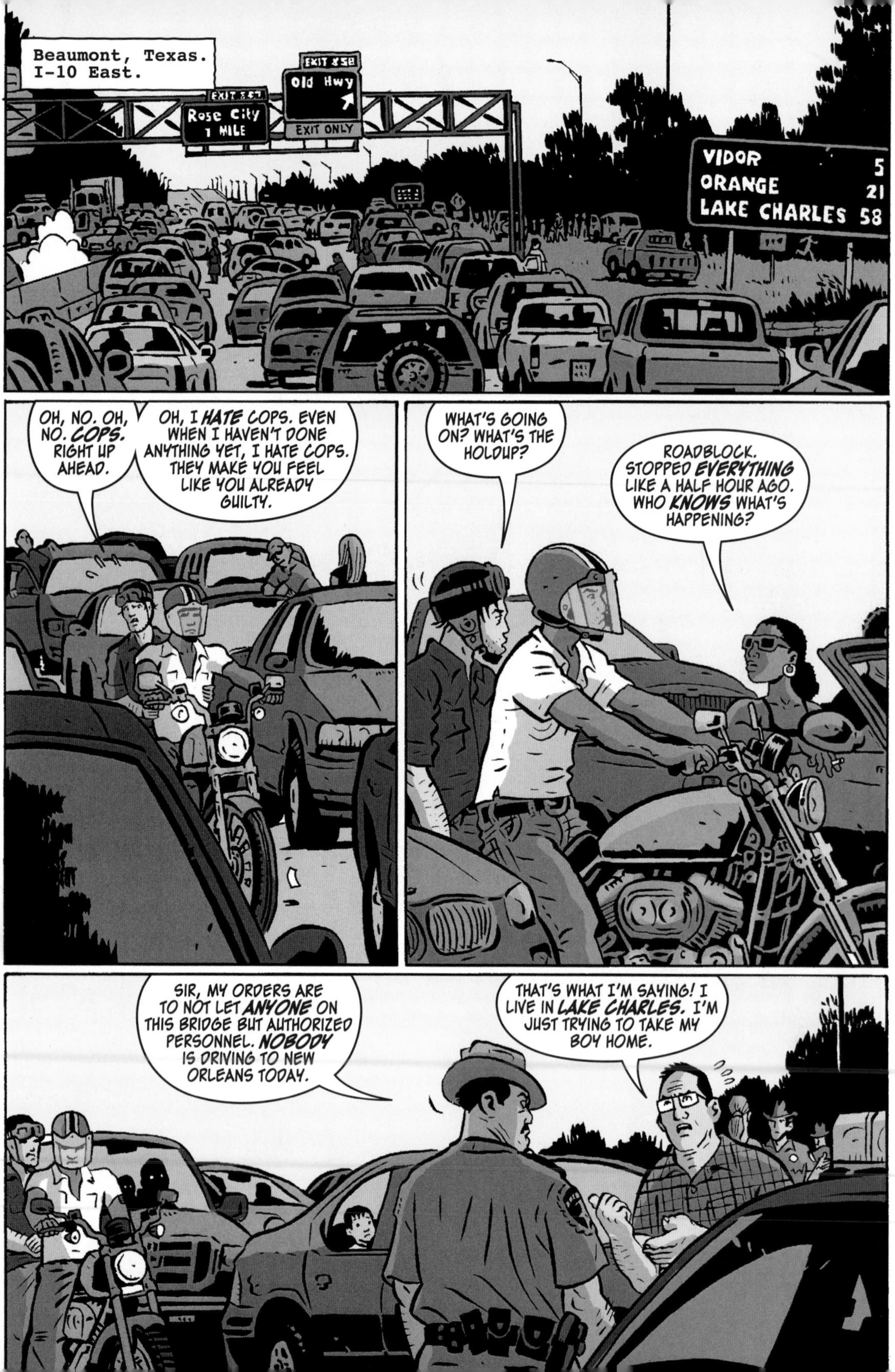
Beaumont, Texas. I-10 East.
EXIT 857
Rose City 1 MILE
EXIT 858
Old Hwy
EXIT ONLY
VIDOR 5
ORANGE 21
LAKE CHARLES 58
OH, NO. OH, NO. COPS. RIGHT UP AHEAD.
OH, I HATE COPS. EVEN WHEN I HAVEN'T DONE ANYTHING YET, I HATE COPS. THEY MAKE YOU FEEL LIKE YOU ALREADY GUILTY.
WHAT'S GOING ON? WHAT'S THE HOLDUP?
ROADBLOCK. STOPPED EVERYTHING LIKE A HALF HOUR AGO. WHO KNOWS WHAT'S HAPPENING?
SIR, MY ORDERS ARE TO NOT LET ANYONE ON THIS BRIDGE BUT AUTHORIZED PERSONNEL. NOBODY IS DRIVING TO NEW ORLEANS TODAY.
THAT'S WHAT I'M SAYING! I LIVE IN LAKE CHARLES. I'M JUST TRYING TO TAKE MY BOY HOME.

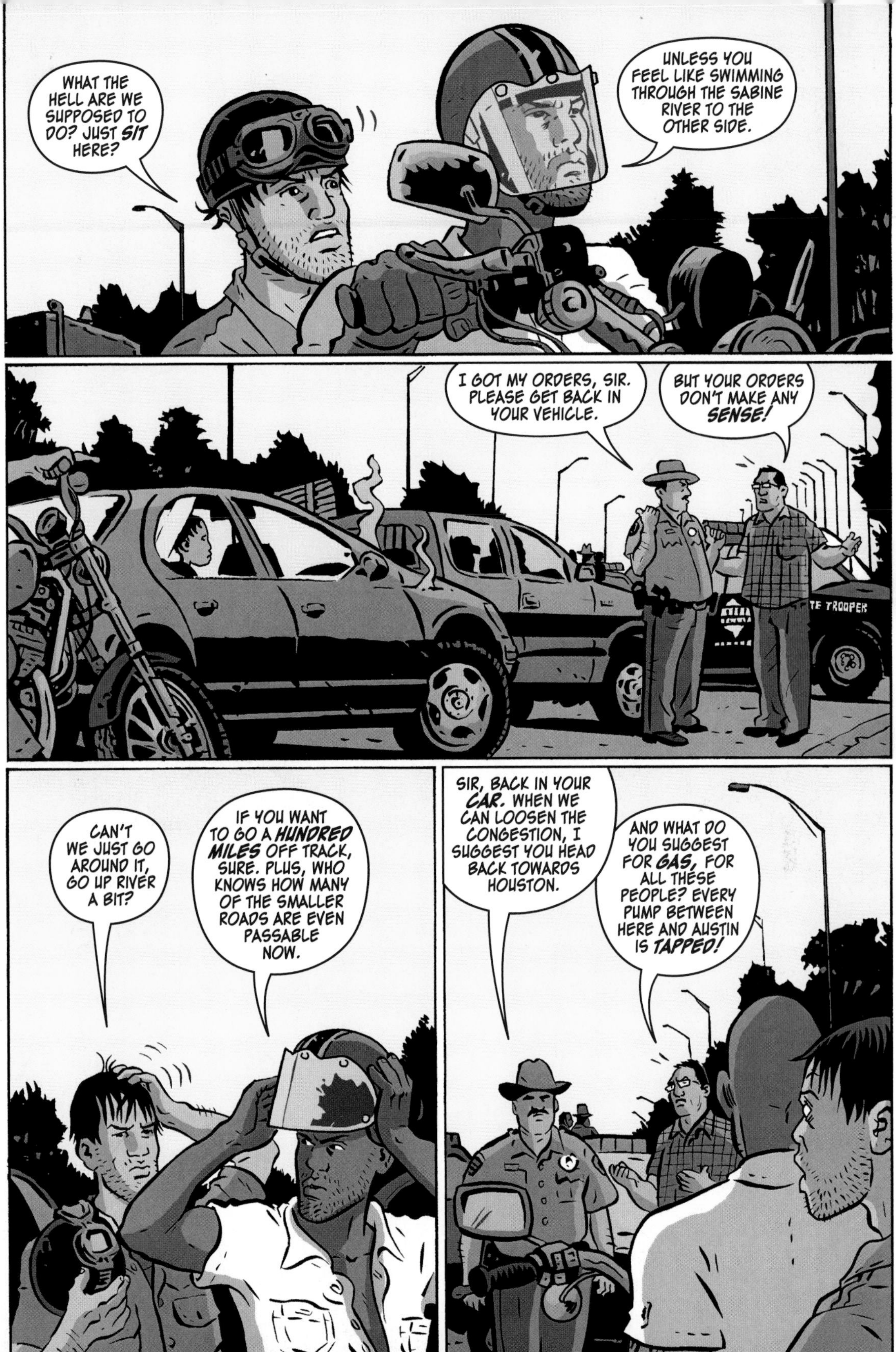
WHAT THE HELL ARE WE SUPPOSED TO DO? JUST SIT HERE?
UNLESS YOU FEEL LIKE SWIMMING THROUGH THE SABINE RIVER TO THE OTHER SIDE.
I GOT MY ORDERS, SIR. PLEASE GET BACK IN YOUR VEHICLE.
BUT YOUR ORDERS DON'T MAKE ANY SENSE!
TE TROOPER
CAN'T WE JUST GO AROUND IT, GO UP RIVER A BIT?
IF YOU WANT TO GO A HUNDRED MILES OFF TRACK, SURE. PLUS, WHO KNOWS HOW MANY OF THE SMALLER ROADS ARE EVEN PASSABLE NOW.
SIR, BACK IN YOUR CAR. WHEN WE CAN LOOSEN THE CONGESTION, I SUGGEST YOU HEAD BACK TOWARDS HOUSTON.
AND WHAT DO YOU SUGGEST FOR GAS, FOR ALL THESE PEOPLE? EVERY PUMP BETWEEN HERE AND AUSTIN IS TAPPED!

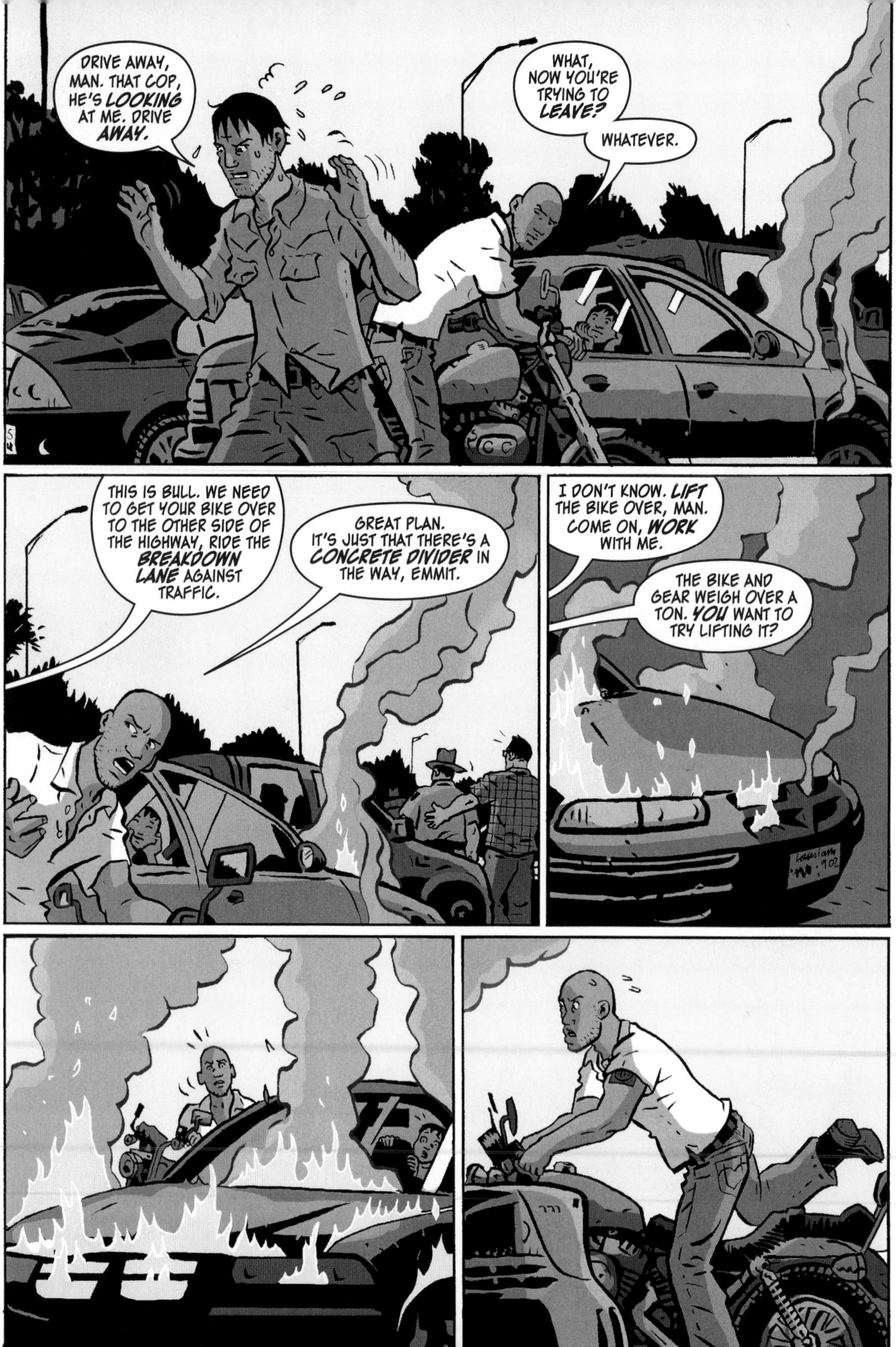
DRIVE AWAY, MAN. THAT COP, HE'S LOOKING AT ME. DRIVE AWAY.
WHAT, NOW YOU'RE TRYING TO LEAVE?
WHATEVER.
THIS IS BULL. WE NEED TO GET YOUR BIKE OVER TO THE OTHER SIDE OF THE HIGHWAY, RIDE THE BREAKDOWN LANE AGAINST TRAFFIC.
GREAT PLAN. IT'S JUST THAT THERE'S A CONCRETE DIVIDER IN THE WAY, EMMIT.
I DON'T KNOW. LIFT THE BIKE OVER, MAN. COME ON, WORK WITH ME.
THE BIKE AND GEAR WEIGH OVER A TON. YOU WANT TO TRY LIFTING IT?

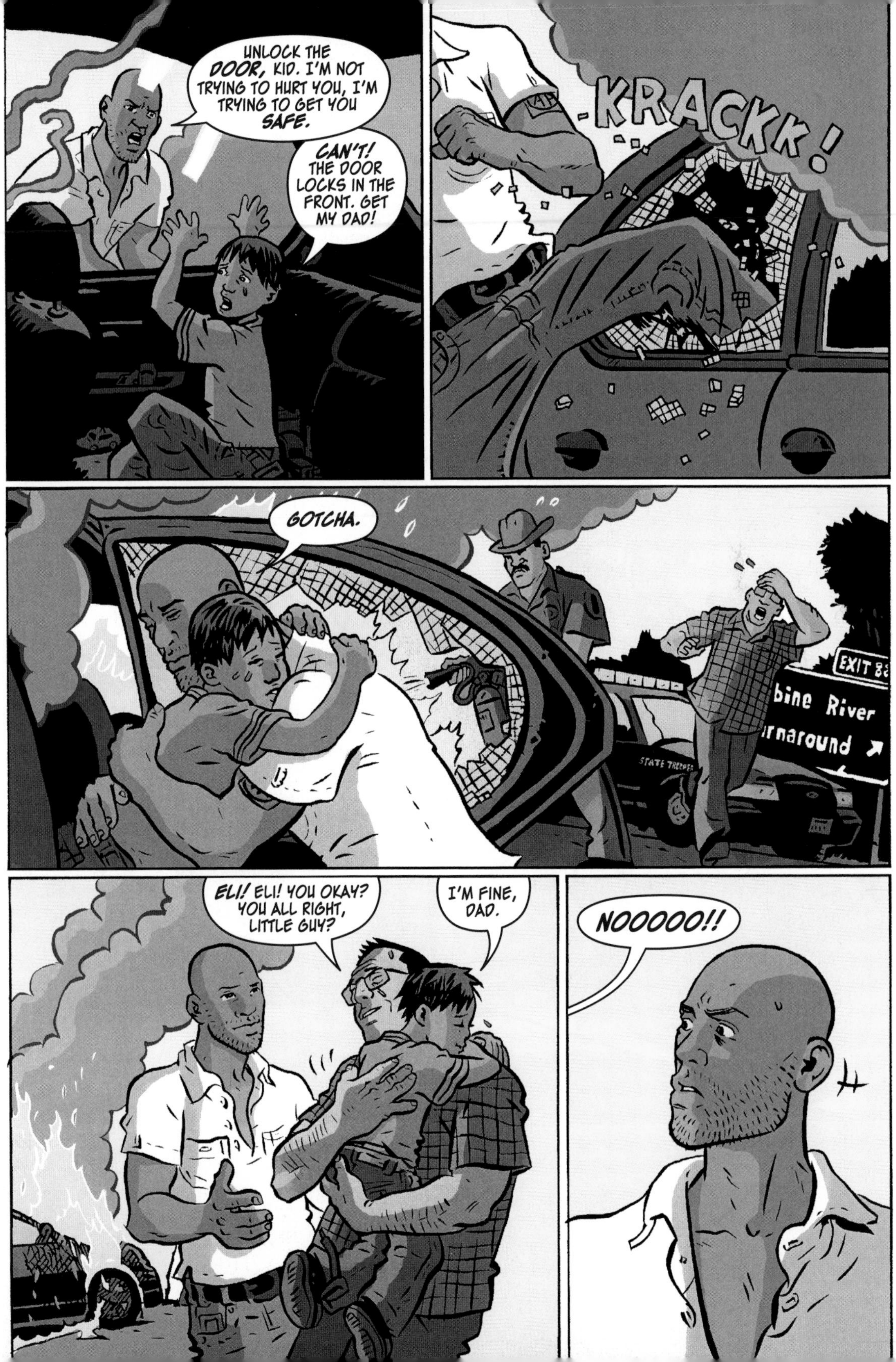
UNLOCK THE DOOR, KID. I'M NOT TRYING TO HURT YOU, I'M TRYING TO GET YOU SAFE.
CAN'T! THE DOOR LOCKS IN THE FRONT. GET MY DAD!
KRACKK!
GOTCHA.
EXIT 82
bine River
rnaround
STATE TROOPER
ELI! ELI! YOU OKAY? YOU ALL RIGHT, LITTLE GUY?
I'M FINE, DAD.
NOOOOO!!

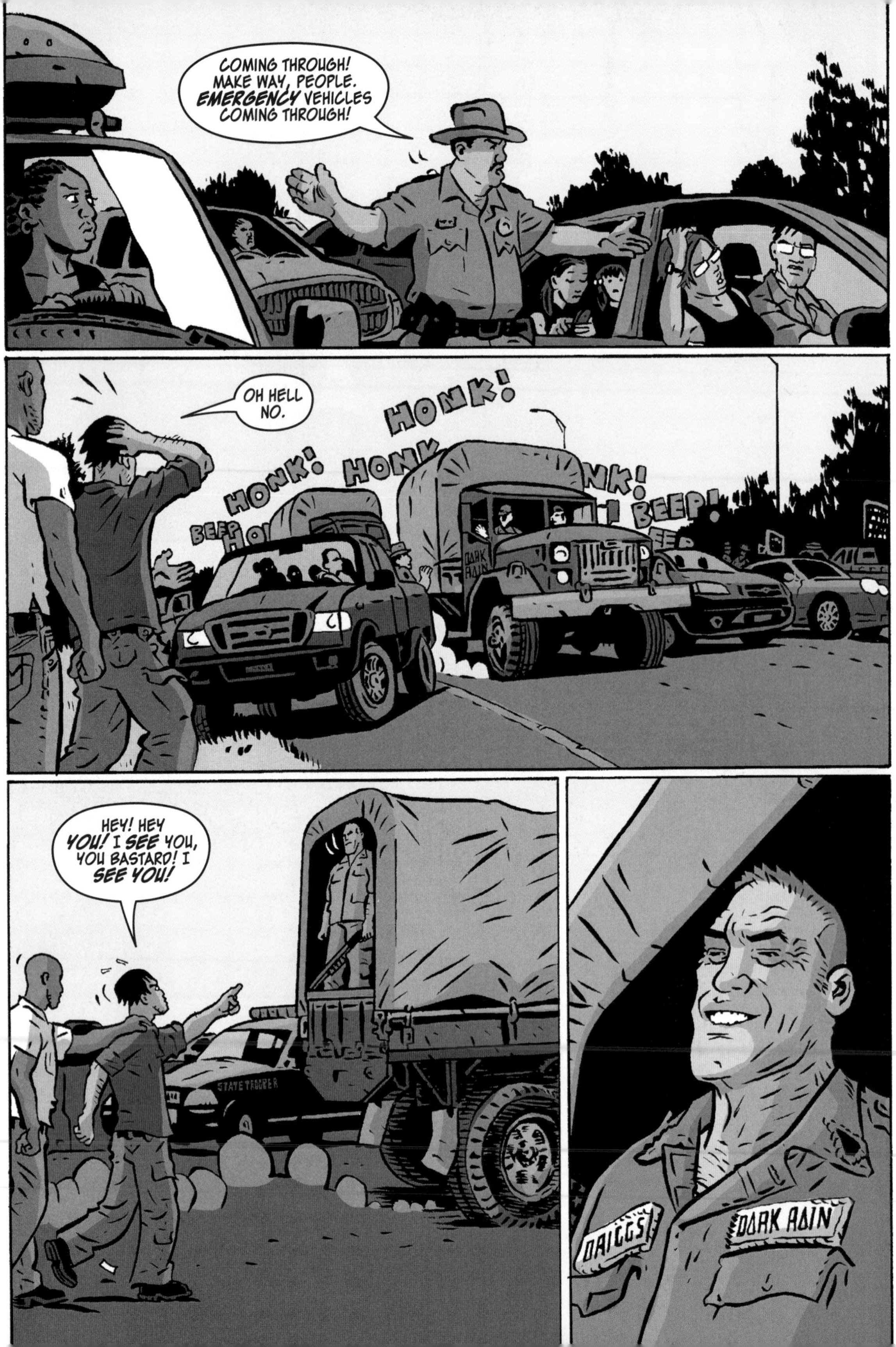
COMING THROUGH! MAKE WAY, PEOPLE. EMERGENCY VEHICLES COMING THROUGH!
OH HELL NO.
HONK!
HONK!
BEEP!
HEY! HEY YOU! I SEE YOU, YOU BASTARD! I SEE YOU!
STATE TROOPER
DRIGGS
DARK RAIN

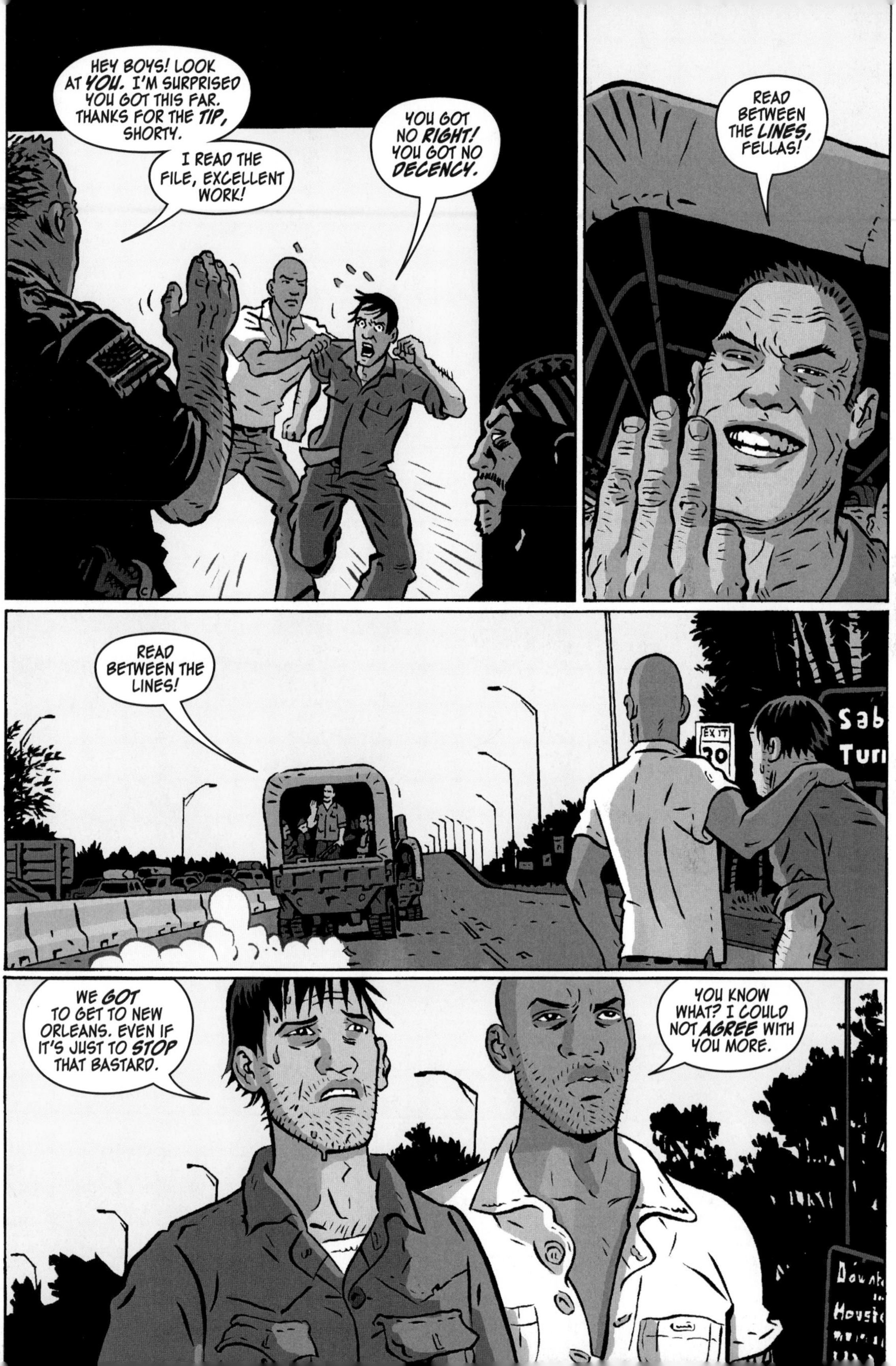
HEY BOYS! LOOK AT YOU. I'M SURPRISED YOU GOT THIS FAR. THANKS FOR THE TIP, SHORTY.
I READ THE FILE, EXCELLENT WORK!
YOU GOT NO RIGHT! YOU GOT NO DECENCY.
READ BETWEEN THE LINES, FELLAS!
READ BETWEEN THE LINES!
EXIT
20
WE GOT TO GET TO NEW ORLEANS. EVEN IF IT'S JUST TO STOP THAT BASTARD.
YOU KNOW WHAT? I COULD NOT AGREE WITH YOU MORE.

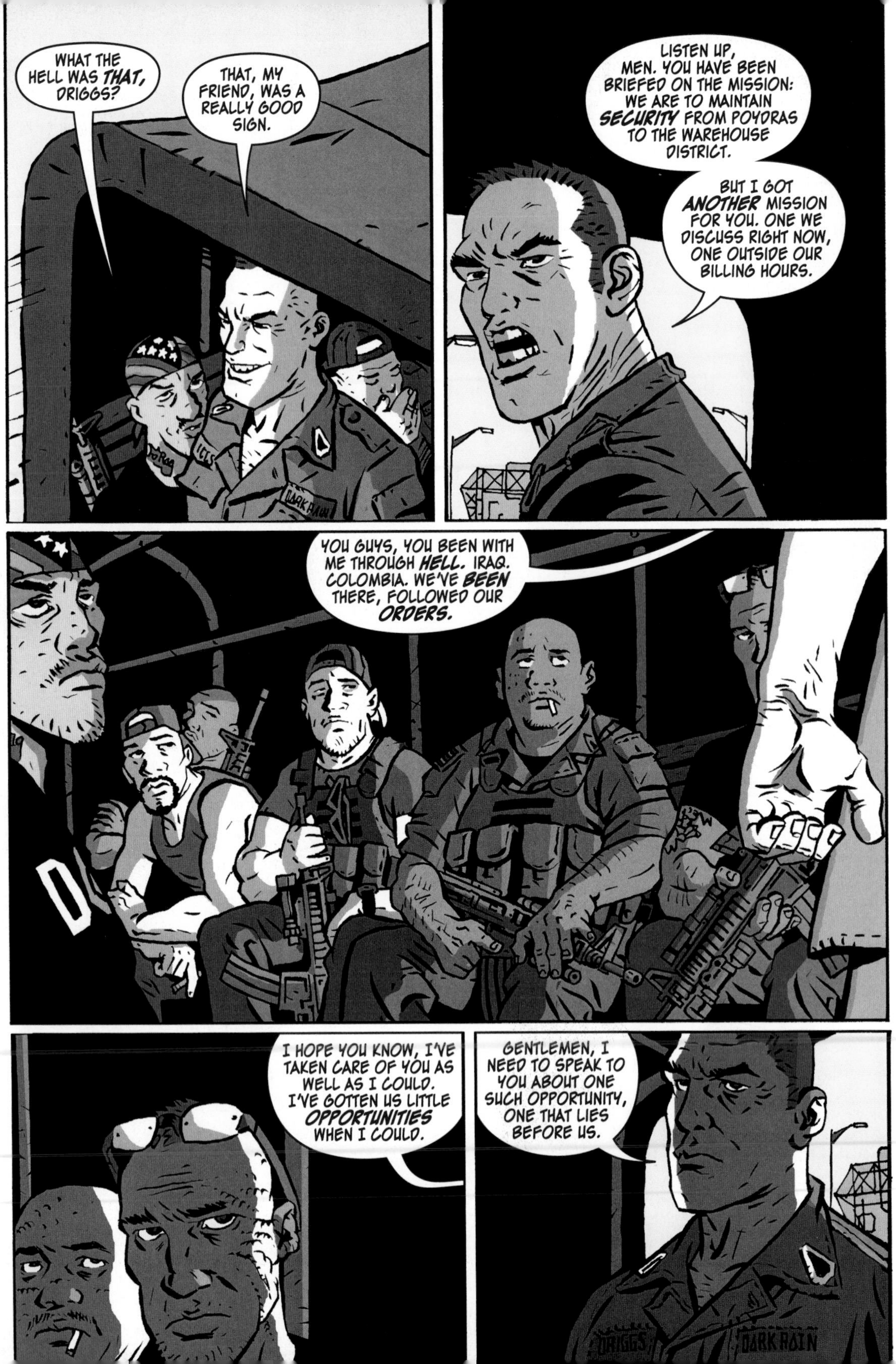
WHAT THE HELL WAS THAT, DRIGGS?
THAT, MY FRIEND, WAS A REALLY GOOD SIGN.
LISTEN UP, MEN. YOU HAVE BEEN BRIEFED ON THE MISSION: WE ARE TO MAINTAIN SECURITY FROM POYDRAS TO THE WAREHOUSE DISTRICT.
BUT I GOT ANOTHER MISSION FOR YOU. ONE WE DISCUSS RIGHT NOW, ONE OUTSIDE OUR BILLING HOURS.
YOU GUYS, YOU BEEN WITH ME THROUGH HELL. IRAQ. COLOMBIA. WE'VE BEEN THERE, FOLLOWED OUR ORDERS.
I HOPE YOU KNOW, I'VE TAKEN CARE OF YOU AS WELL AS I COULD. I'VE GOTTEN US LITTLE OPPORTUNITIES WHEN I COULD.
GENTLEMEN, I NEED TO SPEAK TO YOU ABOUT ONE SUCH OPPORTUNITY, ONE THAT LIES BEFORE US.
DRIGGS
DARK RAIN

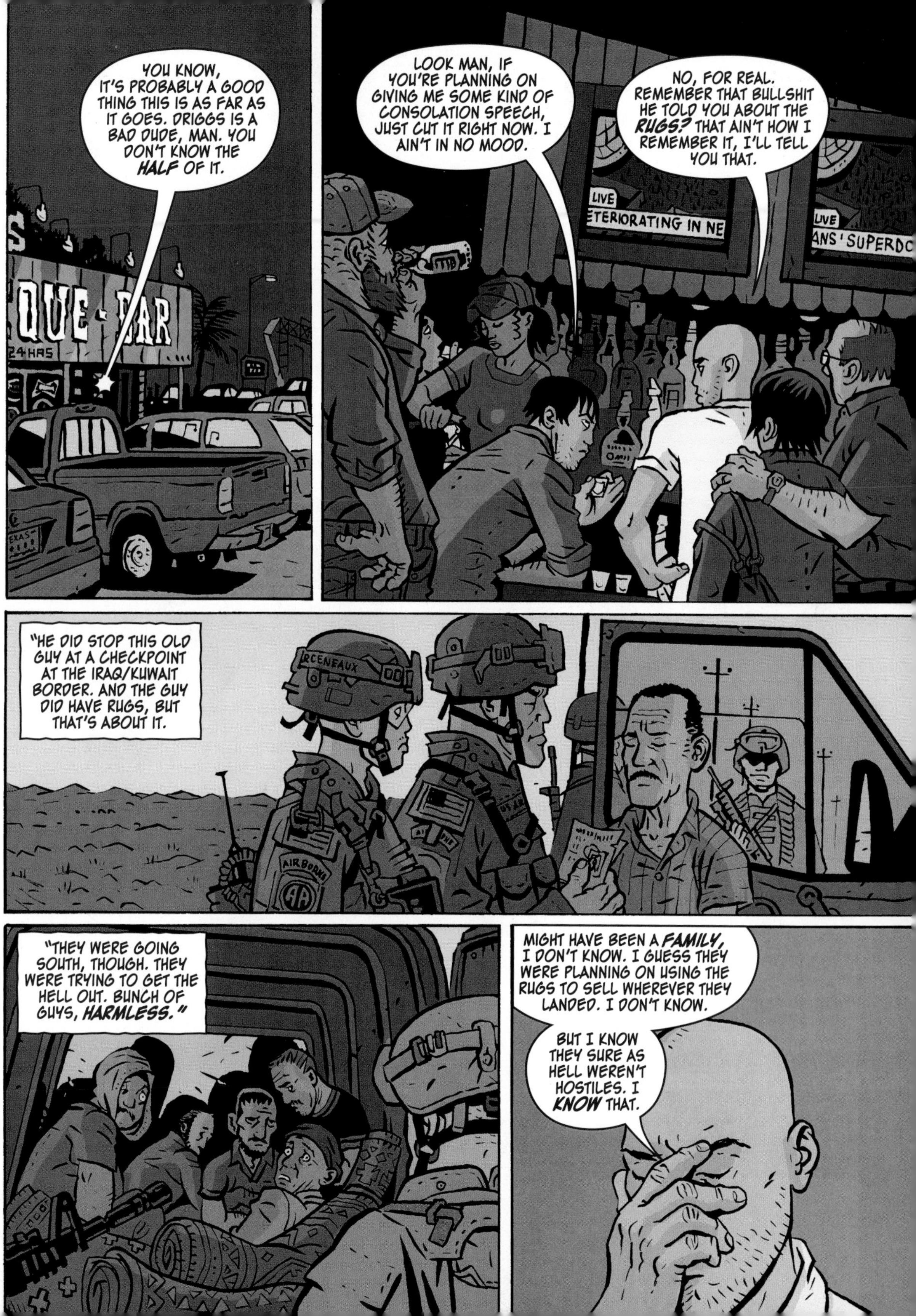
YOU KNOW, IT'S PROBABLY A GOOD THING THIS IS AS FAR AS IT GOES. DRIGGS IS A BAD DUDE, MAN. YOU DON'T KNOW THE HALF OF IT.
-QUE-BAR
24 HRS
LOOK MAN, IF YOU'RE PLANNING ON GIVING ME SOME KIND OF CONSOLATION SPEECH, JUST CUT IT RIGHT NOW. I AIN'T IN NO MOOD.
NO, FOR REAL. REMEMBER THAT BULLSHIT HE TOLD YOU ABOUT THE RUGS? THAT AIN'T HOW I REMEMBER IT, I'LL TELL YOU THAT.
LIVE
ETERIORATING IN NE
LIVE
ANS' SUPERDO
"HE DID STOP THIS OLD GUY AT A CHECKPOINT AT THE IRAQ/KUWAIT BORDER. AND THE GUY DID HAVE RUGS, BUT THAT'S ABOUT IT.
RCENEAUX
AIRBORNE
AA
"THEY WERE GOING SOUTH, THOUGH. THEY WERE TRYING TO GET THE HELL OUT. BUNCH OF GUYS, HARMLESS."
MIGHT HAVE BEEN A FAMILY, I DON'T KNOW. I GUESS THEY WERE PLANNING ON USING THE RUGS TO SELL WHEREVER THEY LANDED. I DON'T KNOW.
BUT I KNOW THEY SURE AS HELL WEREN'T HOSTILES. I KNOW THAT.

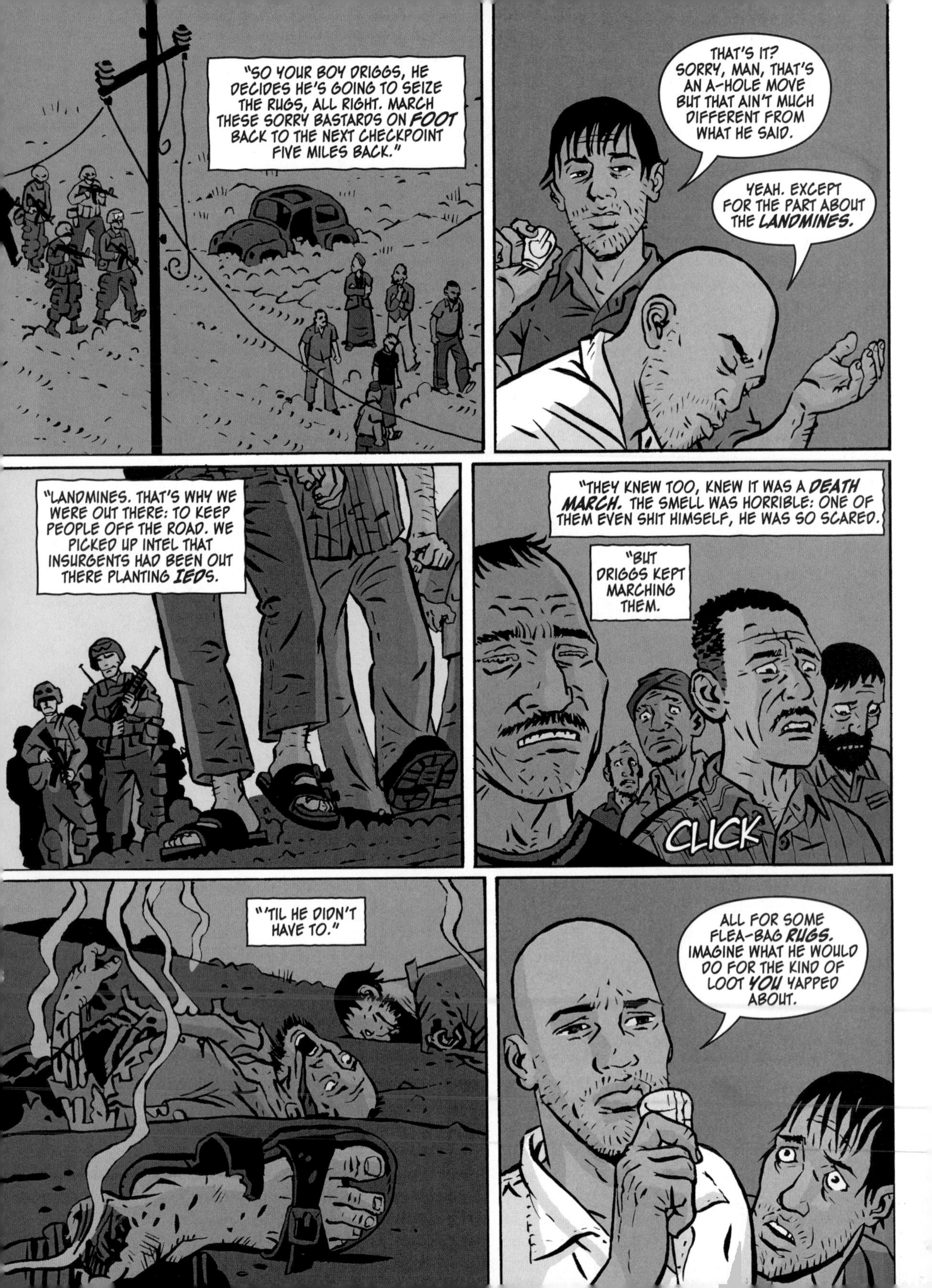
"SO YOUR BOY DRIGGS, HE DECIDES HE'S GOING TO SEIZE THE RUGS, ALL RIGHT. MARCH THESE SORRY BASTARDS ON FOOT BACK TO THE NEXT CHECKPOINT FIVE MILES BACK."
THAT'S IT? SORRY, MAN, THAT'S AN A-HOLE MOVE BUT THAT AIN'T MUCH DIFFERENT FROM WHAT HE SAID.
YEAH. EXCEPT FOR THE PART ABOUT THE LANDMINES.
"LANDMINES. THAT'S WHY WE WERE OUT THERE: TO KEEP PEOPLE OFF THE ROAD. WE PICKED UP INTEL THAT INSURGENTS HAD BEEN OUT THERE PLANTING IEDS.
"THEY KNEW TOO, KNEW IT WAS A DEATH MARCH. THE SMELL WAS HORRIBLE: ONE OF THEM EVEN SHIT HIMSELF, HE WAS SO SCARED.
"BUT DRIGGS KEPT MARCHING THEM.
CLICK
"'TIL HE DIDN'T HAVE TO."
ALL FOR SOME FLEA-BAG RUGS. IMAGINE WHAT HE WOULD DO FOR THE KIND OF LOOT YOU YAPPED ABOUT.

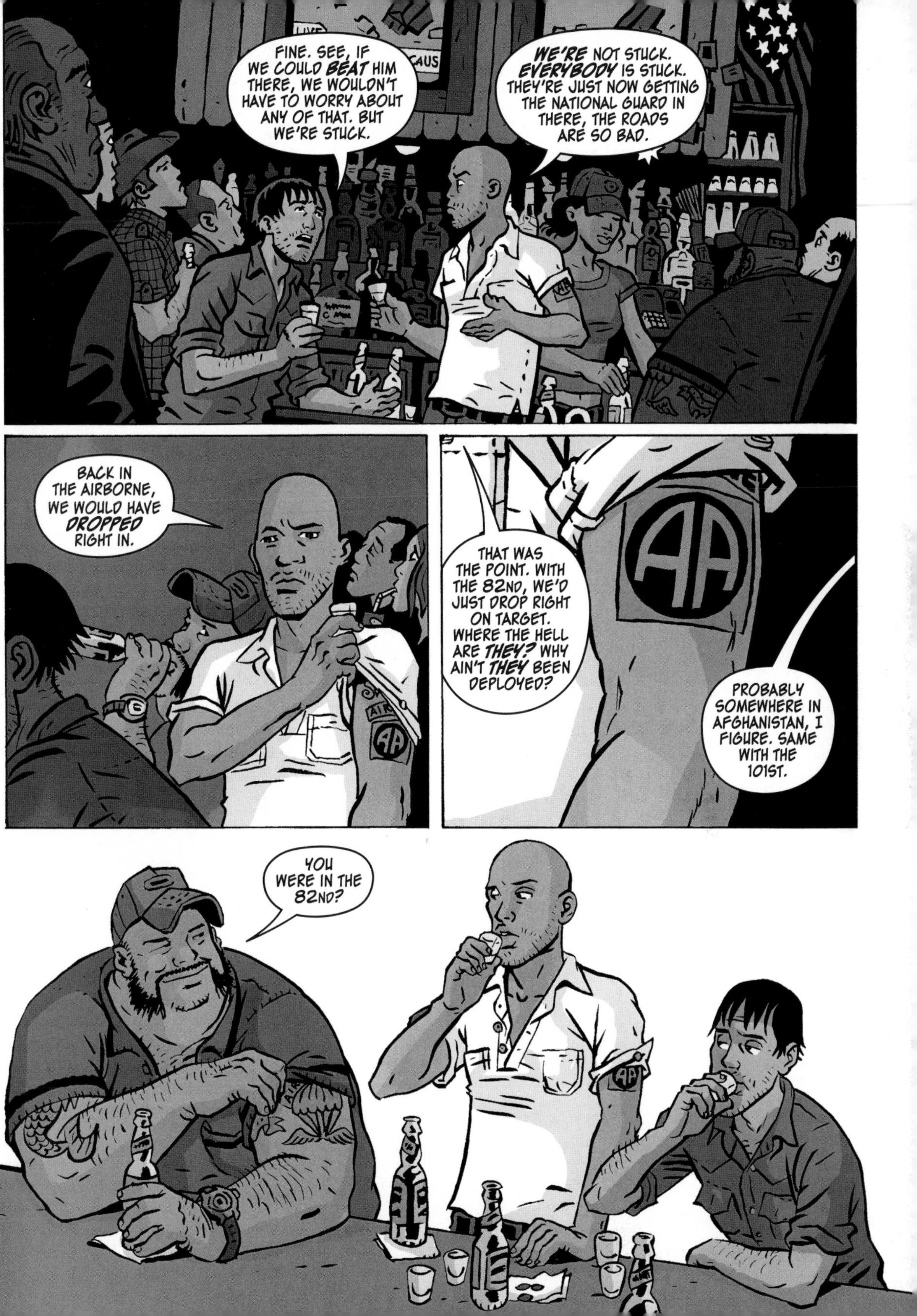
FINE. SEE, IF WE COULD BEAT HIM THERE, WE WOULDN'T HAVE TO WORRY ABOUT ANY OF THAT. BUT WE'RE STUCK.
WE'RE NOT STUCK. EVERYBODY IS STUCK. THEY'RE JUST NOW GETTING THE NATIONAL GUARD IN THERE, THE ROADS ARE SO BAD.
BACK IN THE AIRBORNE, WE WOULD HAVE DROPPED RIGHT IN.
THAT WAS THE POINT. WITH THE 82ND, WE'D JUST DROP RIGHT ON TARGET. WHERE THE HELL ARE THEY? WHY AIN'T THEY BEEN DEPLOYED?
PROBABLY SOMEWHERE IN AFGHANISTAN, I FIGURE. SAME WITH THE 101ST.
YOU WERE IN THE 82ND?

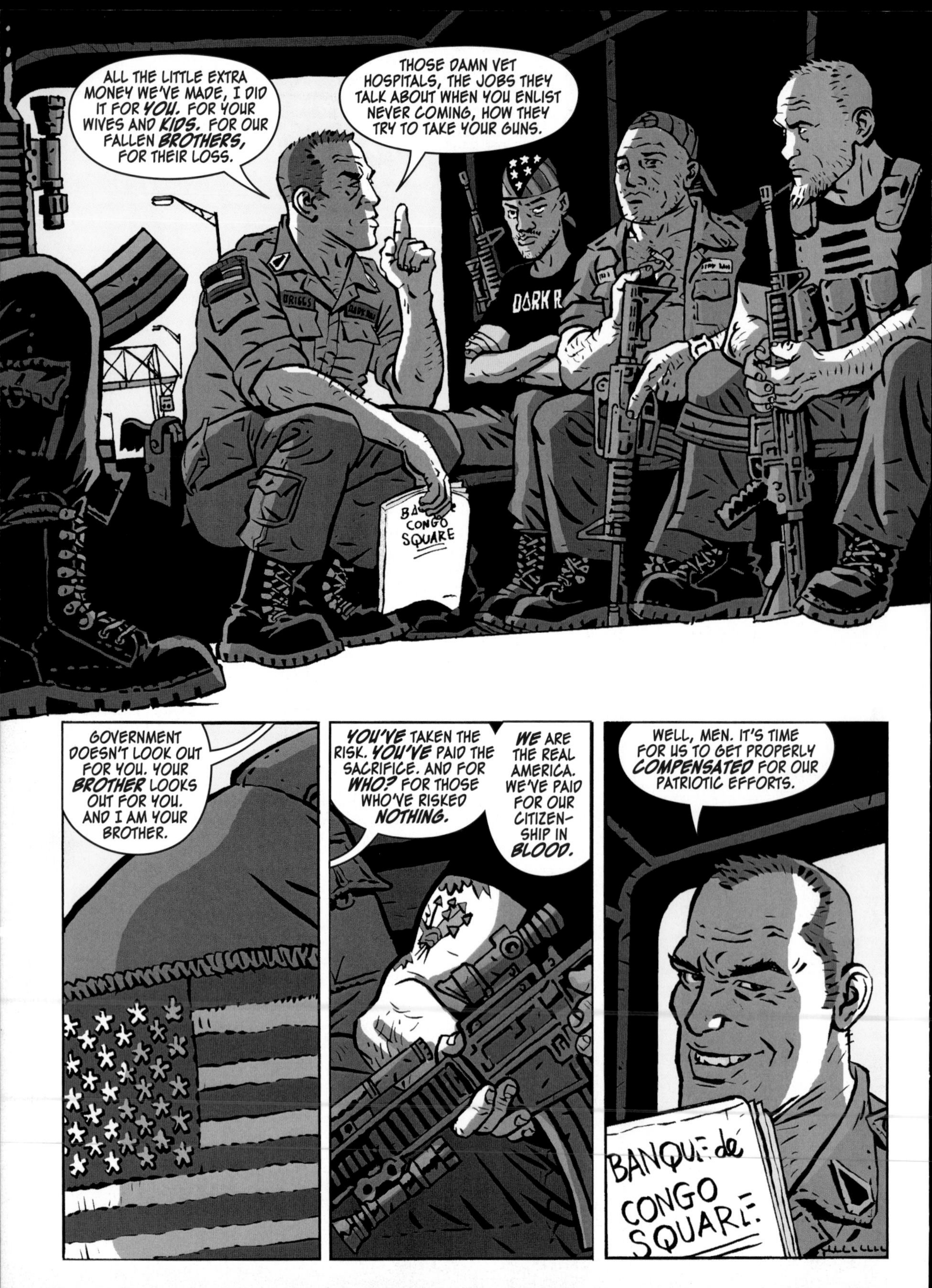
ALL THE LITTLE EXTRA MONEY WE'VE MADE, I DID IT FOR YOU. FOR YOUR WIVES AND KIDS. FOR OUR FALLEN BROTHERS, FOR THEIR LOSS.
THOSE DAMN VET HOSPITALS, THE JOBS THEY TALK ABOUT WHEN YOU ENLIST NEVER COMING, HOW THEY TRY TO TAKE YOUR GUNS.
BRIGGS
DARK R
CONGO SQUARE
GOVERNMENT DOESN'T LOOK OUT FOR YOU. YOUR BROTHER LOOKS OUT FOR YOU. AND I AM YOUR BROTHER.
YOU'VE TAKEN THE RISK. YOU'VE PAID THE SACRIFICE. AND FOR WHO? FOR THOSE WHO'VE RISKED NOTHING.
WE ARE THE REAL AMERICA. WE'VE PAID FOR OUR CITIZEN-SHIP IN BLOOD.
WELL, MEN. IT'S TIME FOR US TO GET PROPERLY COMPENSATED FOR OUR PATRIOTIC EFFORTS.
BANQUE de CONGO SQUARE

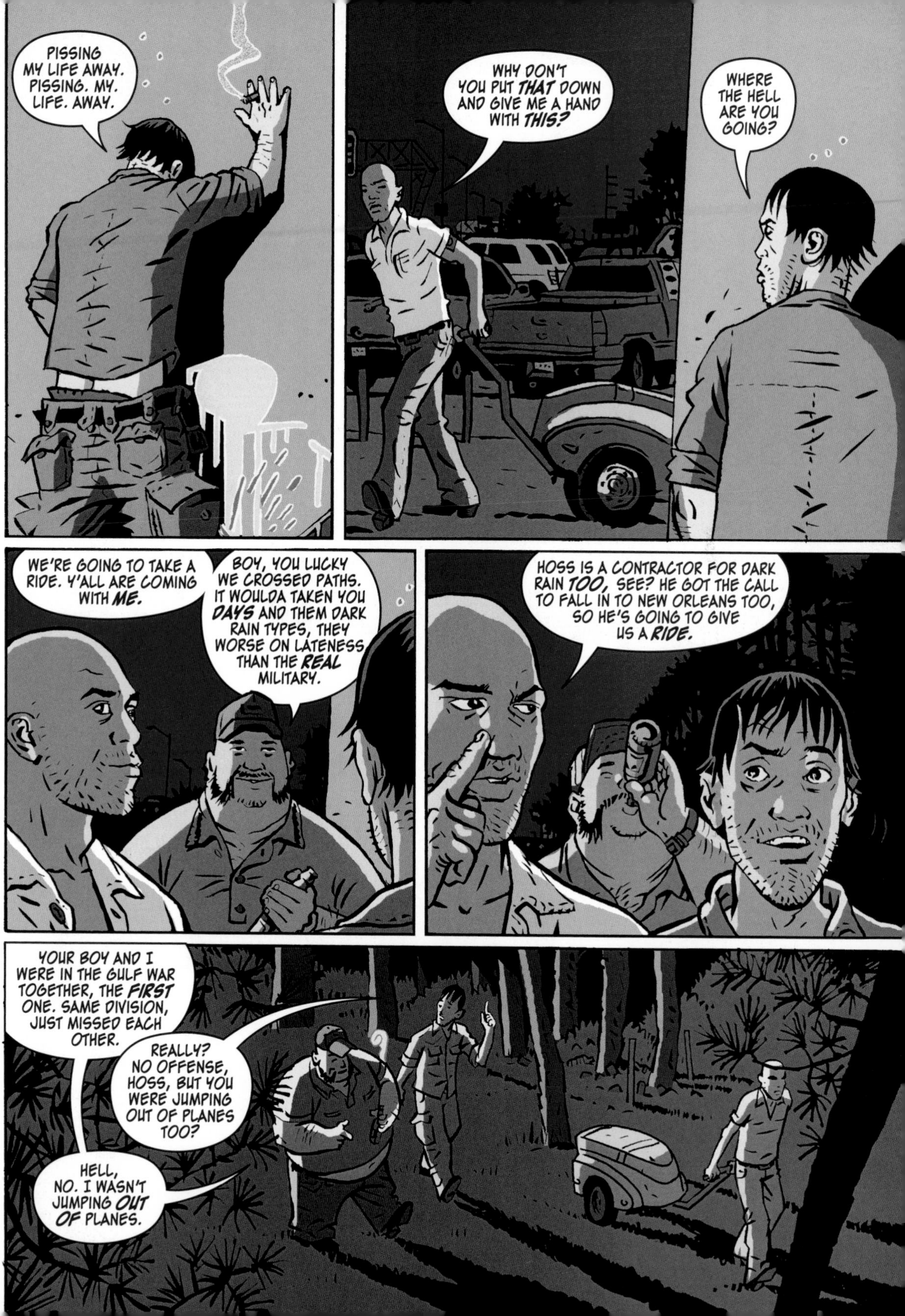
PISSING MY LIFE AWAY. PISSING. MY. LIFE. AWAY.
WHY DON'T YOU PUT THAT DOWN AND GIVE ME A HAND WITH THIS?
WHERE THE HELL ARE YOU GOING?
WE'RE GOING TO TAKE A RIDE. Y'ALL ARE COMING WITH ME.
BOY, YOU LUCKY WE CROSSED PATHS. IT WOULDA TAKEN YOU DAYS AND THEM DARK RAIN TYPES, THEY WORSE ON LATENESS THAN THE REAL MILITARY.
HOSS IS A CONTRACTOR FOR DARK RAIN TOO, SEE? HE GOT THE CALL TO FALL IN TO NEW ORLEANS TOO, SO HE'S GOING TO GIVE US A RIDE.
YOUR BOY AND I WERE IN THE GULF WAR TOGETHER, THE FIRST ONE. SAME DIVISION, JUST MISSED EACH OTHER.
REALLY? NO OFFENSE, HOSS, BUT YOU WERE JUMPING OUT OF PLANES TOO?
HELL, NO. I WASN'T JUMPING OUT OF PLANES.

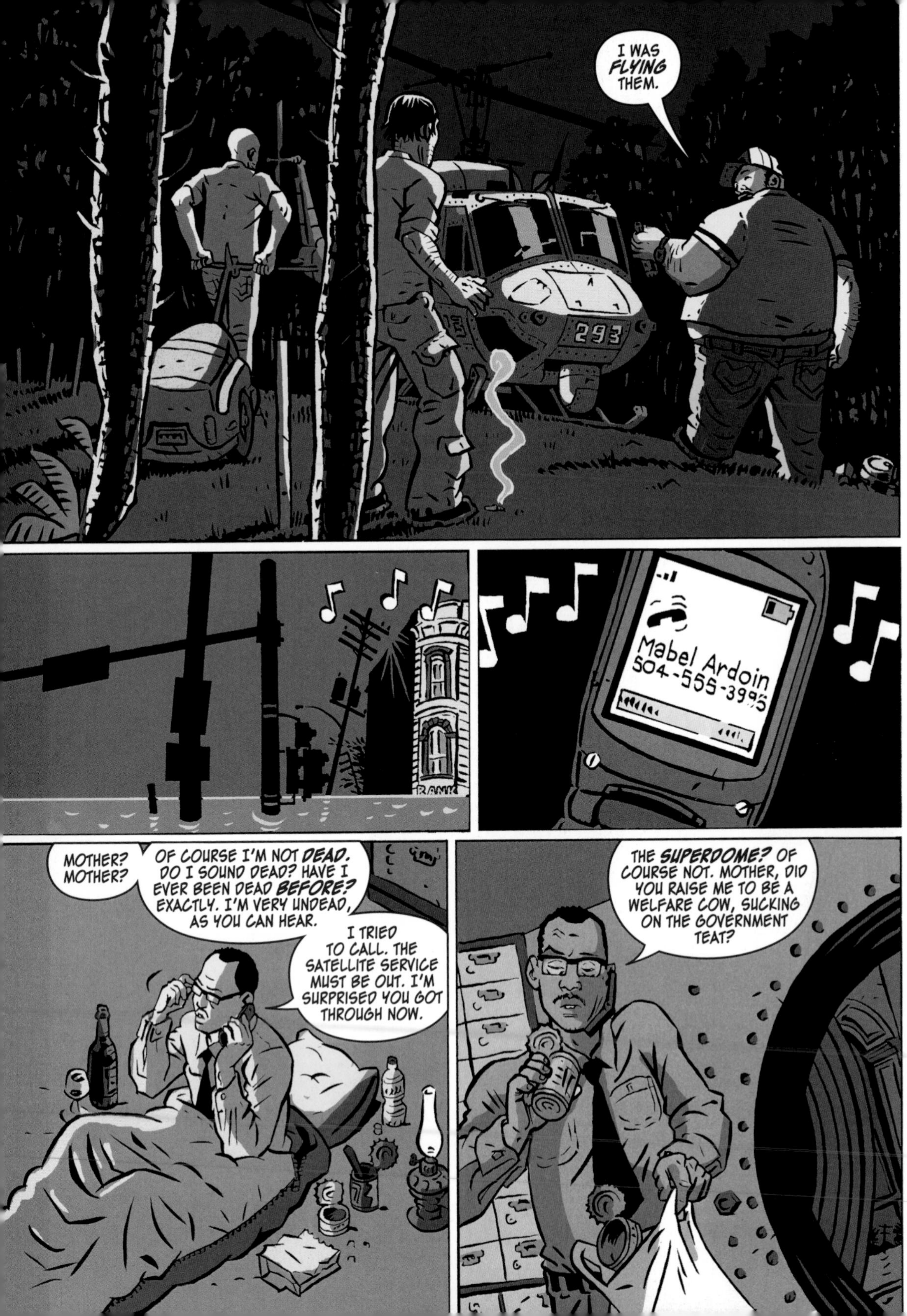
I WAS *FLYING* THEM.
293
Mabel Ardoin
504-555-3995
BANK
MOTHER? MOTHER?
OF COURSE I'M NOT *DEAD.* DO I SOUND DEAD? HAVE I EVER BEEN DEAD *BEFORE?* EXACTLY. I'M VERY UNDEAD, AS YOU CAN HEAR.
I TRIED TO CALL. THE SATELLITE SERVICE MUST BE OUT. I'M SURPRISED YOU GOT THROUGH NOW.
THE *SUPERDOME?* OF COURSE NOT. MOTHER, DID YOU RAISE ME TO BE A WELFARE COW, SUCKING ON THE GOVERNMENT TEAT?

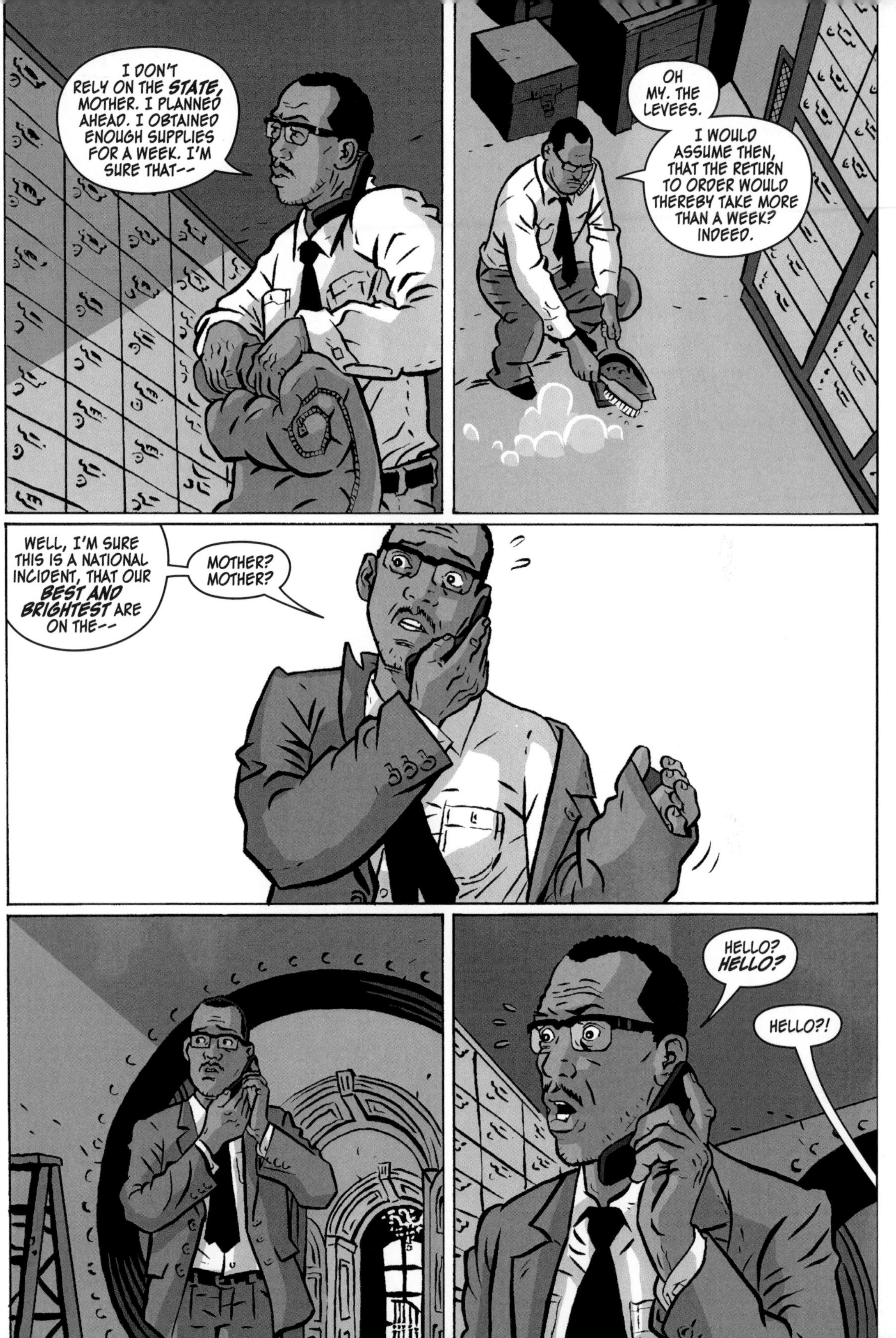
I DON'T RELY ON THE STATE, MOTHER. I PLANNED AHEAD. I OBTAINED ENOUGH SUPPLIES FOR A WEEK. I'M SURE THAT--
OH MY. THE LEVEES.
I WOULD ASSUME THEN, THAT THE RETURN TO ORDER WOULD THEREBY TAKE MORE THAN A WEEK? INDEED.
WELL, I'M SURE THIS IS A NATIONAL INCIDENT, THAT OUR BEST AND BRIGHTEST ARE ON THE--
MOTHER? MOTHER?
HELLO? HELLO?
HELLO?!

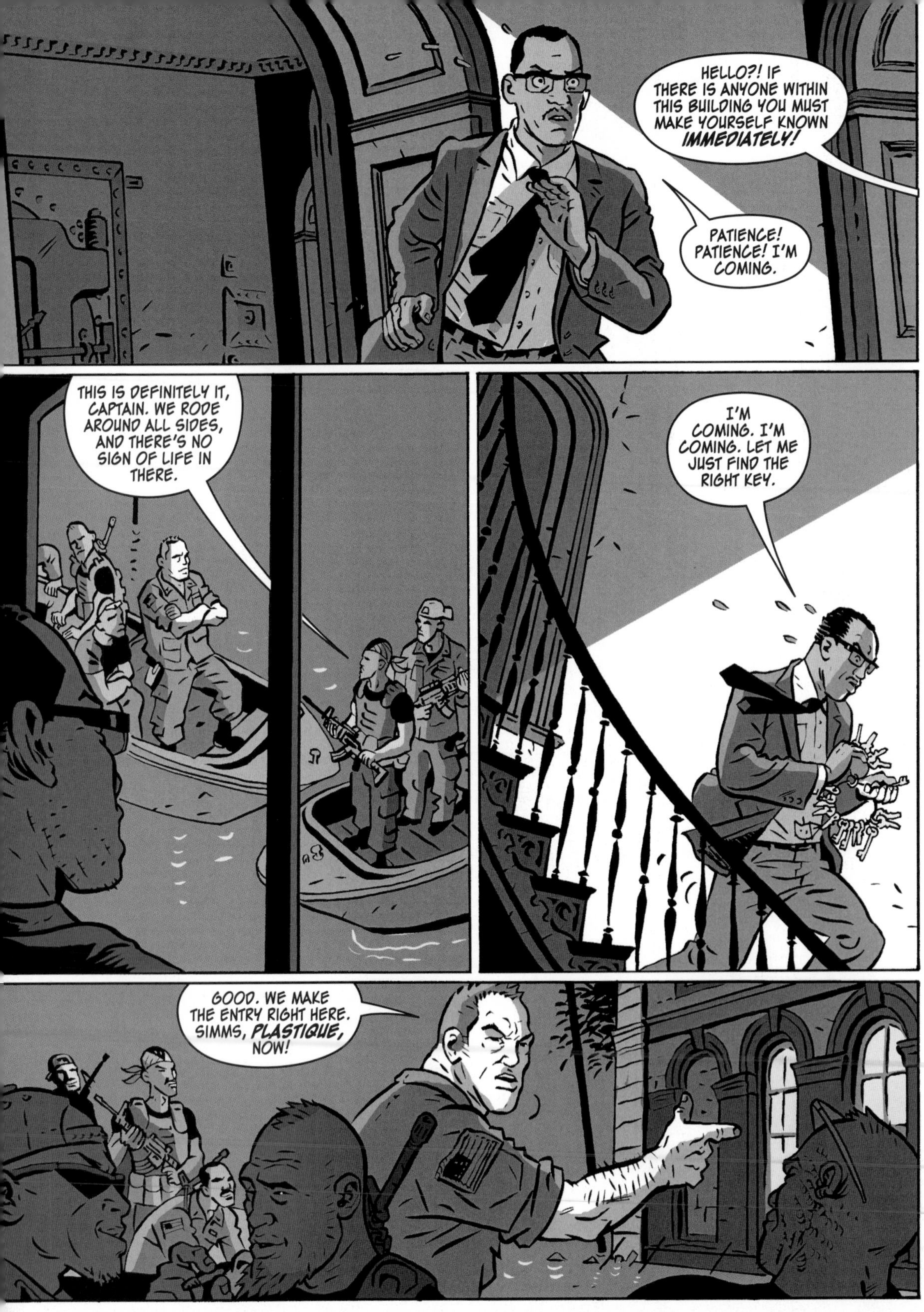
HELLO?! IF THERE IS ANYONE WITHIN THIS BUILDING YOU MUST MAKE YOURSELF KNOWN **IMMEDIATELY!**
PATIENCE! PATIENCE! I'M COMING.
THIS IS DEFINITELY IT, CAPTAIN. WE RODE AROUND ALL SIDES, AND THERE'S NO SIGN OF LIFE IN THERE.
I'M COMING. I'M COMING. LET ME JUST FIND THE RIGHT KEY.
GOOD. WE MAKE THE ENTRY RIGHT HERE. SIMMS, **PLASTIQUE,** NOW!

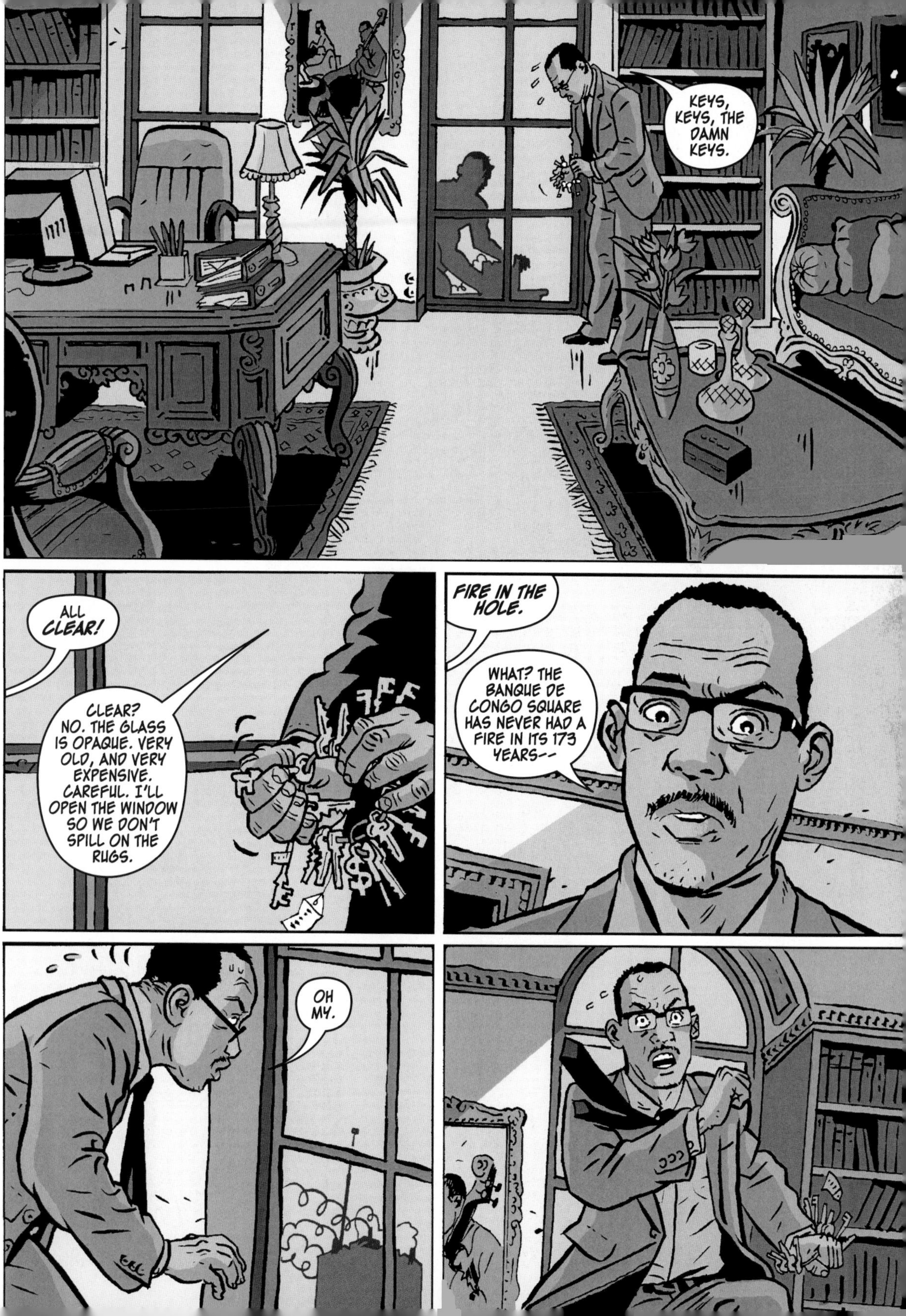
KEYS, KEYS, THE DAMN KEYS.
ALL CLEAR!
CLEAR? NO. THE GLASS IS OPAQUE. VERY OLD, AND VERY EXPENSIVE. CAREFUL. I'LL OPEN THE WINDOW SO WE DON'T SPILL ON THE RUGS.
FIRE IN THE HOLE.
WHAT? THE BANQUE DE CONGO SQUARE HAS NEVER HAD A FIRE IN ITS 173 YEARS--
OH MY.

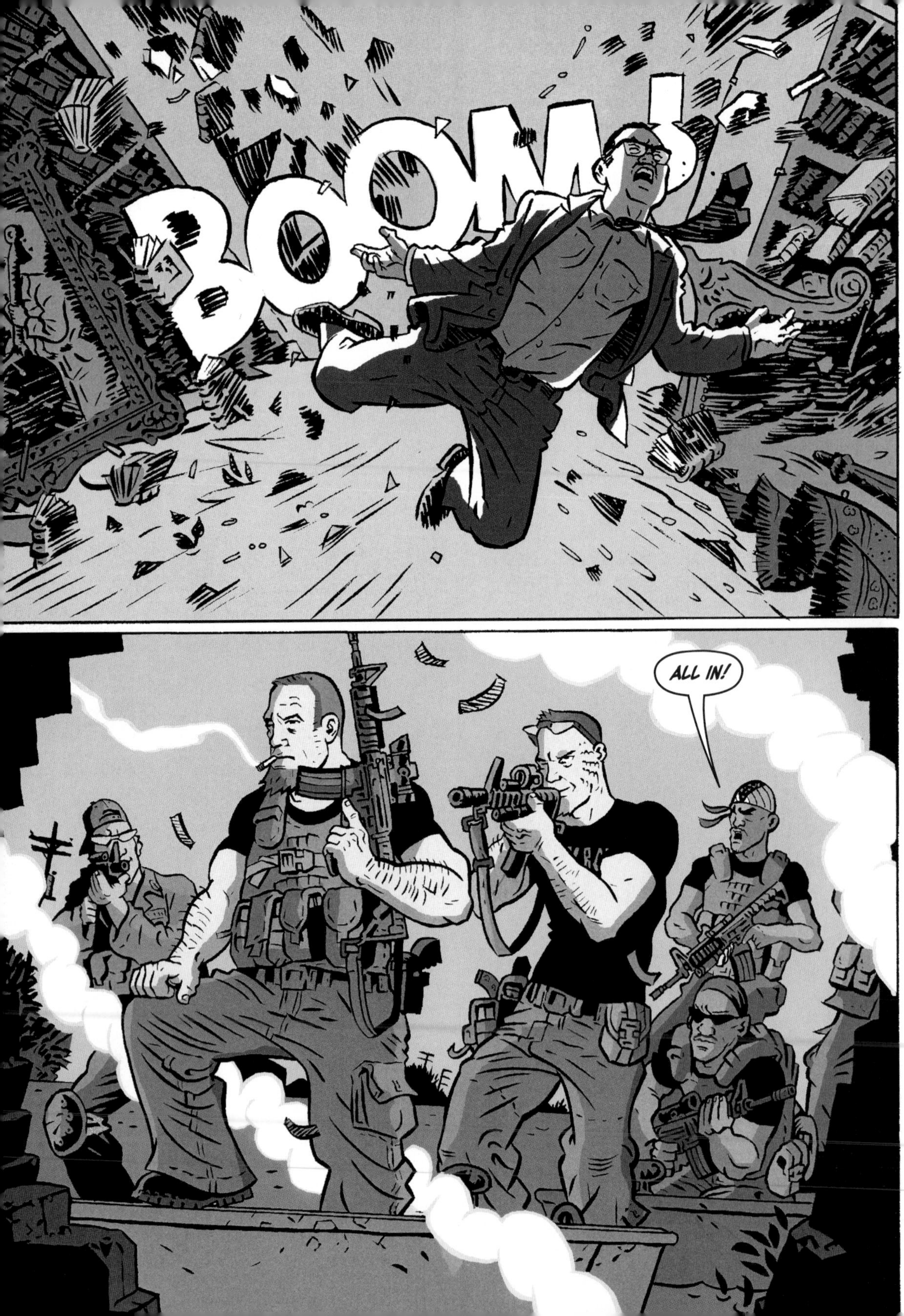
BOOM!
ALL IN!

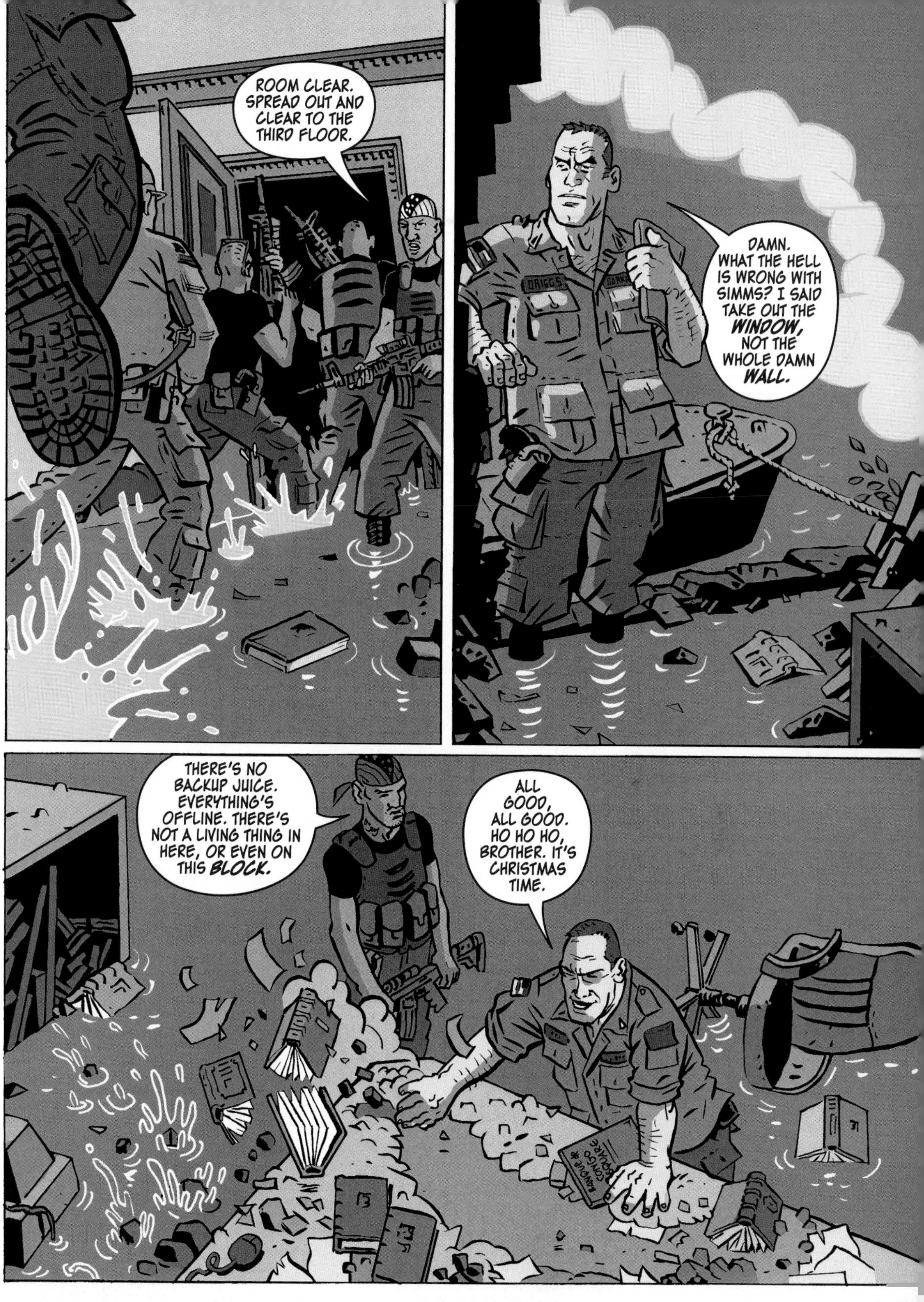
ROOM CLEAR. SPREAD OUT AND CLEAR TO THE THIRD FLOOR.
DAMN. WHAT THE HELL IS WRONG WITH SIMMS? I SAID TAKE OUT THE WINDOW, NOT THE WHOLE DAMN WALL.
THERE'S NO BACKUP JUICE. EVERYTHING'S OFFLINE. THERE'S NOT A LIVING THING IN HERE, OR EVEN ON THIS BLOCK.
ALL GOOD, ALL GOOD. HO HO HO, BROTHER. IT'S CHRISTMAS TIME.

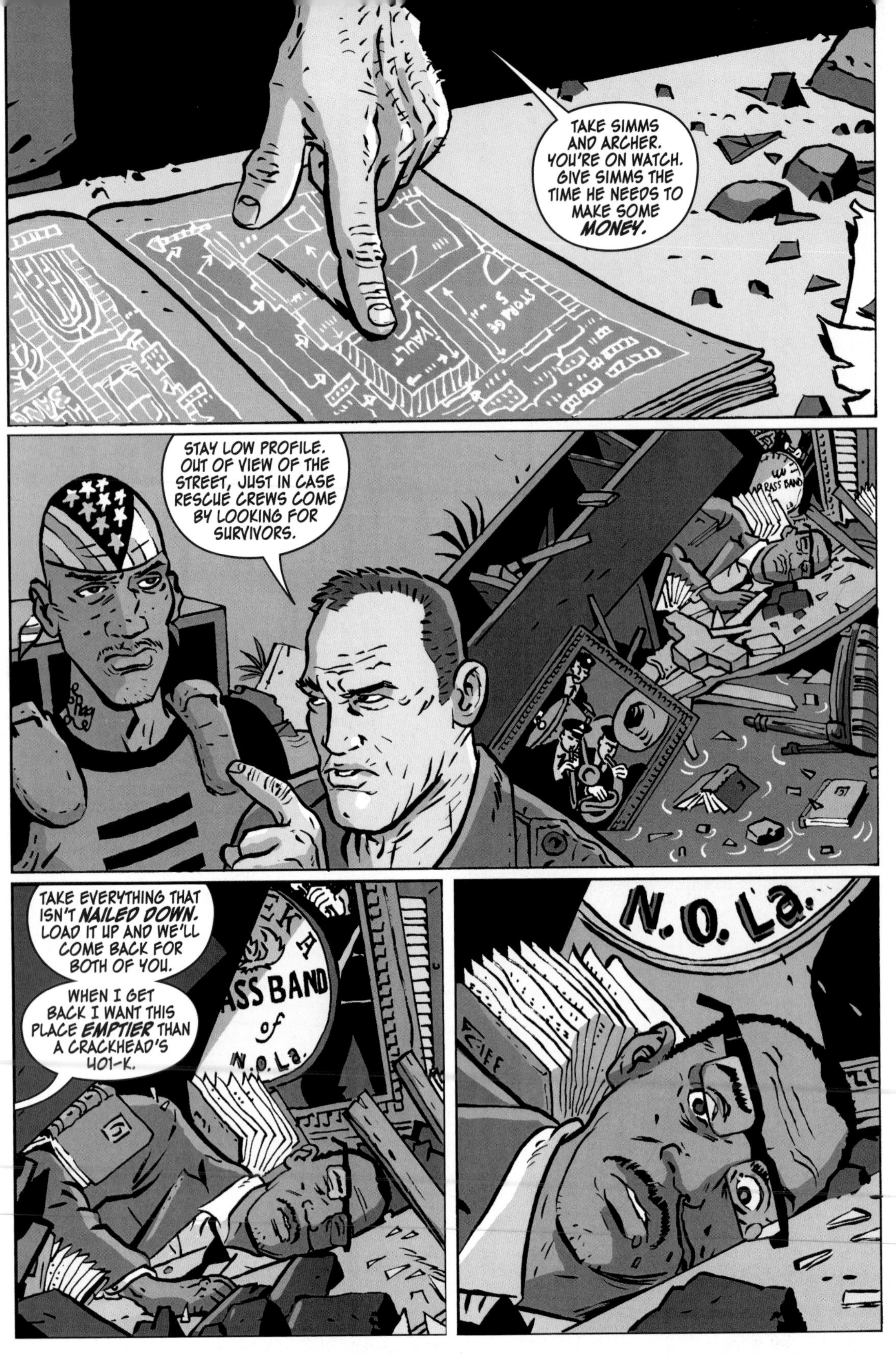
TAKE SIMMS AND ARCHER. YOU'RE ON WATCH. GIVE SIMMS THE TIME HE NEEDS TO MAKE SOME MONEY.
VAULT
STORAGE
STAY LOW PROFILE. OUT OF VIEW OF THE STREET, JUST IN CASE RESCUE CREWS COME BY LOOKING FOR SURVIVORS.
TAKE EVERYTHING THAT ISN'T NAILED DOWN. LOAD IT UP AND WE'LL COME BACK FOR BOTH OF YOU.
WHEN I GET BACK I WANT THIS PLACE EMPTIER THAN A CRACKHEAD'S 401-K.
ASS BAND of N.O. La.
N.O. La.

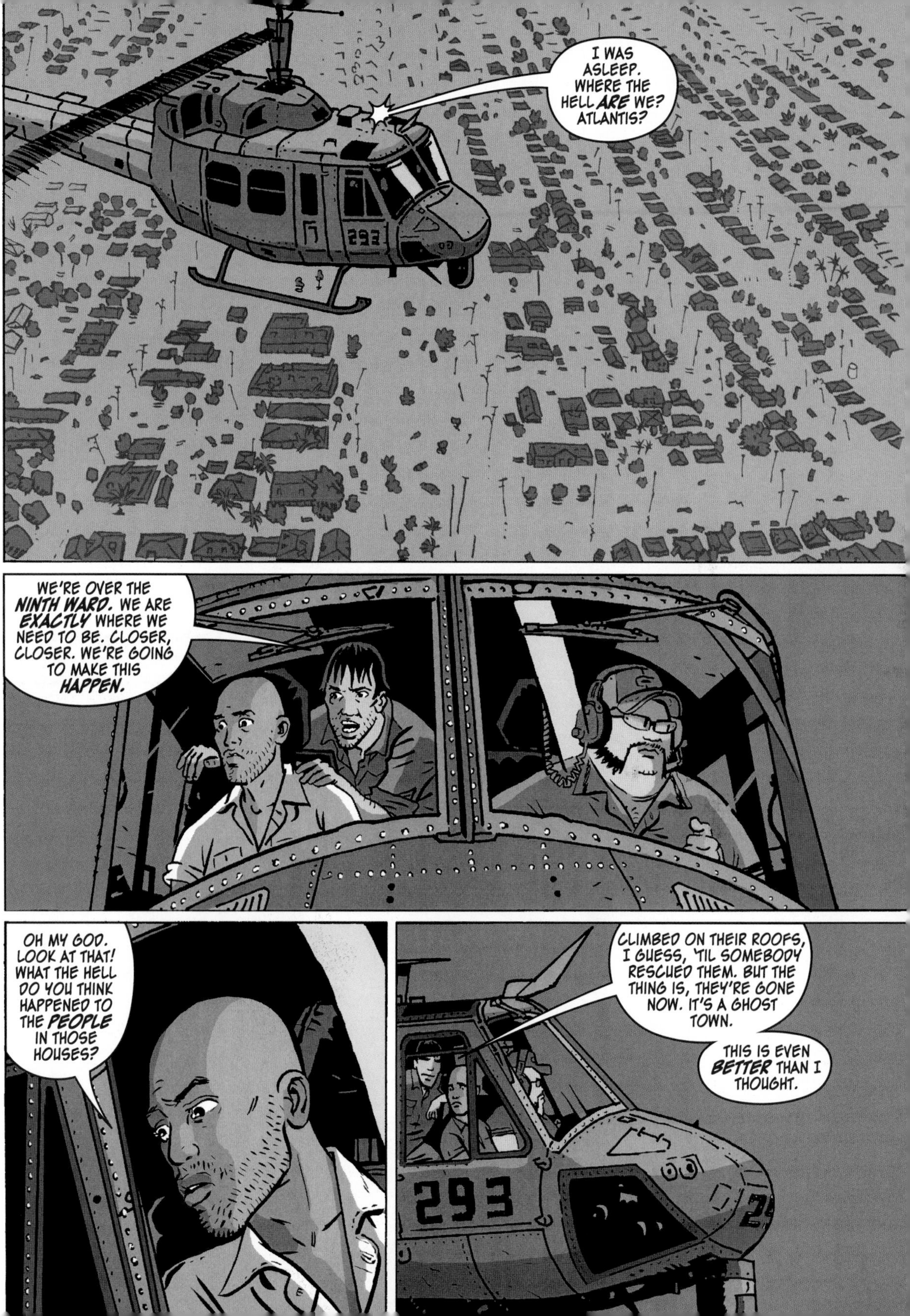
I WAS ASLEEP. WHERE THE HELL ARE WE? ATLANTIS?
293
WE'RE OVER THE NINTH WARD. WE ARE EXACTLY WHERE WE NEED TO BE. CLOSER, CLOSER. WE'RE GOING TO MAKE THIS HAPPEN.
OH MY GOD. LOOK AT THAT! WHAT THE HELL DO YOU THINK HAPPENED TO THE PEOPLE IN THOSE HOUSES?
CLIMBED ON THEIR ROOFS, I GUESS, 'TIL SOMEBODY RESCUED THEM. BUT THE THING IS, THEY'RE GONE NOW. IT'S A GHOST TOWN.
THIS IS EVEN BETTER THAN I THOUGHT.
293

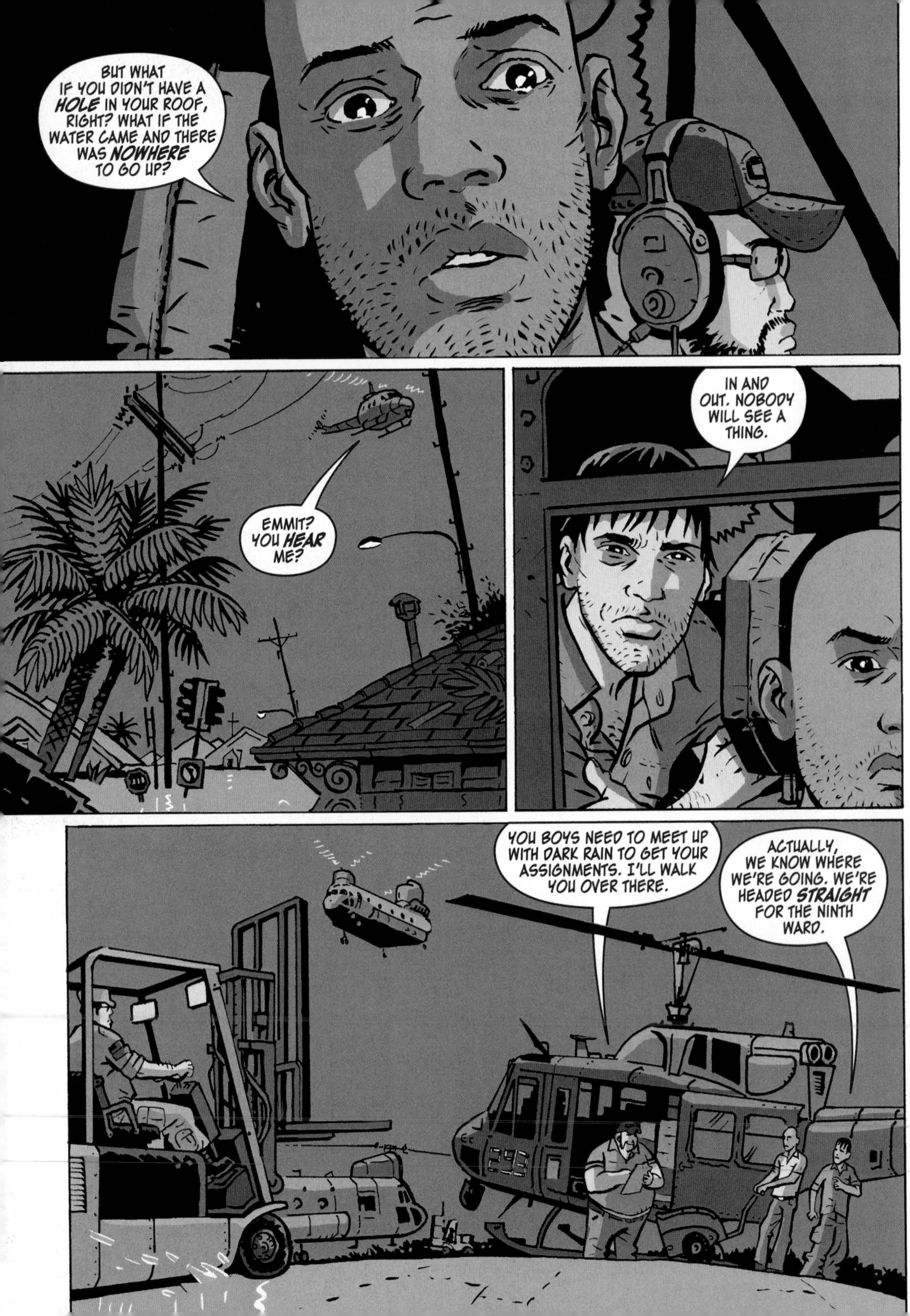
BUT WHAT IF YOU DIDN'T HAVE A ***HOLE*** IN YOUR ROOF, RIGHT? WHAT IF THE WATER CAME AND THERE WAS ***NOWHERE*** TO GO UP?
EMMIT? YOU ***HEAR*** ME?
IN AND OUT. NOBODY WILL SEE A THING.
YOU BOYS NEED TO MEET UP WITH DARK RAIN TO GET YOUR ASSIGNMENTS. I'LL WALK YOU OVER THERE.
ACTUALLY, WE KNOW WHERE WE'RE GOING. WE'RE HEADED ***STRAIGHT*** FOR THE NINTH WARD.

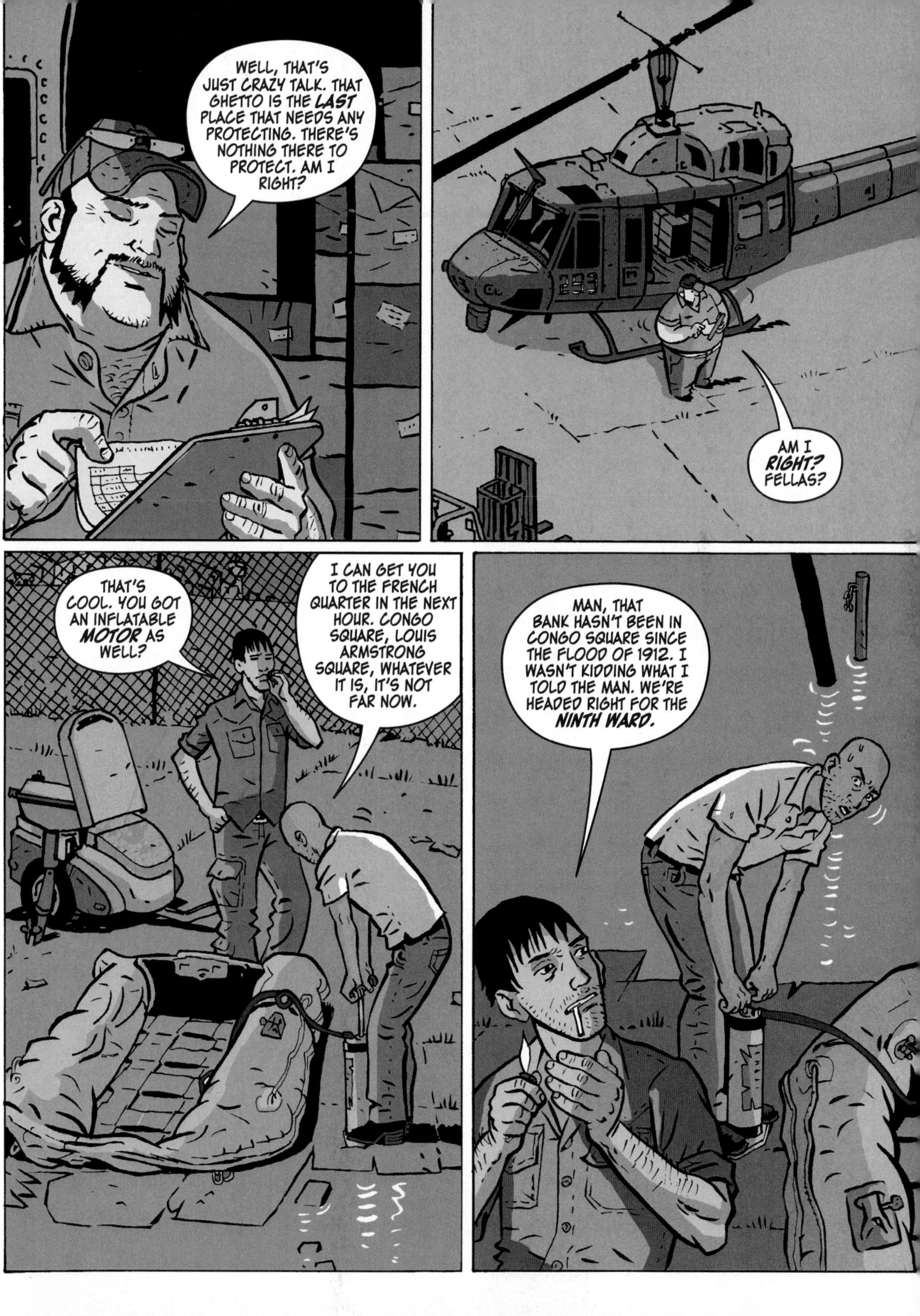
WELL, THAT'S JUST CRAZY TALK. THAT GHETTO IS THE LAST PLACE THAT NEEDS ANY PROTECTING. THERE'S NOTHING THERE TO PROTECT. AM I RIGHT?
AM I RIGHT? FELLAS?
THAT'S COOL. YOU GOT AN INFLATABLE MOTOR AS WELL?
I CAN GET YOU TO THE FRENCH QUARTER IN THE NEXT HOUR. CONGO SQUARE, LOUIS ARMSTRONG SQUARE, WHATEVER IT IS, IT'S NOT FAR NOW.
MAN, THAT BANK HASN'T BEEN IN CONGO SQUARE SINCE THE FLOOD OF 1912. I WASN'T KIDDING WHAT I TOLD THE MAN. WE'RE HEADED RIGHT FOR THE NINTH WARD.

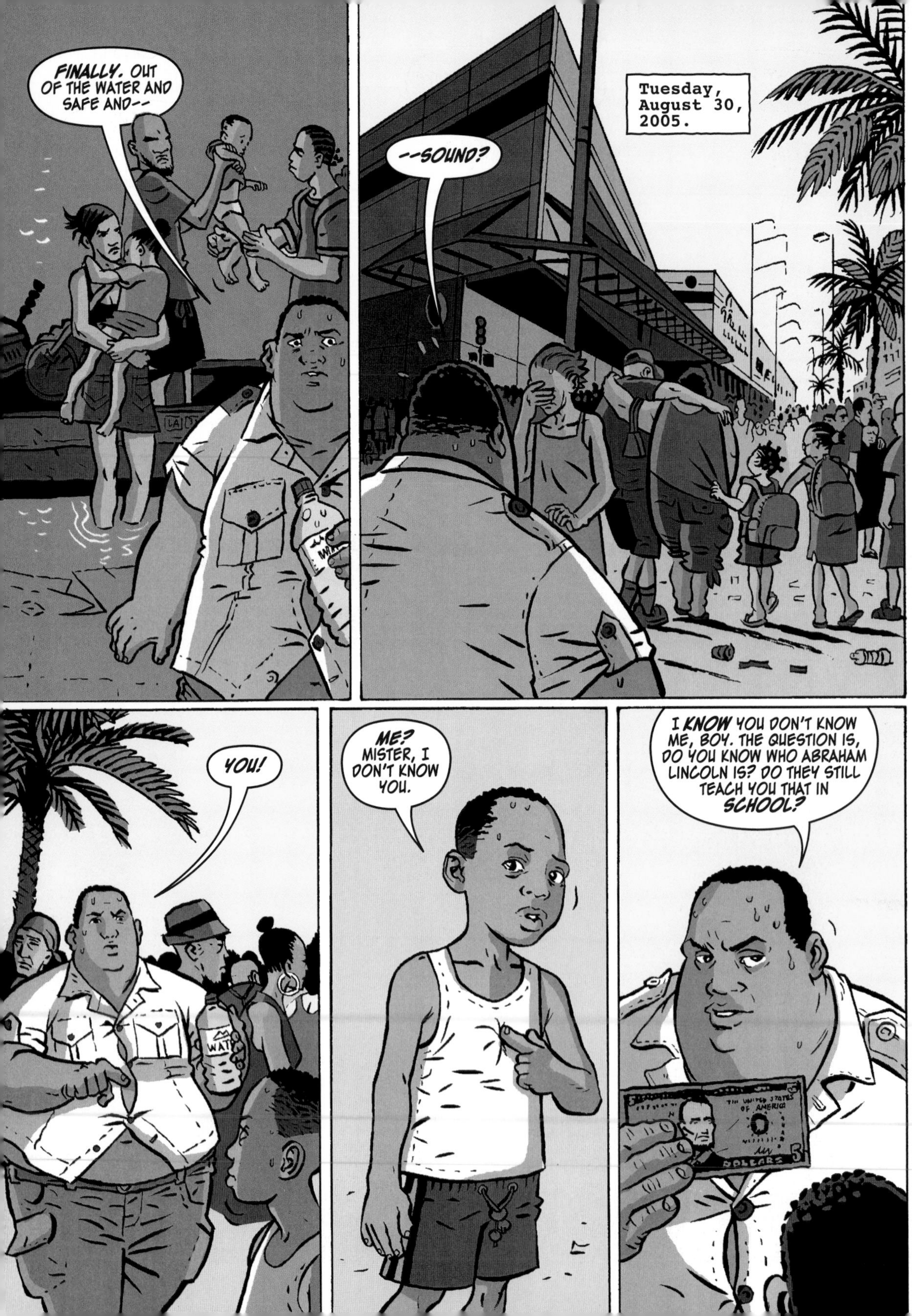
FINALLY. OUT OF THE WATER AND SAFE AND--
Tuesday, August 30, 2005.
--SOUND?
YOU!
ME? MISTER, I DON'T KNOW YOU.
I KNOW YOU DON'T KNOW ME, BOY. THE QUESTION IS, DO YOU KNOW WHO ABRAHAM LINCOLN IS? DO THEY STILL TEACH YOU THAT IN SCHOOL?

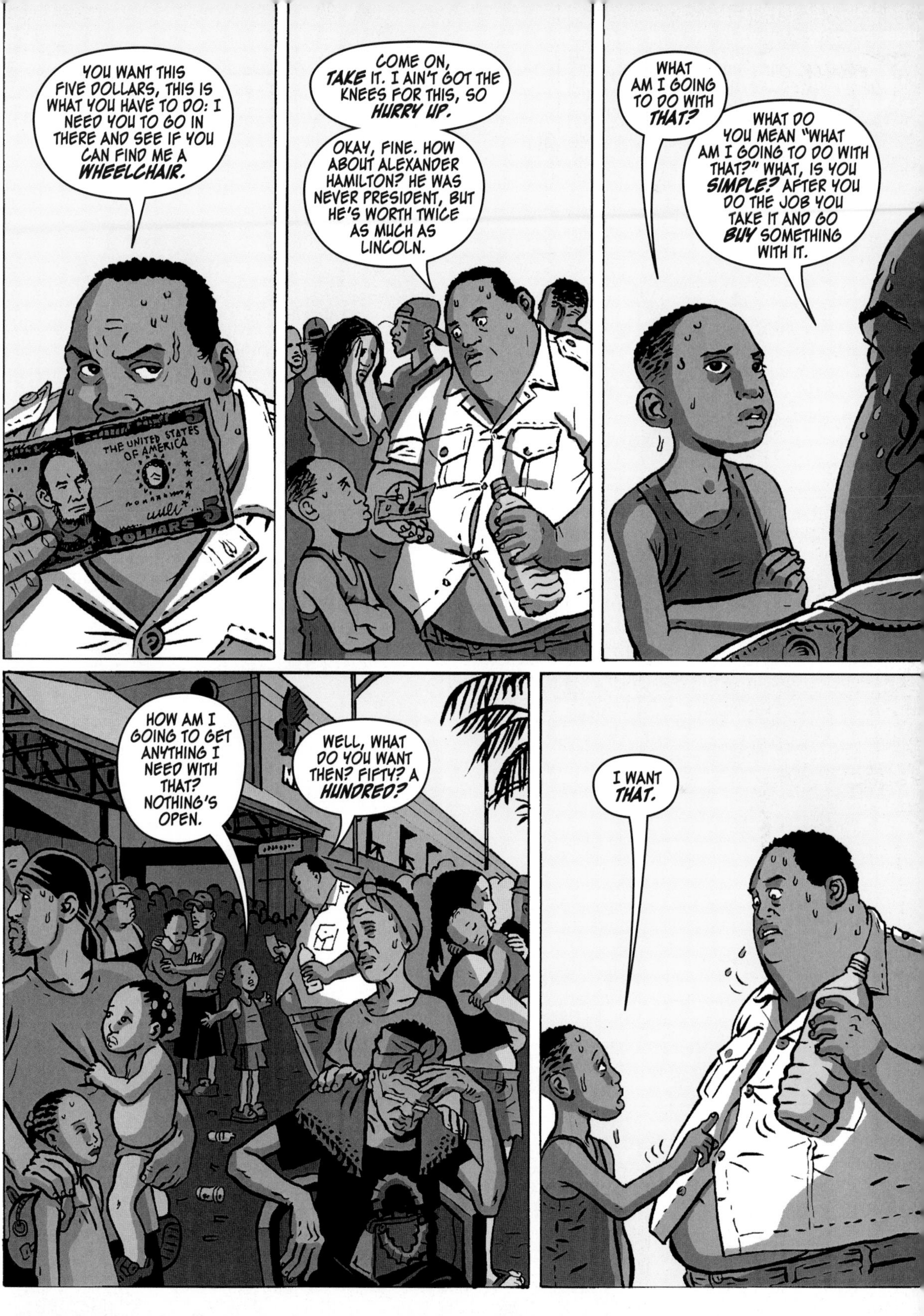
YOU WANT THIS FIVE DOLLARS, THIS IS WHAT YOU HAVE TO DO: I NEED YOU TO GO IN THERE AND SEE IF YOU CAN FIND ME A WHEELCHAIR.
THE UNITED STATES OF AMERICA
DOLLARS
COME ON, TAKE IT. I AIN'T GOT THE KNEES FOR THIS, SO HURRY UP.
OKAY, FINE. HOW ABOUT ALEXANDER HAMILTON? HE WAS NEVER PRESIDENT, BUT HE'S WORTH TWICE AS MUCH AS LINCOLN.
WHAT AM I GOING TO DO WITH THAT?
WHAT DO YOU MEAN "WHAT AM I GOING TO DO WITH THAT?" WHAT, IS YOU SIMPLE? AFTER YOU DO THE JOB YOU TAKE IT AND GO BUY SOMETHING WITH IT.
HOW AM I GOING TO GET ANYTHING I NEED WITH THAT? NOTHING'S OPEN.
WELL, WHAT DO YOU WANT THEN? FIFTY? A HUNDRED?
I WANT THAT.

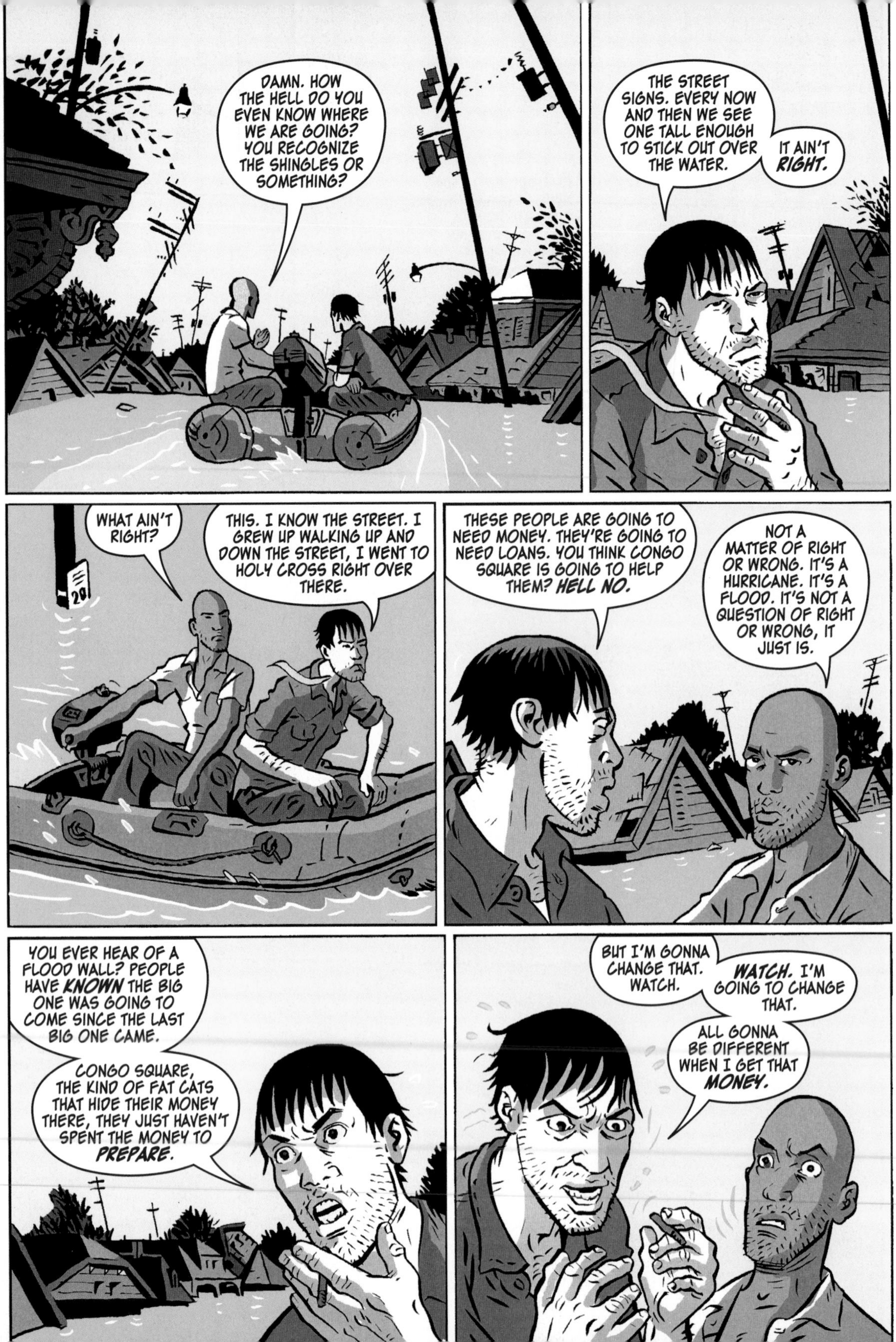
DAMN. HOW THE HELL DO YOU EVEN KNOW WHERE WE ARE GOING? YOU RECOGNIZE THE SHINGLES OR SOMETHING?
THE STREET SIGNS. EVERY NOW AND THEN WE SEE ONE TALL ENOUGH TO STICK OUT OVER THE WATER.
IT AIN'T *RIGHT.*
WHAT AIN'T RIGHT?
THIS. I KNOW THE STREET. I GREW UP WALKING UP AND DOWN THE STREET, I WENT TO HOLY CROSS RIGHT OVER THERE.
THESE PEOPLE ARE GOING TO NEED MONEY. THEY'RE GOING TO NEED LOANS. YOU THINK CONGO SQUARE IS GOING TO HELP THEM? *HELL NO.*
NOT A MATTER OF RIGHT OR WRONG. IT'S A HURRICANE. IT'S A FLOOD. IT'S NOT A QUESTION OF RIGHT OR WRONG, IT JUST IS.
YOU EVER HEAR OF A FLOOD WALL? PEOPLE HAVE *KNOWN* THE BIG ONE WAS GOING TO COME SINCE THE LAST BIG ONE CAME.
CONGO SQUARE, THE KIND OF FAT CATS THAT HIDE THEIR MONEY THERE, THEY JUST HAVEN'T SPENT THE MONEY TO *PREPARE*.
BUT I'M GONNA CHANGE THAT. WATCH.
WATCH. I'M GOING TO CHANGE THAT.
ALL GONNA BE DIFFERENT WHEN I GET THAT *MONEY.*

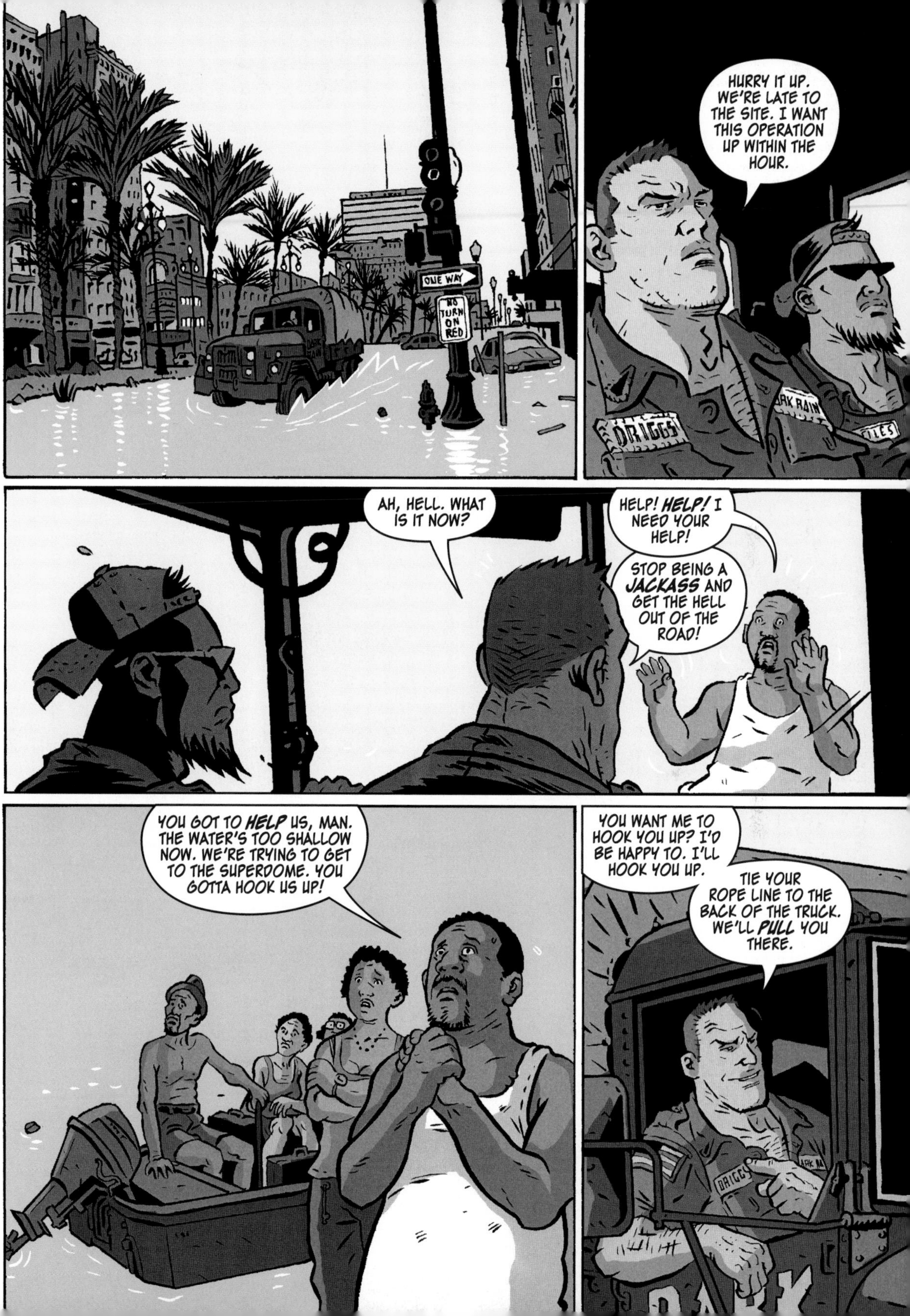
ONE WAY
NO TURN ON RED
HURRY IT UP. WE'RE LATE TO THE SITE. I WANT THIS OPERATION UP WITHIN THE HOUR.
DRIGGS
AH, HELL. WHAT IS IT NOW?
HELP! HELP! I NEED YOUR HELP!
STOP BEING A JACKASS AND GET THE HELL OUT OF THE ROAD!
YOU GOT TO HELP US, MAN. THE WATER'S TOO SHALLOW NOW. WE'RE TRYING TO GET TO THE SUPERDOME. YOU GOTTA HOOK US UP!
YOU WANT ME TO HOOK YOU UP? I'D BE HAPPY TO. I'LL HOOK YOU UP.
TIE YOUR ROPE LINE TO THE BACK OF THE TRUCK. WE'LL PULL YOU THERE.
DRIGGS

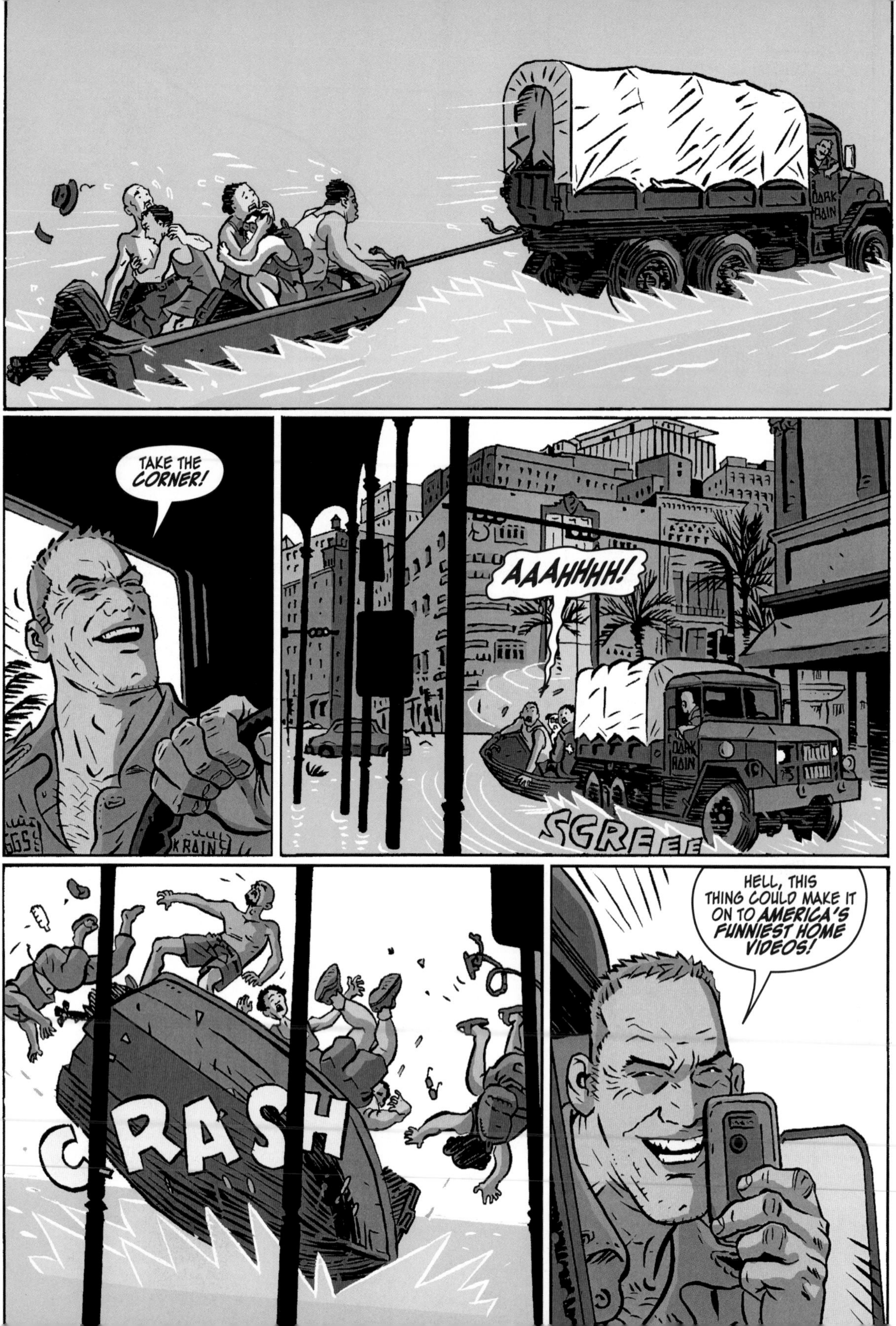
DARK RAIN
TAKE THE CORNER!
AAAHHHH!
DARK RAIN
SCREEE
CRASH
HELL, THIS THING COULD MAKE IT ON TO AMERICA'S FUNNIEST HOME VIDEOS!

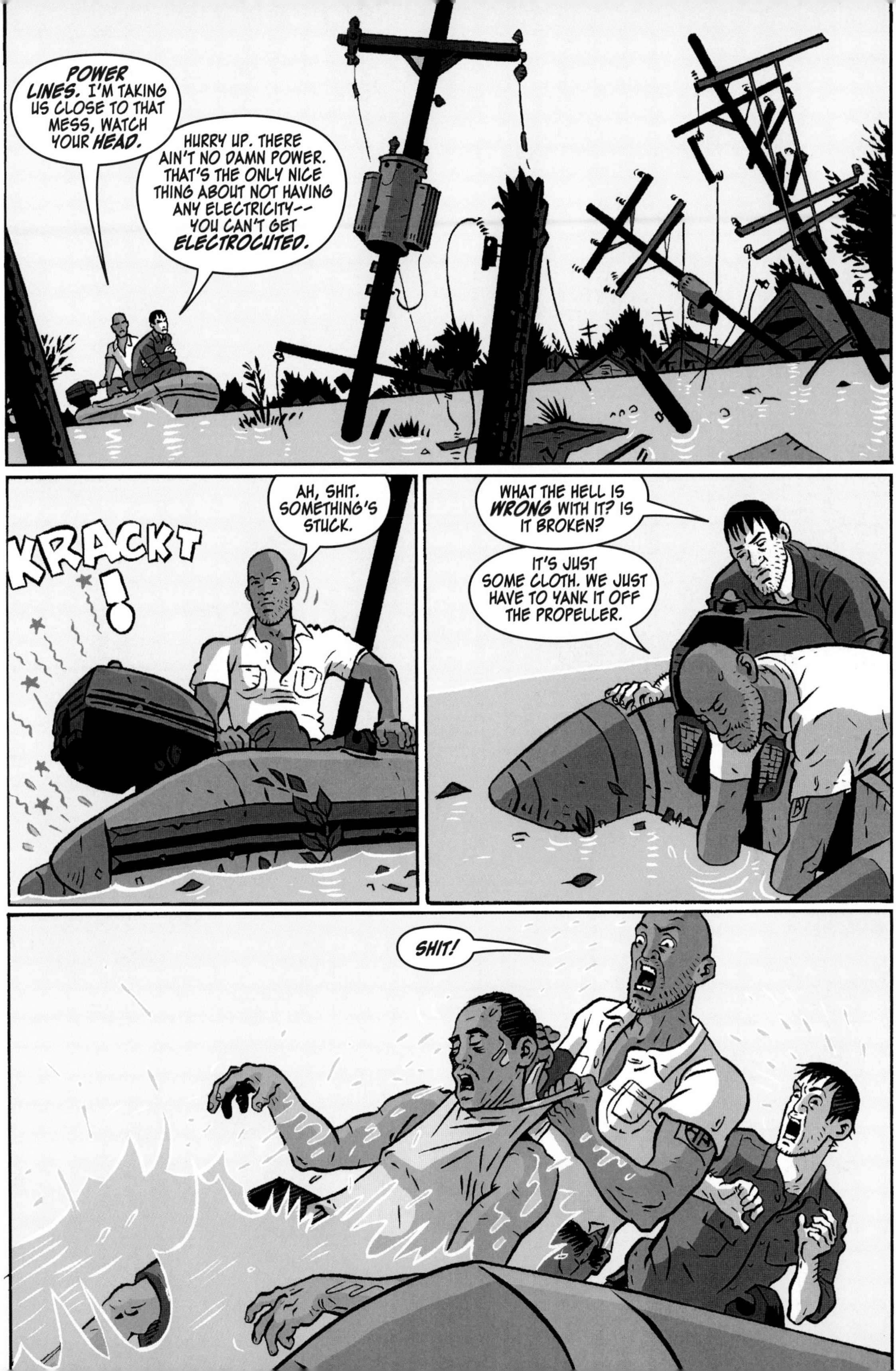
POWER LINES. I'M TAKING US CLOSE TO THAT MESS, WATCH YOUR HEAD.
HURRY UP. THERE AIN'T NO DAMN POWER. THAT'S THE ONLY NICE THING ABOUT NOT HAVING ANY ELECTRICITY-- YOU CAN'T GET ELECTROCUTED.
KRACKT
AH, SHIT. SOMETHING'S STUCK.
WHAT THE HELL IS WRONG WITH IT? IS IT BROKEN?
IT'S JUST SOME CLOTH. WE JUST HAVE TO YANK IT OFF THE PROPELLER.
SHIT!

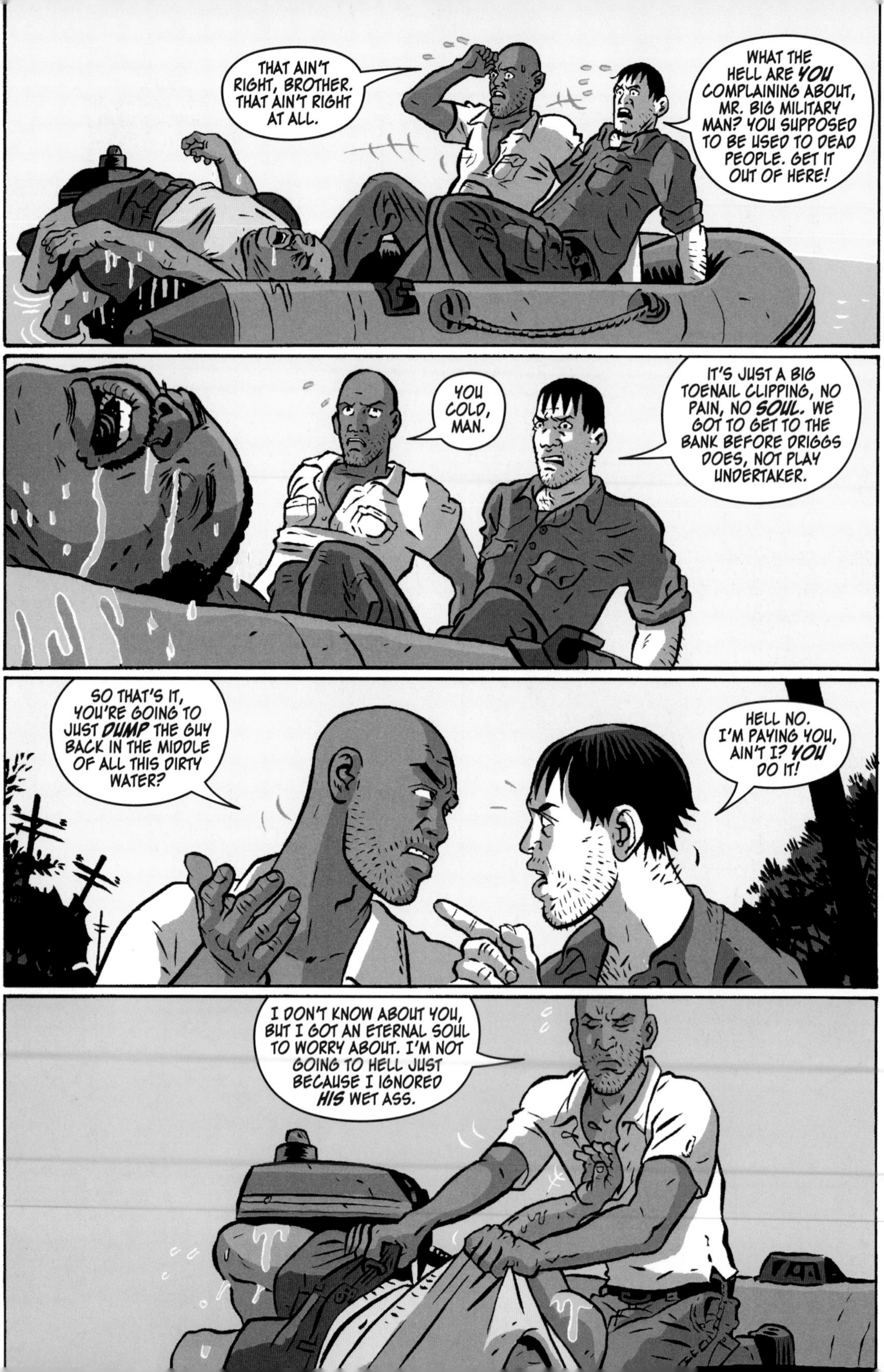

THAT AIN'T RIGHT, BROTHER. THAT AIN'T RIGHT AT ALL.
WHAT THE HELL ARE YOU COMPLAINING ABOUT, MR. BIG MILITARY MAN? YOU SUPPOSED TO BE USED TO DEAD PEOPLE. GET IT OUT OF HERE!
YOU COLD, MAN.
IT'S JUST A BIG TOENAIL CLIPPING, NO PAIN, NO SOUL. WE GOT TO GET TO THE BANK BEFORE DRIGGS DOES, NOT PLAY UNDERTAKER.
SO THAT'S IT, YOU'RE GOING TO JUST DUMP THE GUY BACK IN THE MIDDLE OF ALL THIS DIRTY WATER?
HELL NO. I'M PAYING YOU, AIN'T I? YOU DO IT!
I DON'T KNOW ABOUT YOU, BUT I GOT AN ETERNAL SOUL TO WORRY ABOUT. I'M NOT GOING TO HELL JUST BECAUSE I IGNORED HIS WET ASS.

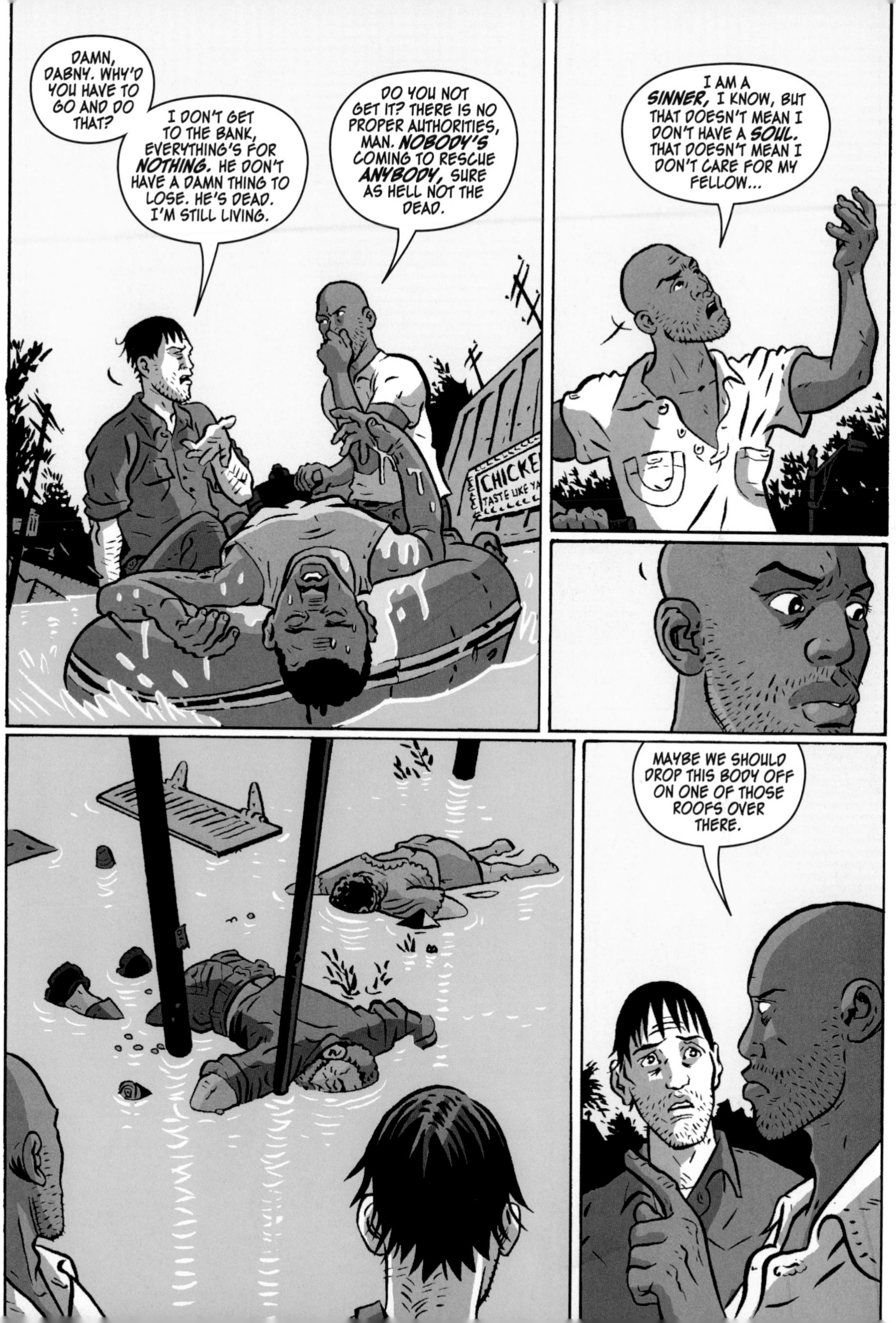
DAMN, DABNY. WHY'D YOU HAVE TO GO AND DO THAT?
I DON'T GET TO THE BANK, EVERYTHING'S FOR NOTHING. HE DON'T HAVE A DAMN THING TO LOSE. HE'S DEAD. I'M STILL LIVING.
DO YOU NOT GET IT? THERE IS NO PROPER AUTHORITIES, MAN. NOBODY'S COMING TO RESCUE ANYBODY, SURE AS HELL NOT THE DEAD.
CHICKE
TASTE LIKE YA
I AM A SINNER, I KNOW, BUT THAT DOESN'T MEAN I DON'T HAVE A SOUL. THAT DOESN'T MEAN I DON'T CARE FOR MY FELLOW...
MAYBE WE SHOULD DROP THIS BODY OFF ON ONE OF THOSE ROOFS OVER THERE.

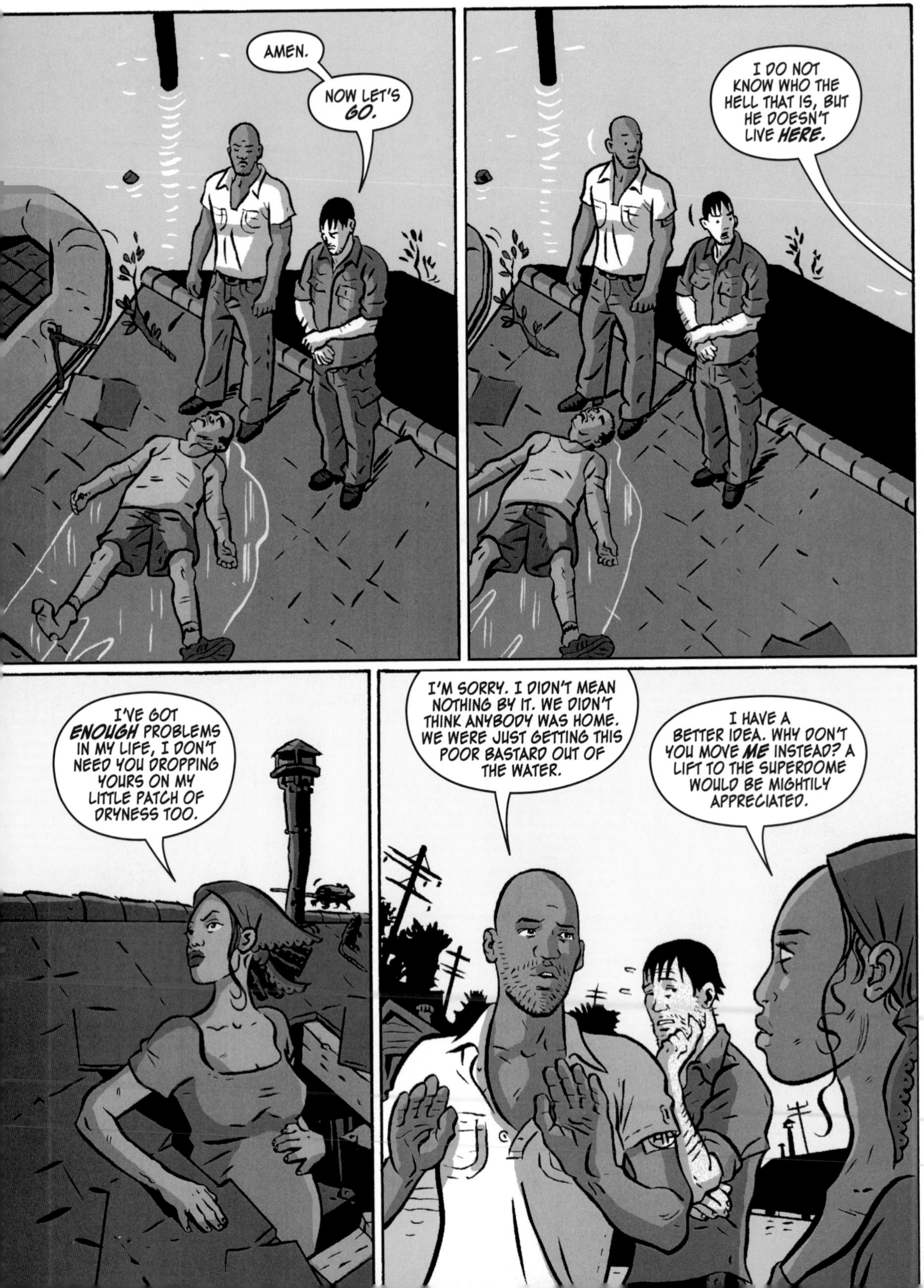
AMEN.
NOW LET'S GO.
I DO NOT KNOW WHO THE HELL THAT IS, BUT HE DOESN'T LIVE HERE.
I'VE GOT ENOUGH PROBLEMS IN MY LIFE, I DON'T NEED YOU DROPPING YOURS ON MY LITTLE PATCH OF DRYNESS TOO.
I'M SORRY. I DIDN'T MEAN NOTHING BY IT. WE DIDN'T THINK ANYBODY WAS HOME. WE WERE JUST GETTING THIS POOR BASTARD OUT OF THE WATER.
I HAVE A BETTER IDEA. WHY DON'T YOU MOVE ME INSTEAD? A LIFT TO THE SUPERDOME WOULD BE MIGHTILY APPRECIATED.

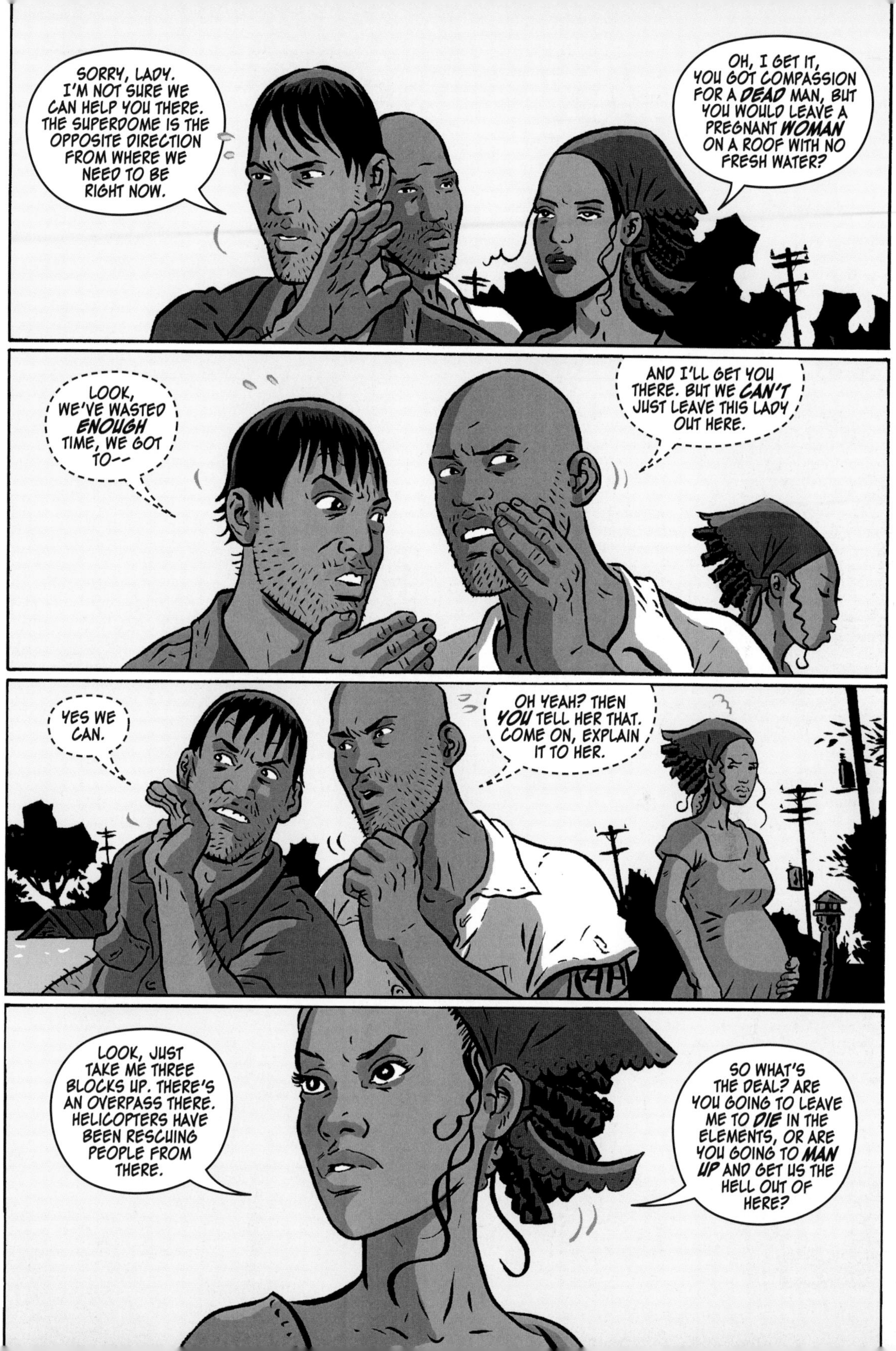
SORRY, LADY. I'M NOT SURE WE CAN HELP YOU THERE. THE SUPERDOME IS THE OPPOSITE DIRECTION FROM WHERE WE NEED TO BE RIGHT NOW.
OH, I GET IT, YOU GOT COMPASSION FOR A DEAD MAN, BUT YOU WOULD LEAVE A PREGNANT WOMAN ON A ROOF WITH NO FRESH WATER?
LOOK, WE'VE WASTED ENOUGH TIME, WE GOT TO--
AND I'LL GET YOU THERE. BUT WE CAN'T JUST LEAVE THIS LADY OUT HERE.
YES WE CAN.
OH YEAH? THEN YOU TELL HER THAT. COME ON, EXPLAIN IT TO HER.
LOOK, JUST TAKE ME THREE BLOCKS UP. THERE'S AN OVERPASS THERE. HELICOPTERS HAVE BEEN RESCUING PEOPLE FROM THERE.
SO WHAT'S THE DEAL? ARE YOU GOING TO LEAVE ME TO DIE IN THE ELEMENTS, OR ARE YOU GOING TO MAN UP AND GET US THE HELL OUT OF HERE?

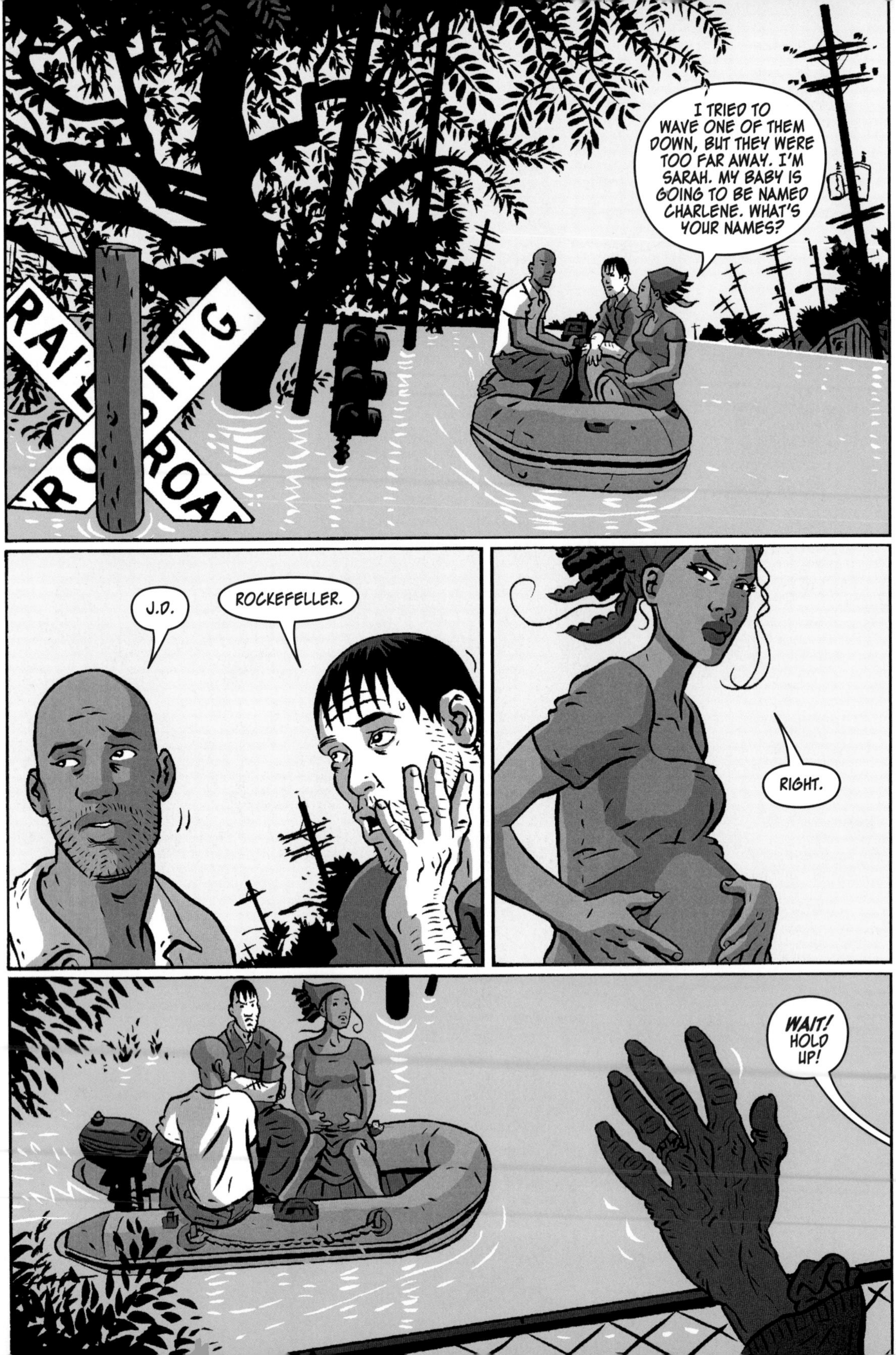

I TRIED TO WAVE ONE OF THEM DOWN, BUT THEY WERE TOO FAR AWAY. I'M SARAH. MY BABY IS GOING TO BE NAMED CHARLENE. WHAT'S YOUR NAMES?
RAILROAD CROSSING
J.D.
ROCKEFELLER.
RIGHT.
WAIT! HOLD UP!

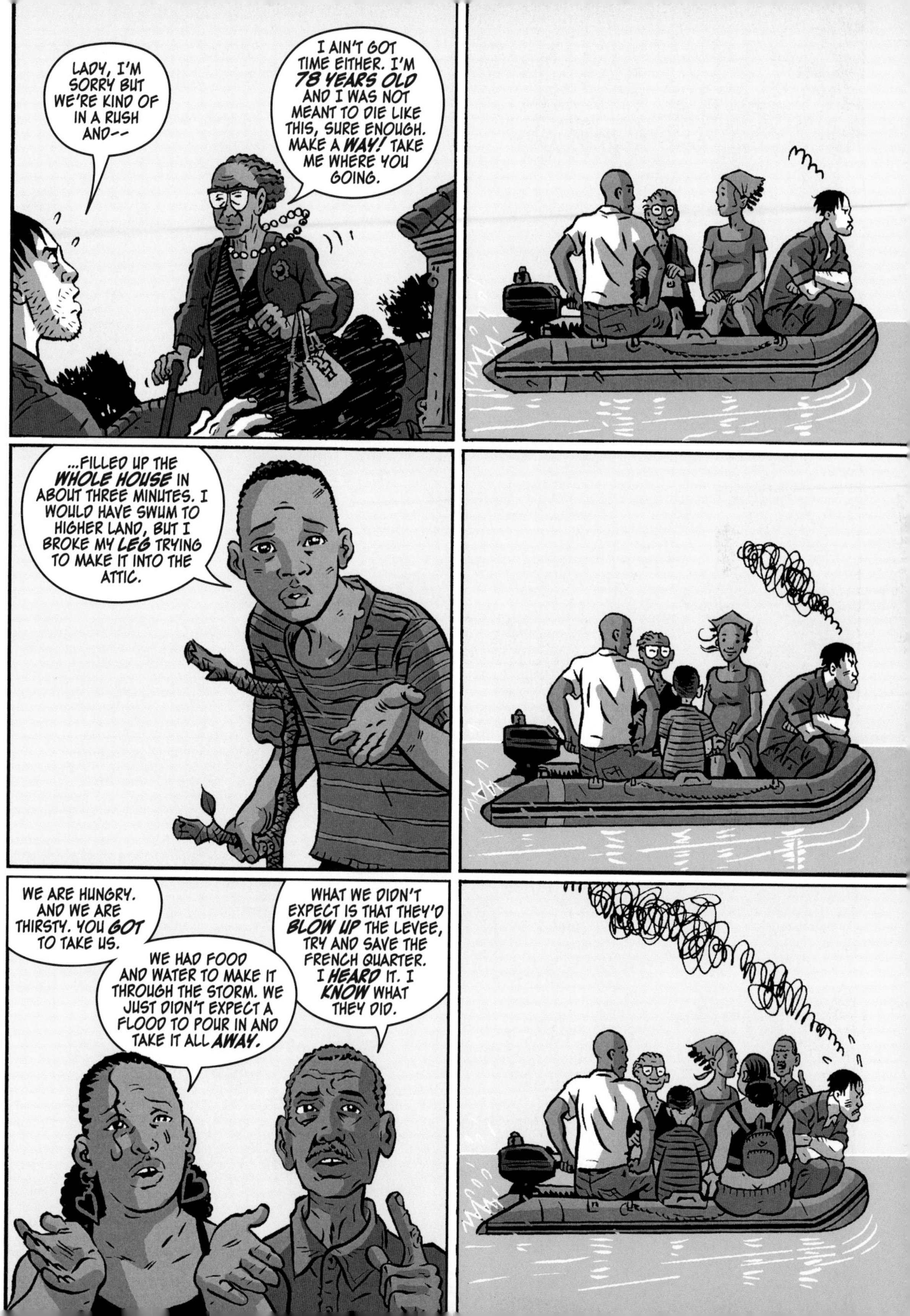

LADY, I'M SORRY BUT WE'RE KIND OF IN A RUSH AND--
I AIN'T GOT TIME EITHER. I'M 78 YEARS OLD AND I WAS NOT MEANT TO DIE LIKE THIS, SURE ENOUGH. MAKE A WAY! TAKE ME WHERE YOU GOING.
...FILLED UP THE WHOLE HOUSE IN ABOUT THREE MINUTES. I WOULD HAVE SWUM TO HIGHER LAND, BUT I BROKE MY LEG TRYING TO MAKE IT INTO THE ATTIC.
WE ARE HUNGRY. AND WE ARE THIRSTY. YOU GOT TO TAKE US.
WE HAD FOOD AND WATER TO MAKE IT THROUGH THE STORM. WE JUST DIDN'T EXPECT A FLOOD TO POUR IN AND TAKE IT ALL AWAY.
WHAT WE DIDN'T EXPECT IS THAT THEY'D BLOW UP THE LEVEE, TRY AND SAVE THE FRENCH QUARTER. I HEARD IT. I KNOW WHAT THEY DID.

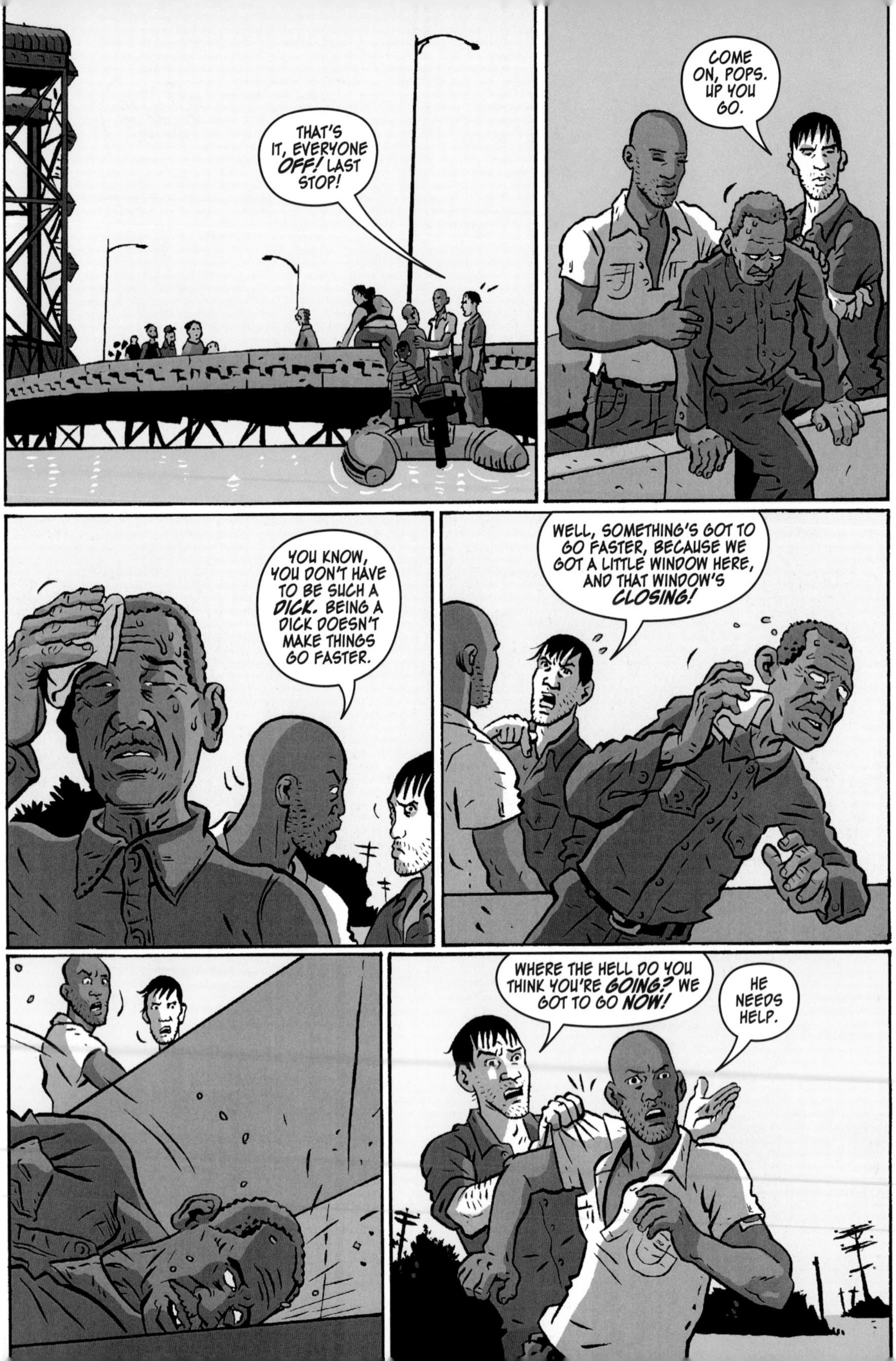
THAT'S IT, EVERYONE OFF! LAST STOP!
COME ON, POPS. UP YOU GO.
YOU KNOW, YOU DON'T HAVE TO BE SUCH A DICK. BEING A DICK DOESN'T MAKE THINGS GO FASTER.
WELL, SOMETHING'S GOT TO GO FASTER, BECAUSE WE GOT A LITTLE WINDOW HERE, AND THAT WINDOW'S CLOSING!
WHERE THE HELL DO YOU THINK YOU'RE GOING? WE GOT TO GO NOW!
HE NEEDS HELP.

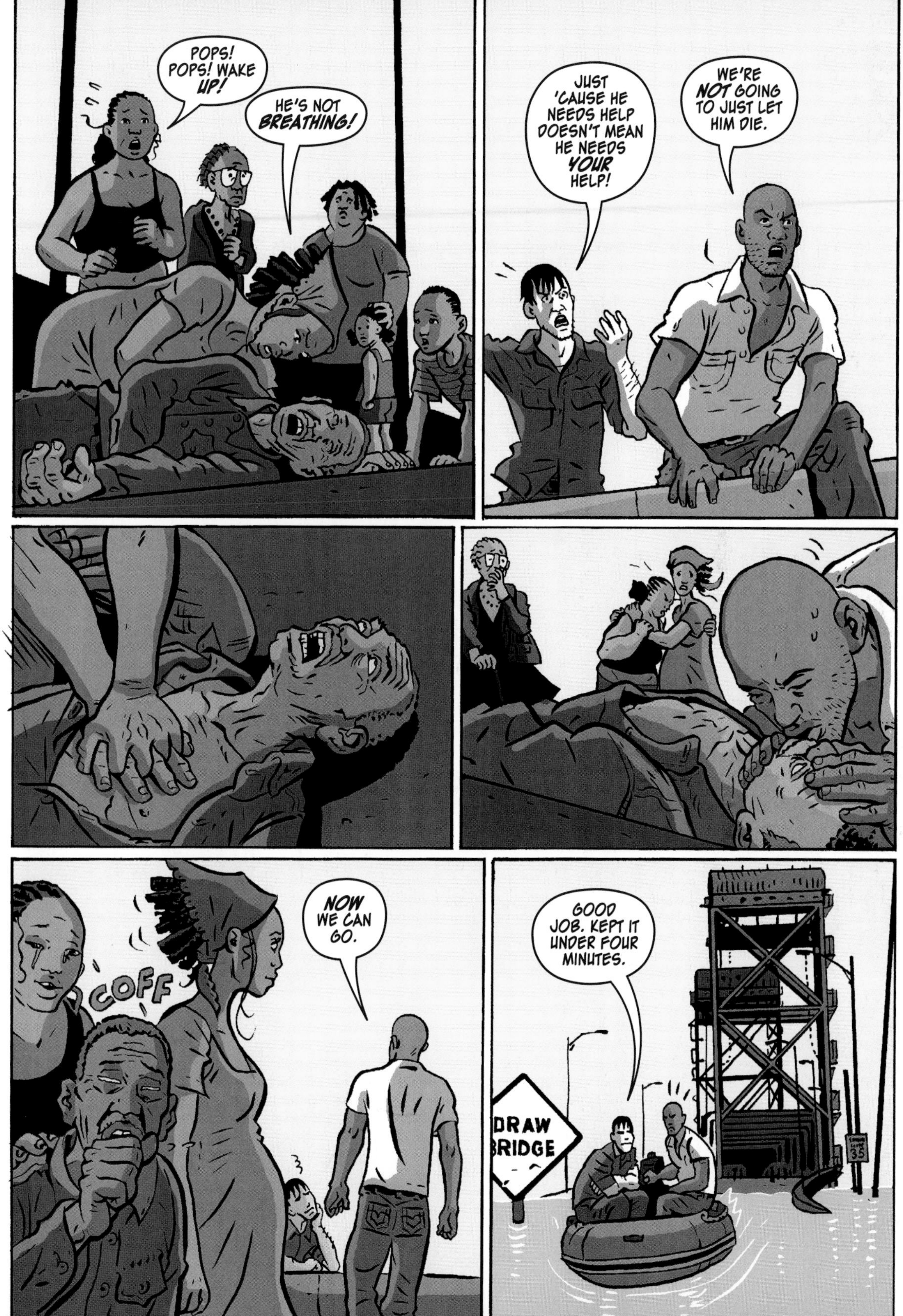
POPS! POPS! WAKE UP!
HE'S NOT BREATHING!
JUST 'CAUSE HE NEEDS HELP DOESN'T MEAN HE NEEDS YOUR HELP!
WE'RE NOT GOING TO JUST LET HIM DIE.
COFF
NOW WE CAN GO.
GOOD JOB. KEPT IT UNDER FOUR MINUTES.
DRAW BRIDGE

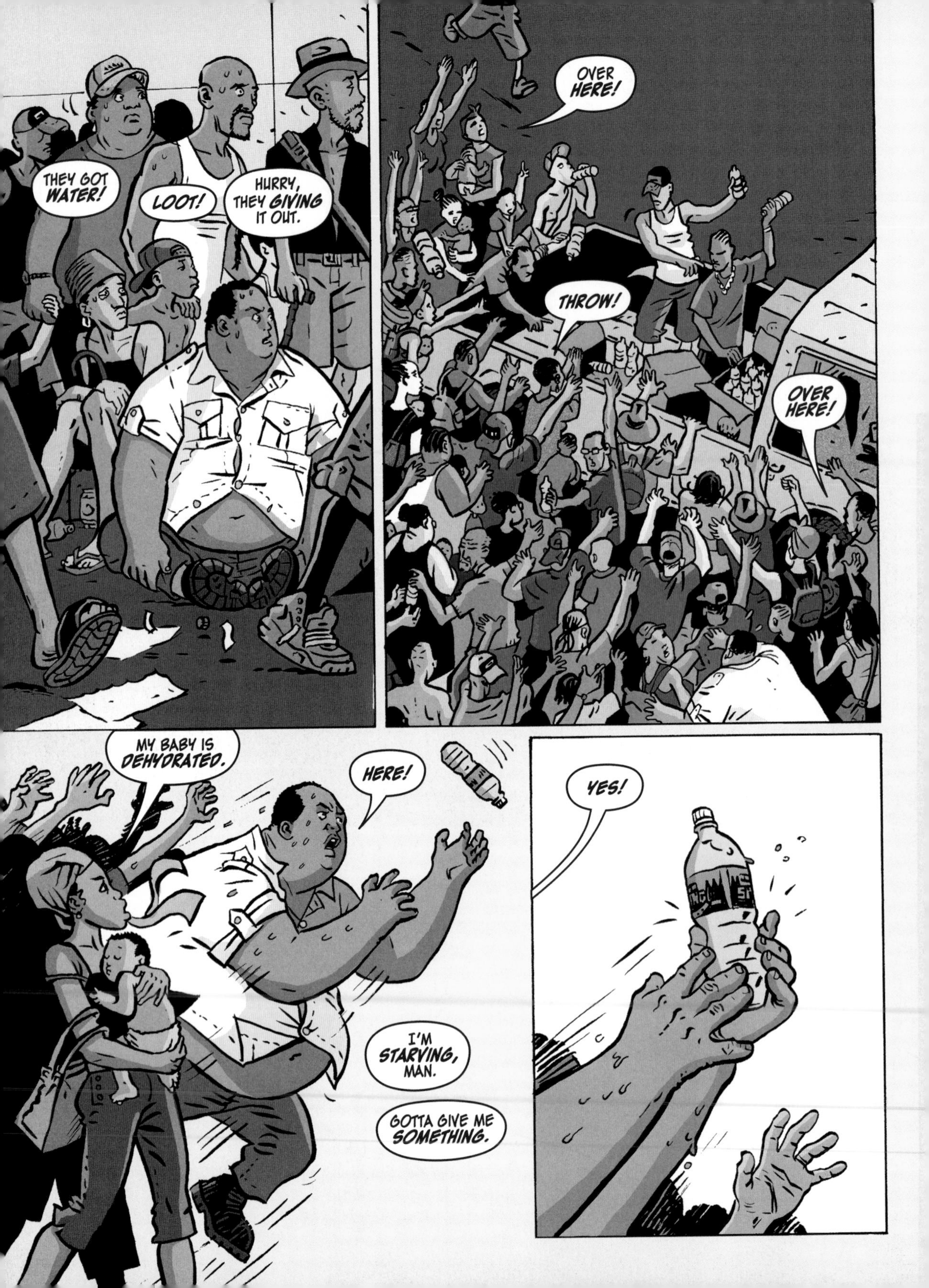
THEY GOT WATER!
LOOT!
HURRY, THEY GIVING IT OUT.
OVER HERE!
THROW!
OVER HERE!
MY BABY IS DEHYDRATED.
HERE!
I'M STARVING, MAN.
GOTTA GIVE ME SOMETHING.
YES!

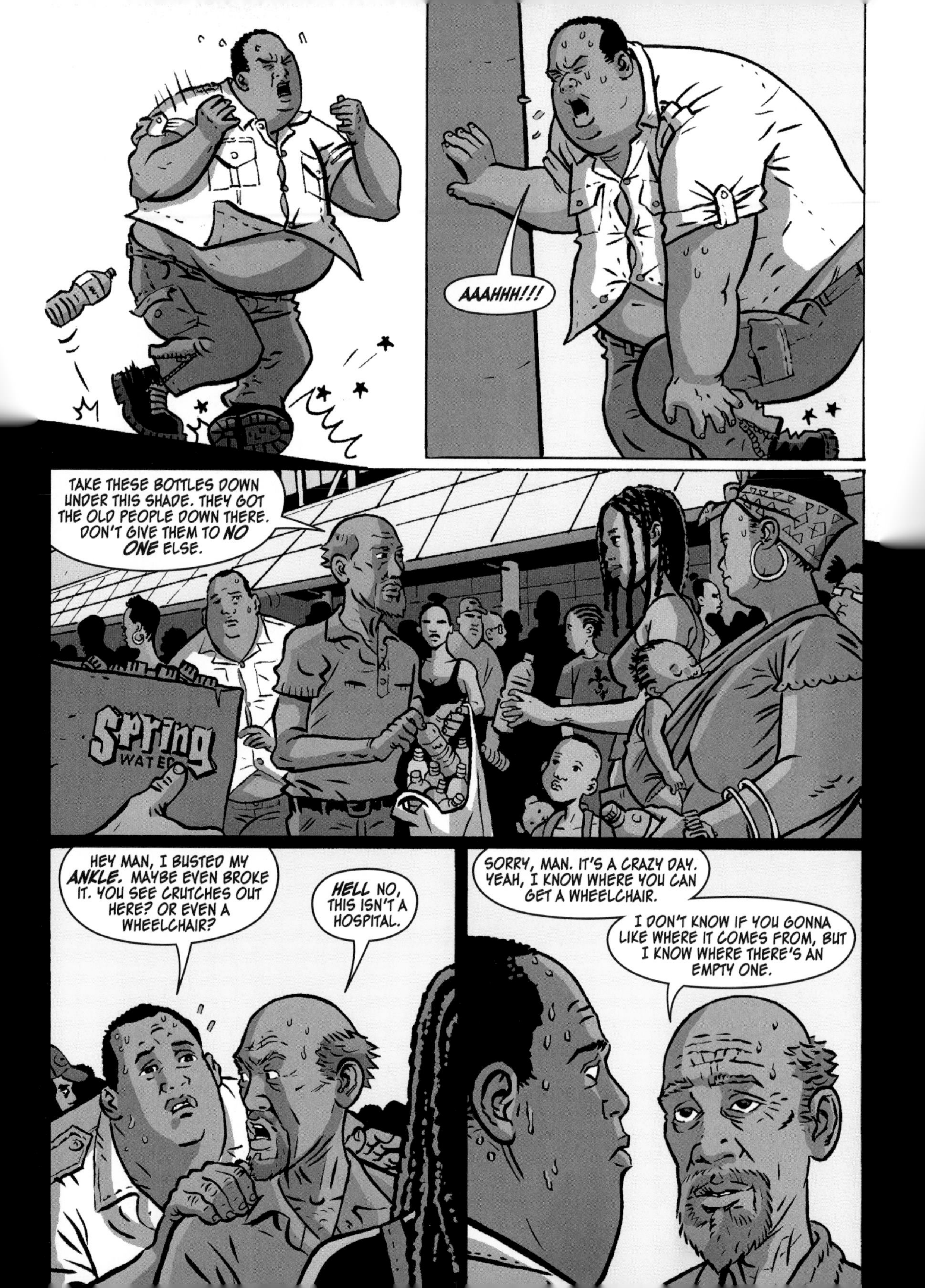
AAAHHH!!!
TAKE THESE BOTTLES DOWN UNDER THIS SHADE. THEY GOT THE OLD PEOPLE DOWN THERE. DON'T GIVE THEM TO NO ONE ELSE.
SPRING WATER
HEY MAN, I BUSTED MY ANKLE. MAYBE EVEN BROKE IT. YOU SEE CRUTCHES OUT HERE? OR EVEN A WHEELCHAIR?
HELL NO, THIS ISN'T A HOSPITAL.
SORRY, MAN. IT'S A CRAZY DAY. YEAH, I KNOW WHERE YOU CAN GET A WHEELCHAIR.
I DON'T KNOW IF YOU GONNA LIKE WHERE IT COMES FROM, BUT I KNOW WHERE THERE'S AN EMPTY ONE.

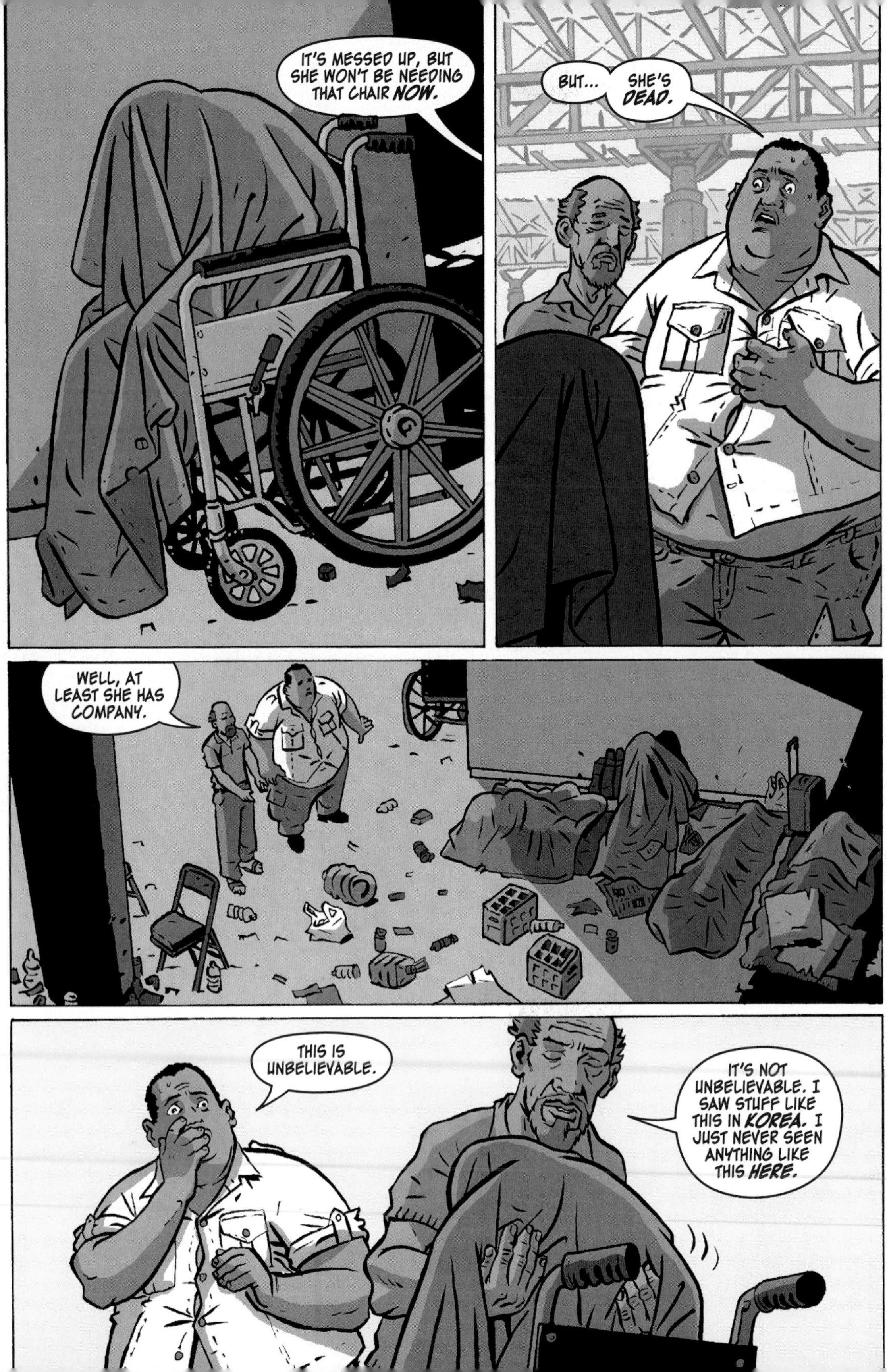
IT'S MESSED UP, BUT SHE WON'T BE NEEDING THAT CHAIR NOW.
BUT...
SHE'S DEAD.
WELL, AT LEAST SHE HAS COMPANY.
THIS IS UNBELIEVABLE.
IT'S NOT UNBELIEVABLE. I SAW STUFF LIKE THIS IN KOREA. I JUST NEVER SEEN ANYTHING LIKE THIS HERE.

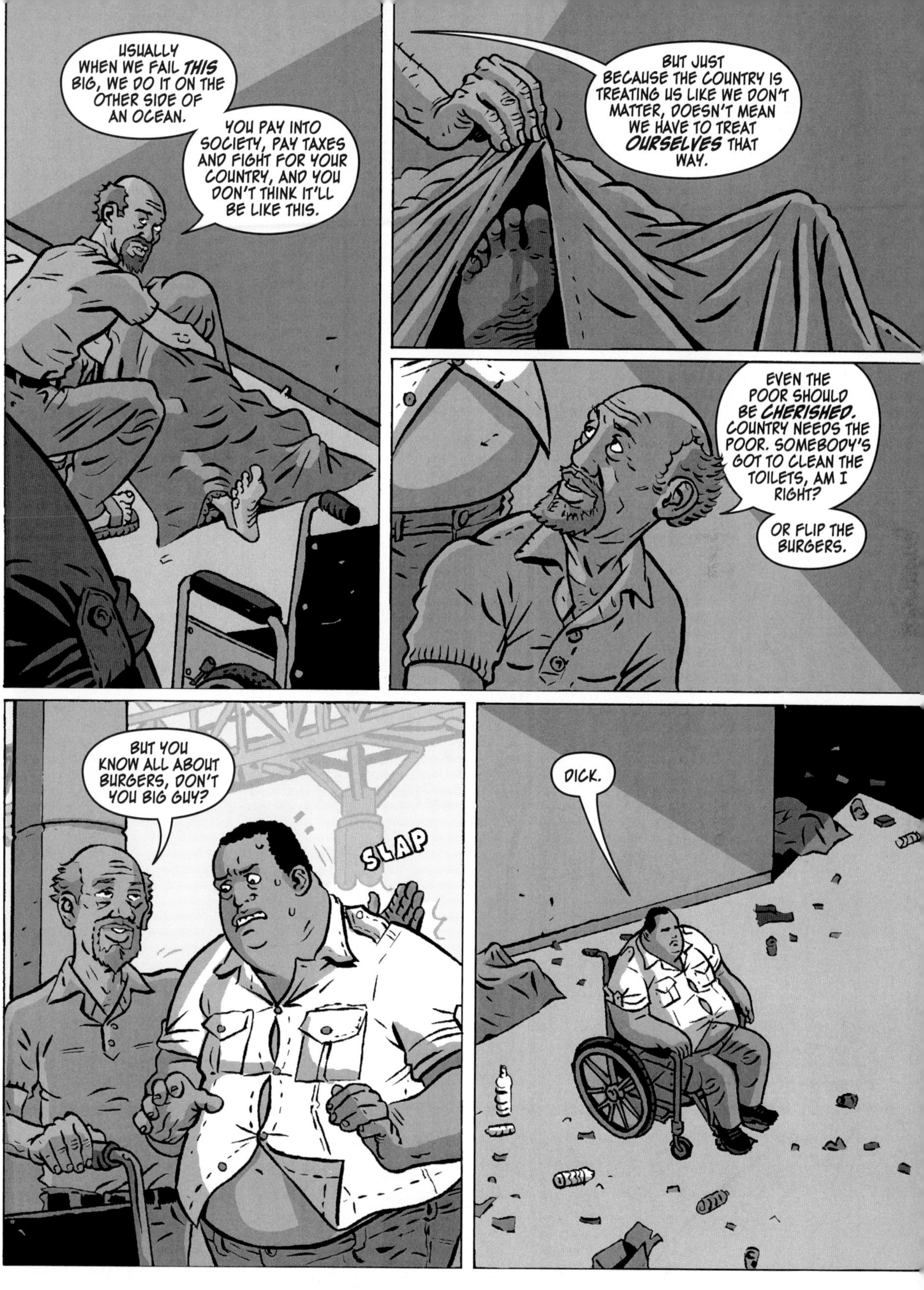

USUALLY WHEN WE FAIL THIS BIG, WE DO IT ON THE OTHER SIDE OF AN OCEAN.
YOU PAY INTO SOCIETY, PAY TAXES AND FIGHT FOR YOUR COUNTRY, AND YOU DON'T THINK IT'LL BE LIKE THIS.
BUT JUST BECAUSE THE COUNTRY IS TREATING US LIKE WE DON'T MATTER, DOESN'T MEAN WE HAVE TO TREAT OURSELVES THAT WAY.
EVEN THE POOR SHOULD BE CHERISHED. COUNTRY NEEDS THE POOR. SOMEBODY'S GOT TO CLEAN THE TOILETS, AM I RIGHT?
OR FLIP THE BURGERS.
BUT YOU KNOW ALL ABOUT BURGERS, DON'T YOU BIG GUY?
SLAP
DICK.

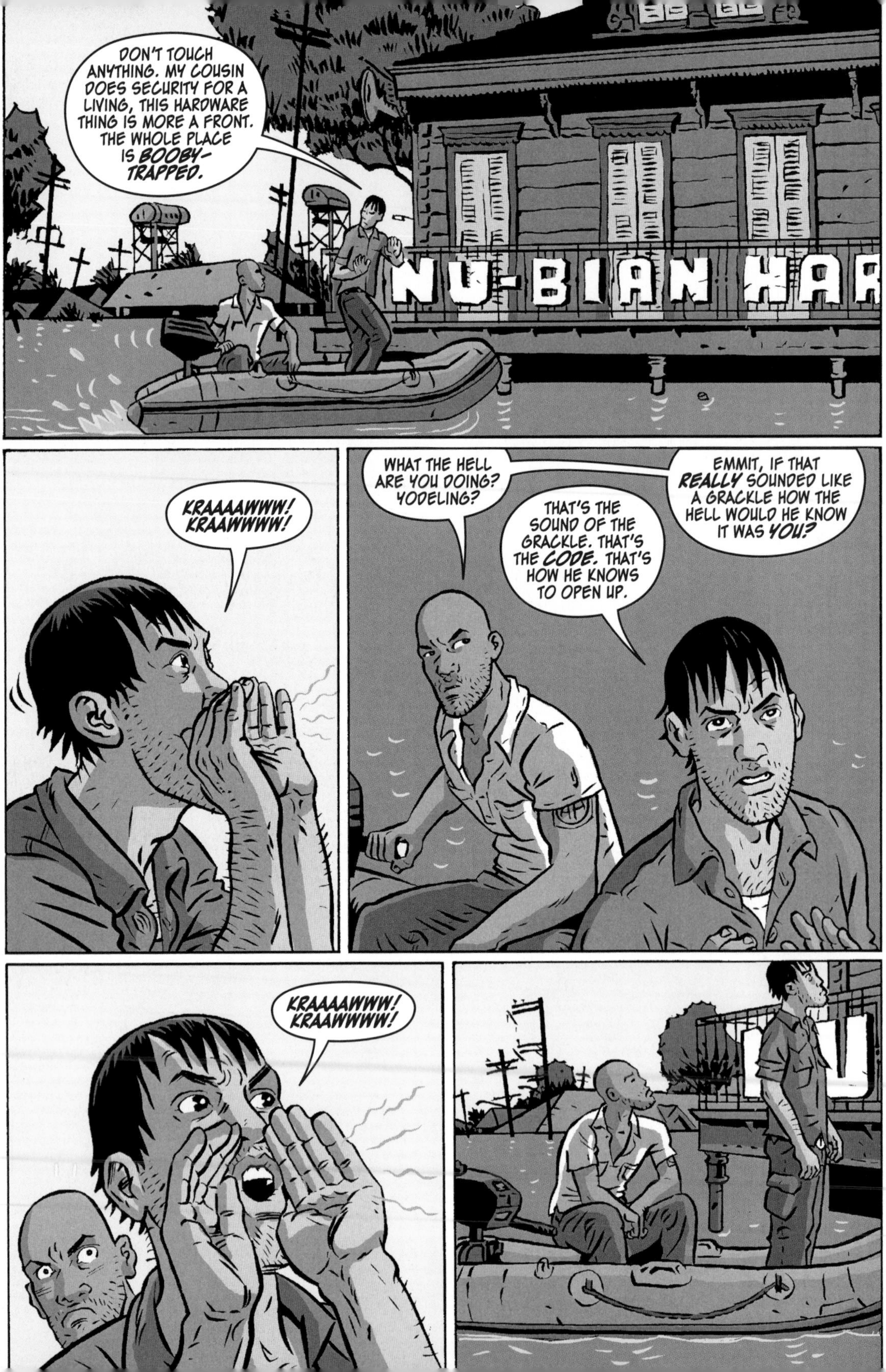
DON'T TOUCH ANYTHING. MY COUSIN DOES SECURITY FOR A LIVING, THIS HARDWARE THING IS MORE A FRONT. THE WHOLE PLACE IS BOOBY-TRAPPED.
NU-BIAN HAR
KRAAAAWWW! KRAAWWWW!
WHAT THE HELL ARE YOU DOING? YODELING?
THAT'S THE SOUND OF THE GRACKLE. THAT'S THE CODE. THAT'S HOW HE KNOWS TO OPEN UP.
EMMIT, IF THAT REALLY SOUNDED LIKE A GRACKLE HOW THE HELL WOULD HE KNOW IT WAS YOU?
KRAAAAWWW! KRAAWWWW!
NU

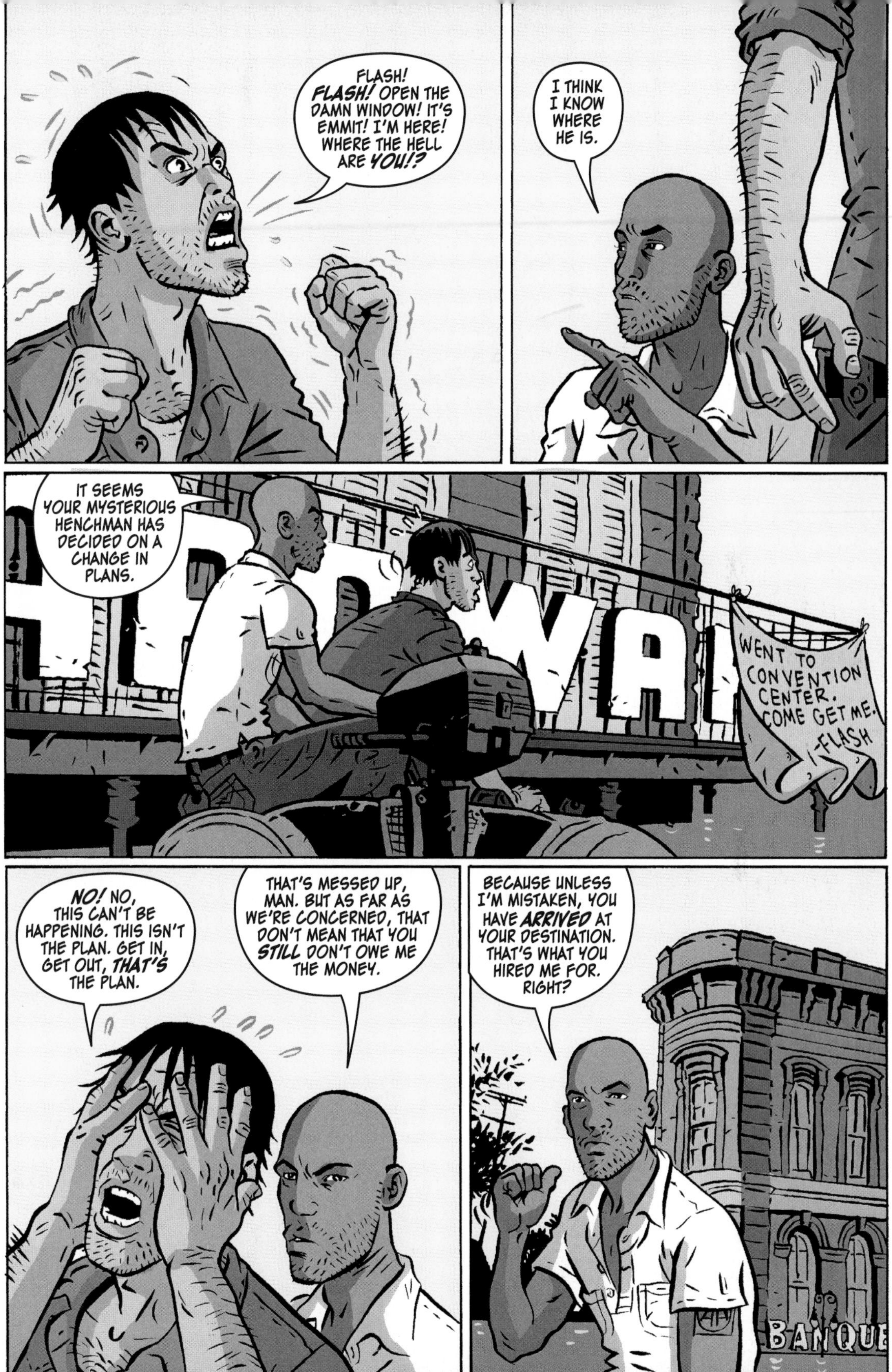
FLASH! FLASH! OPEN THE DAMN WINDOW! IT'S EMMIT! I'M HERE! WHERE THE HELL ARE YOU!?
I THINK I KNOW WHERE HE IS.
IT SEEMS YOUR MYSTERIOUS HENCHMAN HAS DECIDED ON A CHANGE IN PLANS.
WENT TO CONVENTION CENTER. COME GET ME. -FLASH
NO! NO, THIS CAN'T BE HAPPENING. THIS ISN'T THE PLAN. GET IN, GET OUT, THAT'S THE PLAN.
THAT'S MESSED UP, MAN. BUT AS FAR AS WE'RE CONCERNED, THAT DON'T MEAN THAT YOU STILL DON'T OWE ME THE MONEY.
BECAUSE UNLESS I'M MISTAKEN, YOU HAVE ARRIVED AT YOUR DESTINATION. THAT'S WHAT YOU HIRED ME FOR. RIGHT?
BANQUE

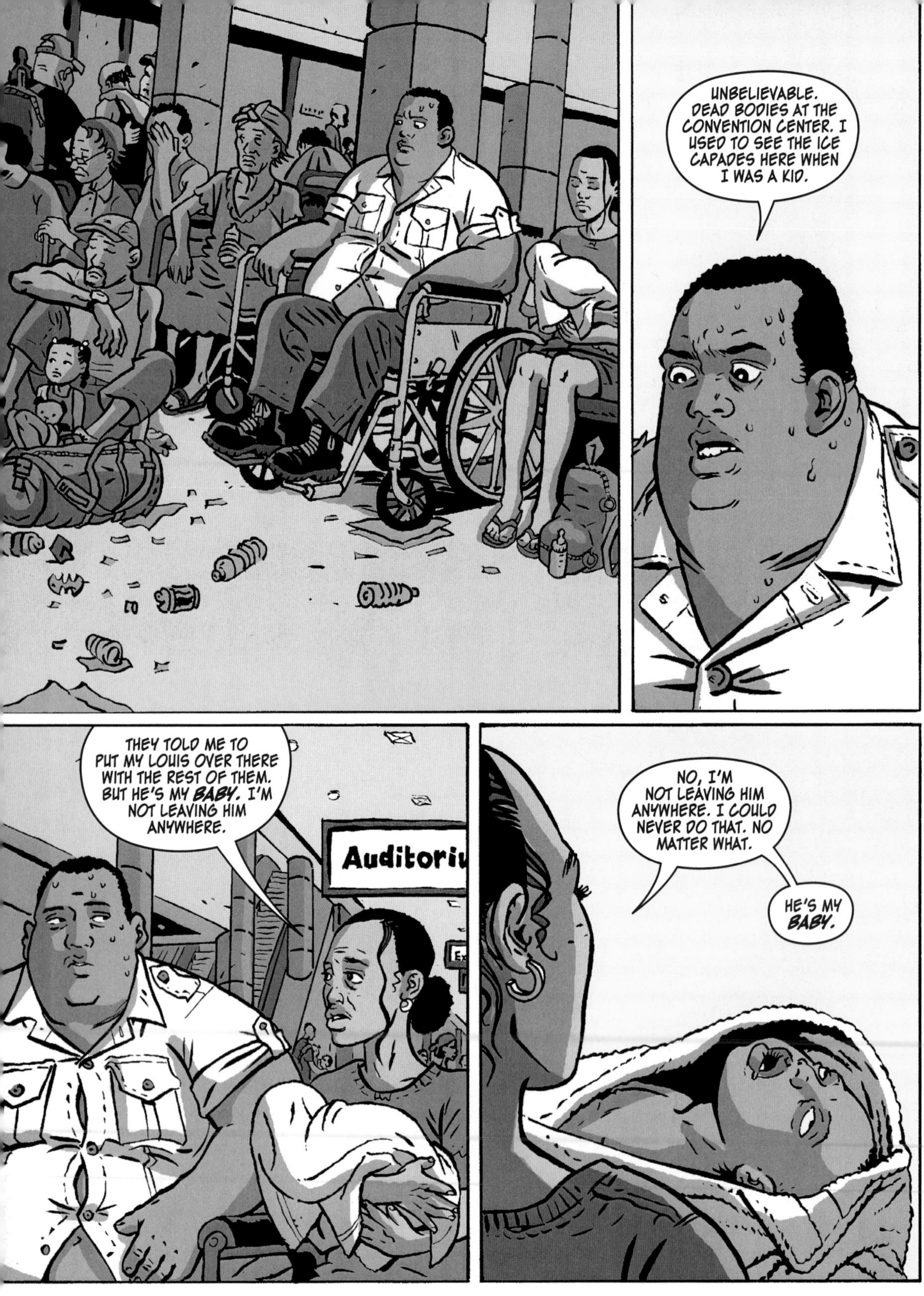
UNBELIEVABLE. DEAD BODIES AT THE CONVENTION CENTER. I USED TO SEE THE ICE CAPADES HERE WHEN I WAS A KID.
THEY TOLD ME TO PUT MY LOUIS OVER THERE WITH THE REST OF THEM. BUT HE'S MY BABY. I'M NOT LEAVING HIM ANYWHERE.
Auditoriu
NO, I'M NOT LEAVING HIM ANYWHERE. I COULD NEVER DO THAT. NO MATTER WHAT.
HE'S MY BABY.

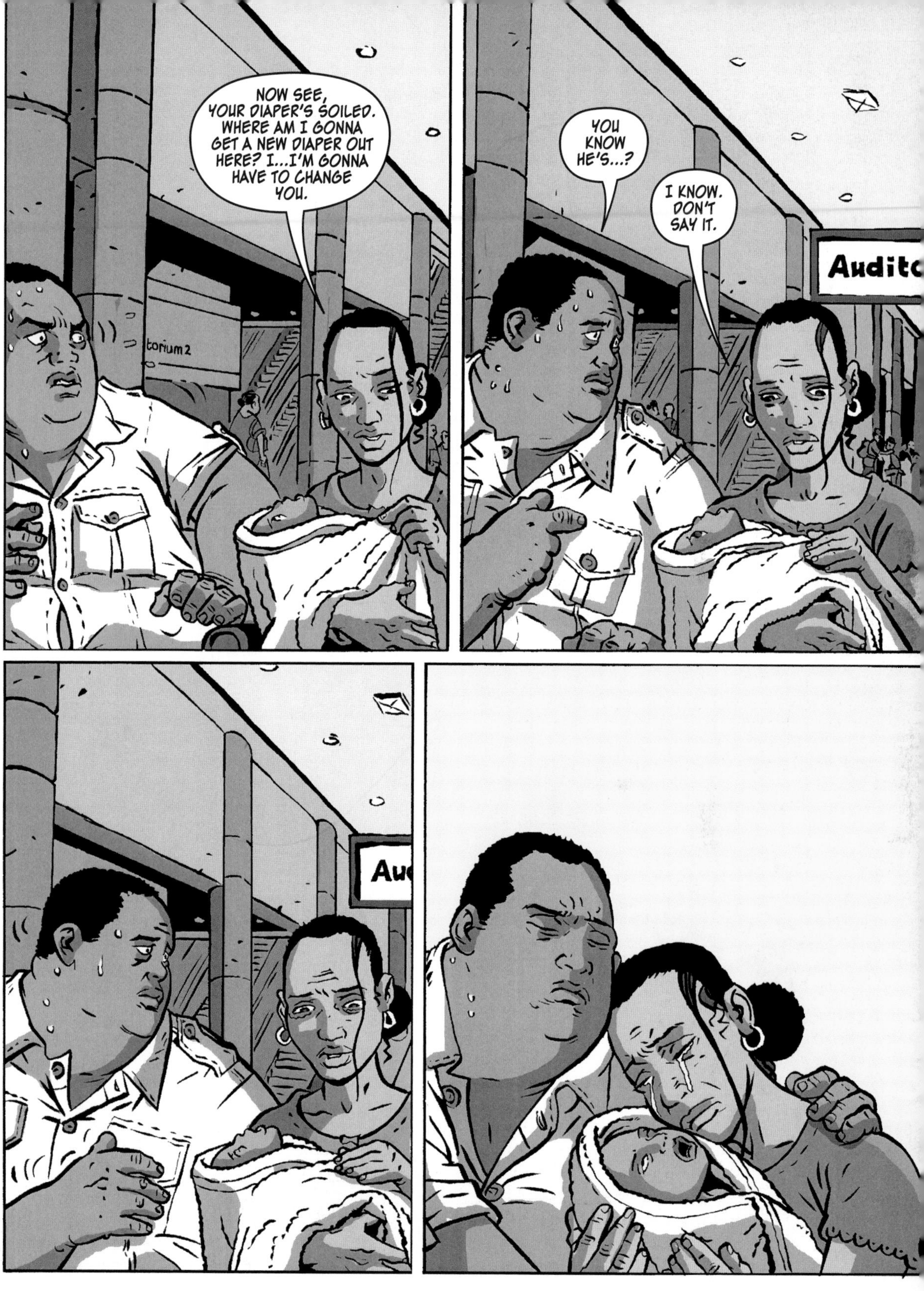
NOW SEE, YOUR DIAPER'S SOILED. WHERE AM I GONNA GET A NEW DIAPER OUT HERE? I...I'M GONNA HAVE TO CHANGE YOU.
torium 2
YOU KNOW HE'S...?
I KNOW. DON'T SAY IT.
Audito
Au

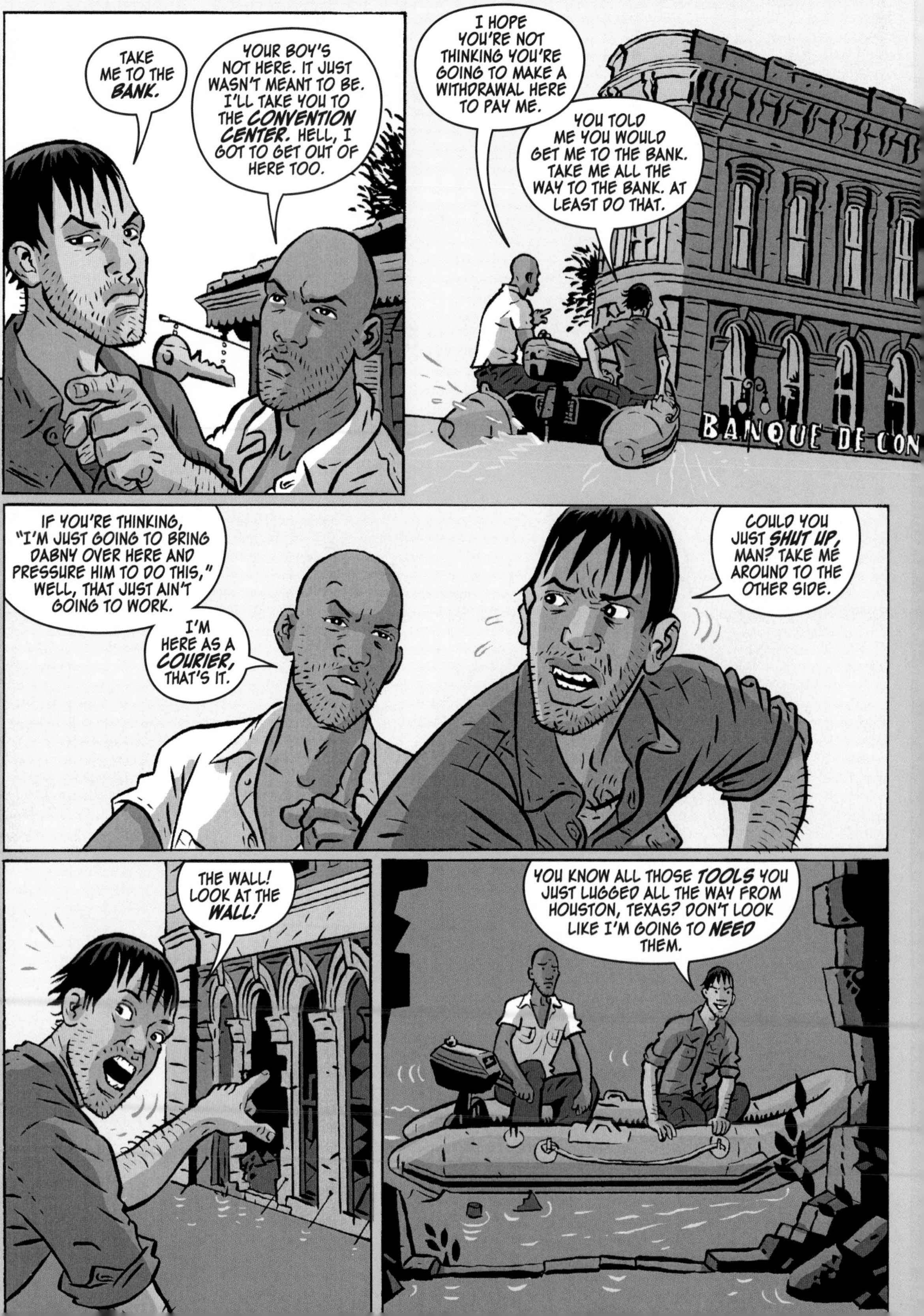
TAKE ME TO THE BANK.
YOUR BOY'S NOT HERE. IT JUST WASN'T MEANT TO BE. I'LL TAKE YOU TO THE CONVENTION CENTER. HELL, I GOT TO GET OUT OF HERE TOO.
I HOPE YOU'RE NOT THINKING YOU'RE GOING TO MAKE A WITHDRAWAL HERE TO PAY ME.
YOU TOLD ME YOU WOULD GET ME TO THE BANK. TAKE ME ALL THE WAY TO THE BANK. AT LEAST DO THAT.
BANQUE DE CON
IF YOU'RE THINKING, "I'M JUST GOING TO BRING DABNY OVER HERE AND PRESSURE HIM TO DO THIS," WELL, THAT JUST AIN'T GOING TO WORK.
I'M HERE AS A COURIER, THAT'S IT.
COULD YOU JUST SHUT UP, MAN? TAKE ME AROUND TO THE OTHER SIDE.
THE WALL! LOOK AT THE WALL!
YOU KNOW ALL THOSE TOOLS YOU JUST LUGGED ALL THE WAY FROM HOUSTON, TEXAS? DON'T LOOK LIKE I'M GOING TO NEED THEM.

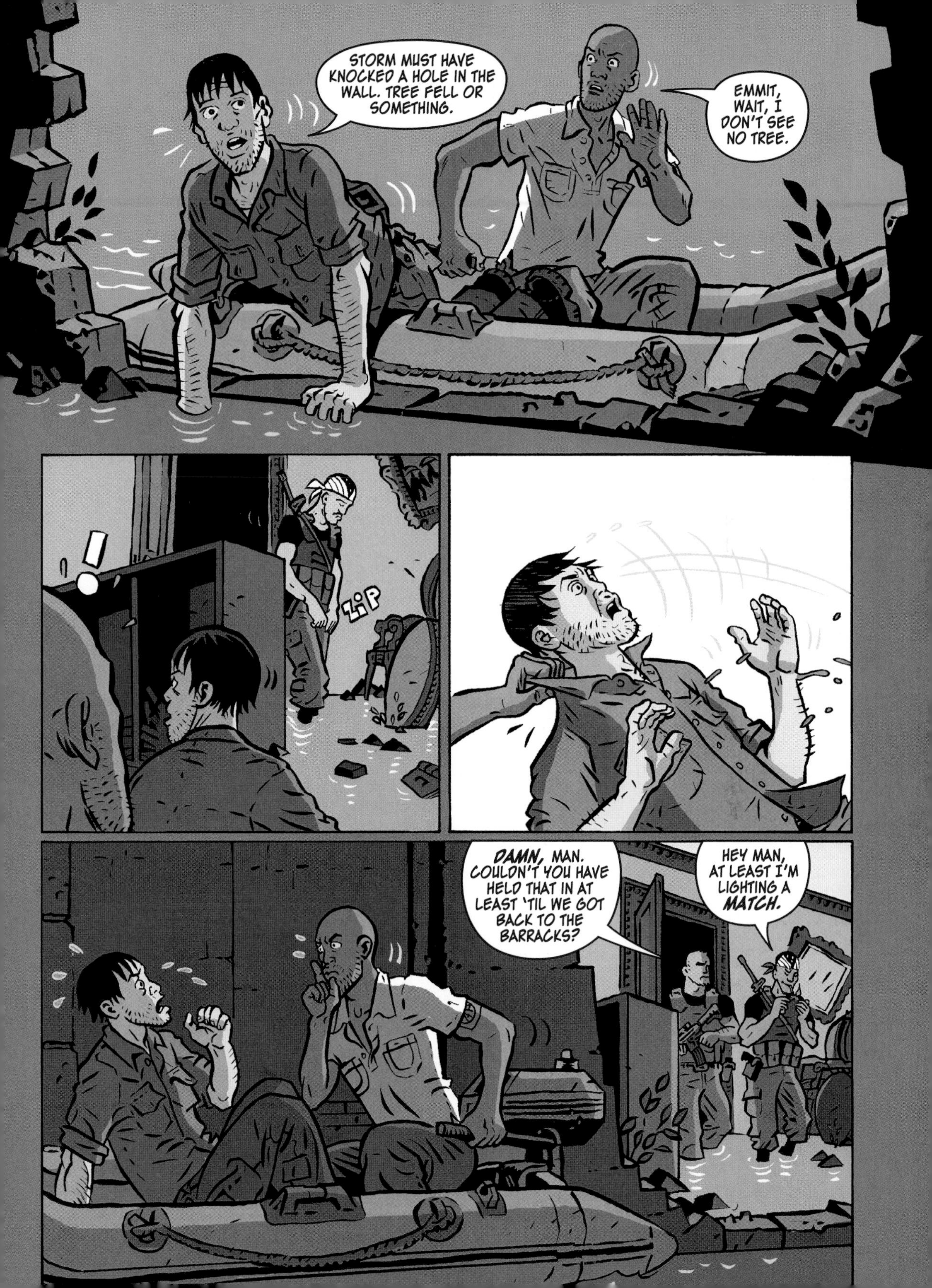
STORM MUST HAVE KNOCKED A HOLE IN THE WALL. TREE FELL OR SOMETHING.
EMMIT, WAIT, I DON'T SEE NO TREE.
!
ZIP
DAMN, MAN. COULDN'T YOU HAVE HELD THAT IN AT LEAST 'TIL WE GOT BACK TO THE BARRACKS?
HEY MAN, AT LEAST I'M LIGHTING A MATCH.

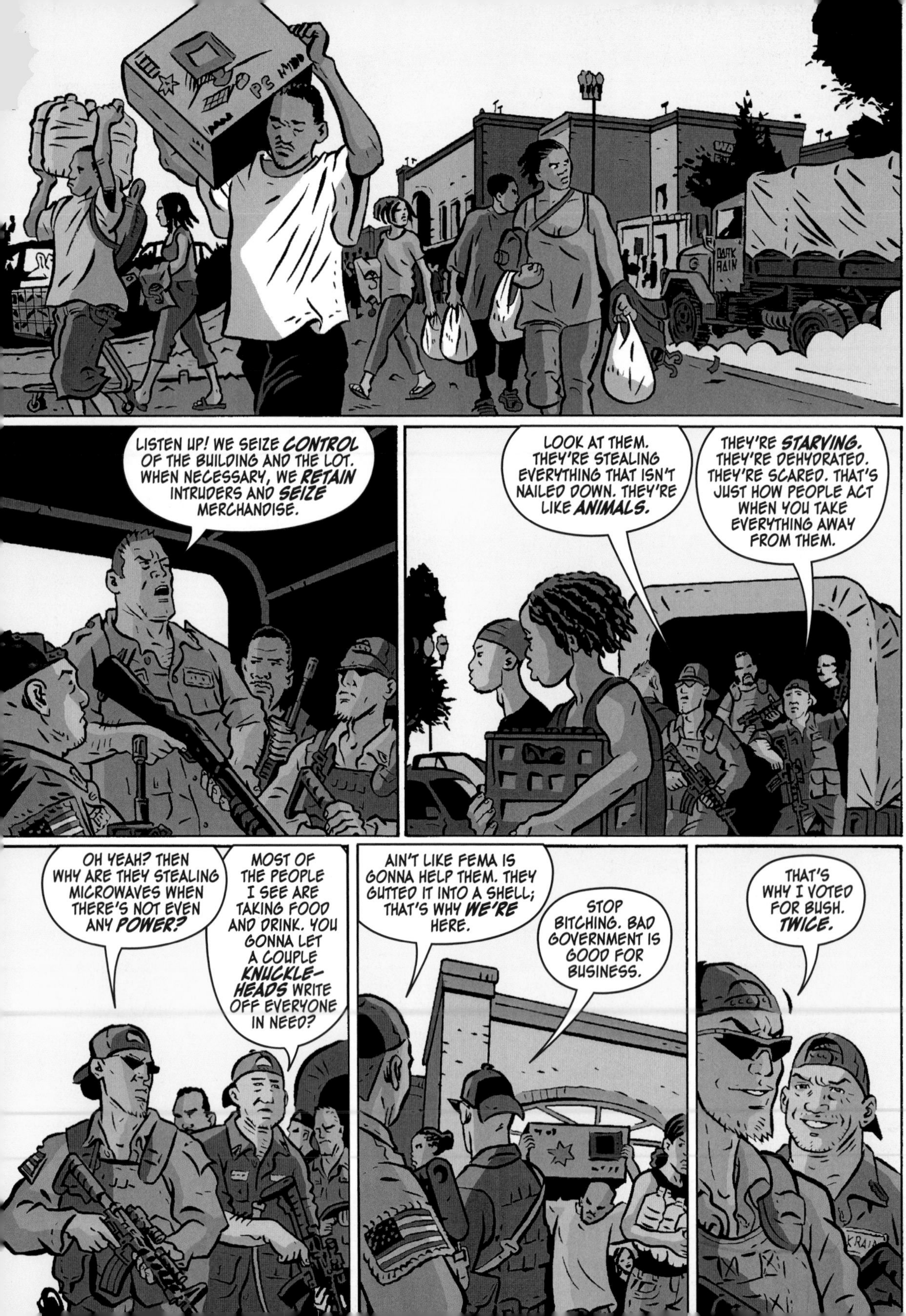

DARK RAIN
LISTEN UP! WE SEIZE CONTROL OF THE BUILDING AND THE LOT. WHEN NECESSARY, WE RETAIN INTRUDERS AND SEIZE MERCHANDISE.
LOOK AT THEM. THEY'RE STEALING EVERYTHING THAT ISN'T NAILED DOWN. THEY'RE LIKE ANIMALS.
THEY'RE STARVING. THEY'RE DEHYDRATED. THEY'RE SCARED. THAT'S JUST HOW PEOPLE ACT WHEN YOU TAKE EVERYTHING AWAY FROM THEM.
OH YEAH? THEN WHY ARE THEY STEALING MICROWAVES WHEN THERE'S NOT EVEN ANY POWER?
MOST OF THE PEOPLE I SEE ARE TAKING FOOD AND DRINK. YOU GONNA LET A COUPLE KNUCKLE-HEADS WRITE OFF EVERYONE IN NEED?
AIN'T LIKE FEMA IS GONNA HELP THEM. THEY GUTTED IT INTO A SHELL; THAT'S WHY WE'RE HERE.
STOP BITCHING. BAD GOVERNMENT IS GOOD FOR BUSINESS.
THAT'S WHY I VOTED FOR BUSH. TWICE.

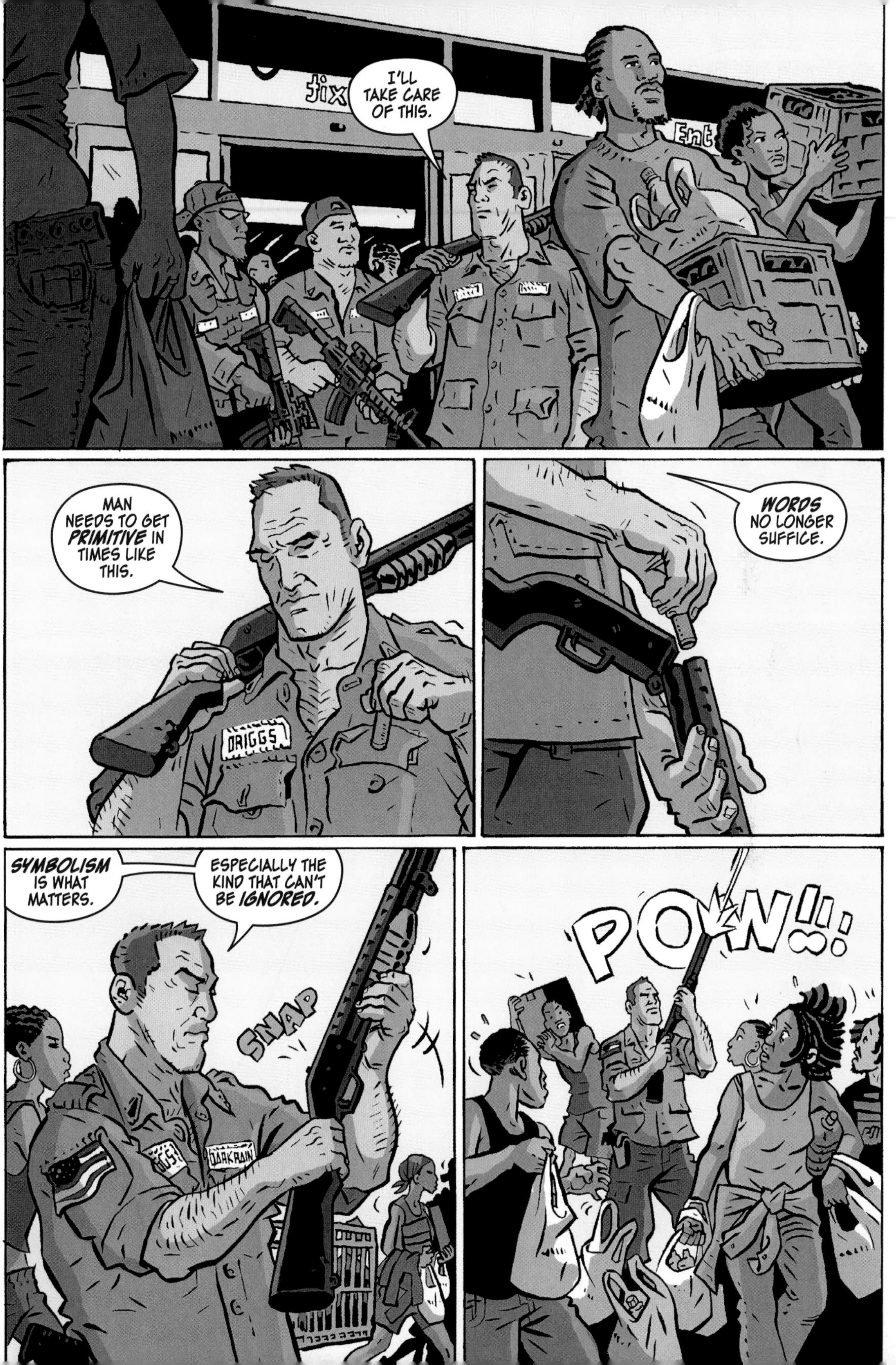
tix
Ent
I'LL TAKE CARE OF THIS.
MAN NEEDS TO GET *PRIMITIVE* IN TIMES LIKE THIS.
DRIGGS
WORDS NO LONGER SUFFICE.
SYMBOLISM IS WHAT MATTERS.
ESPECIALLY THE KIND THAT CAN'T BE *IGNORED.*
SNAP
POW!!!

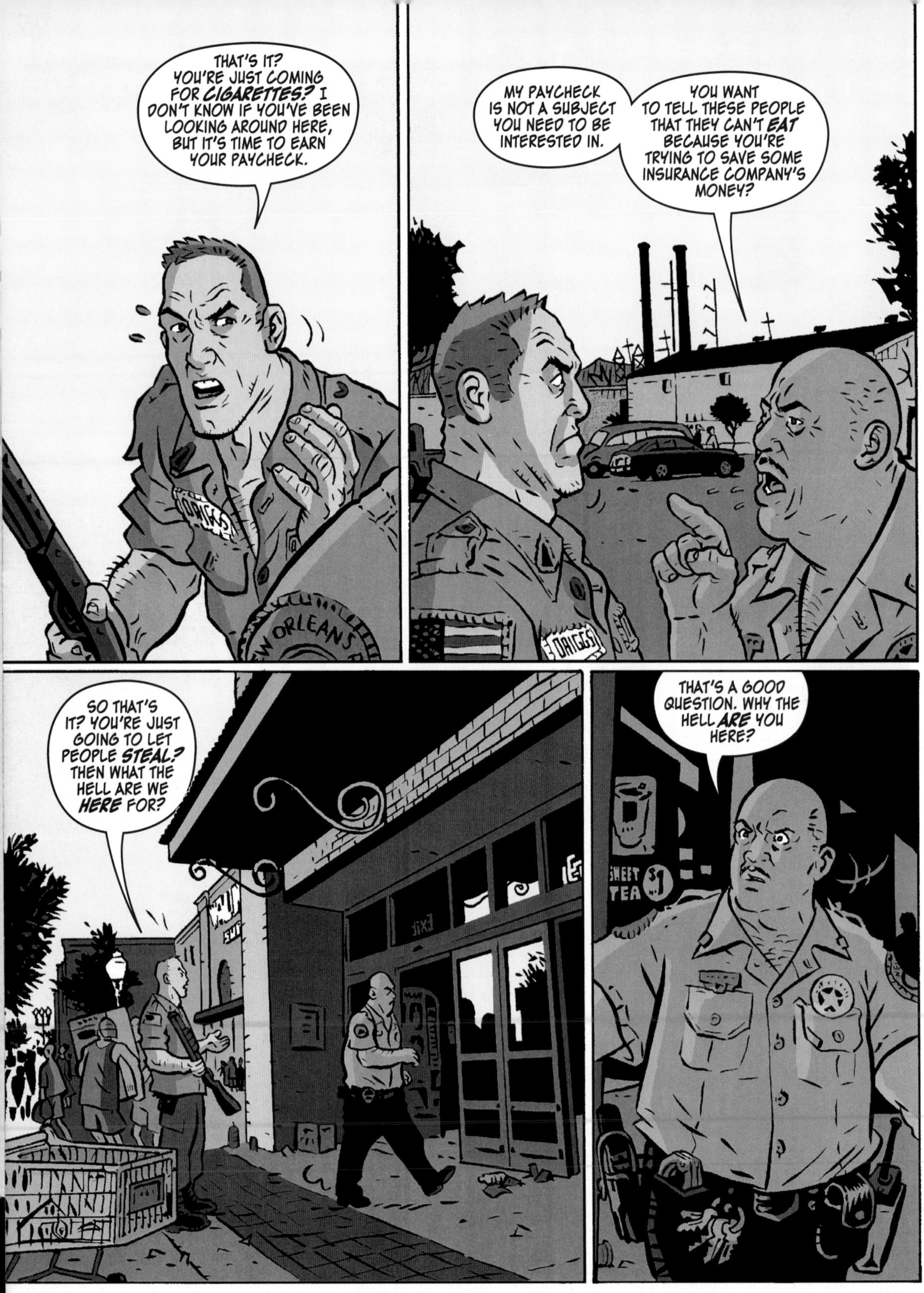
THAT'S IT? YOU'RE JUST COMING FOR CIGARETTES? I DON'T KNOW IF YOU'VE BEEN LOOKING AROUND HERE, BUT IT'S TIME TO EARN YOUR PAYCHECK.
DRIGGS
NEW ORLEANS
MY PAYCHECK IS NOT A SUBJECT YOU NEED TO BE INTERESTED IN.
YOU WANT TO TELL THESE PEOPLE THAT THEY CAN'T EAT BECAUSE YOU'RE TRYING TO SAVE SOME INSURANCE COMPANY'S MONEY?
DRIGGS
SO THAT'S IT? YOU'RE JUST GOING TO LET PEOPLE STEAL? THEN WHAT THE HELL ARE WE HERE FOR?
EXIT
THAT'S A GOOD QUESTION. WHY THE HELL ARE YOU HERE?
SWEET TEA
$1

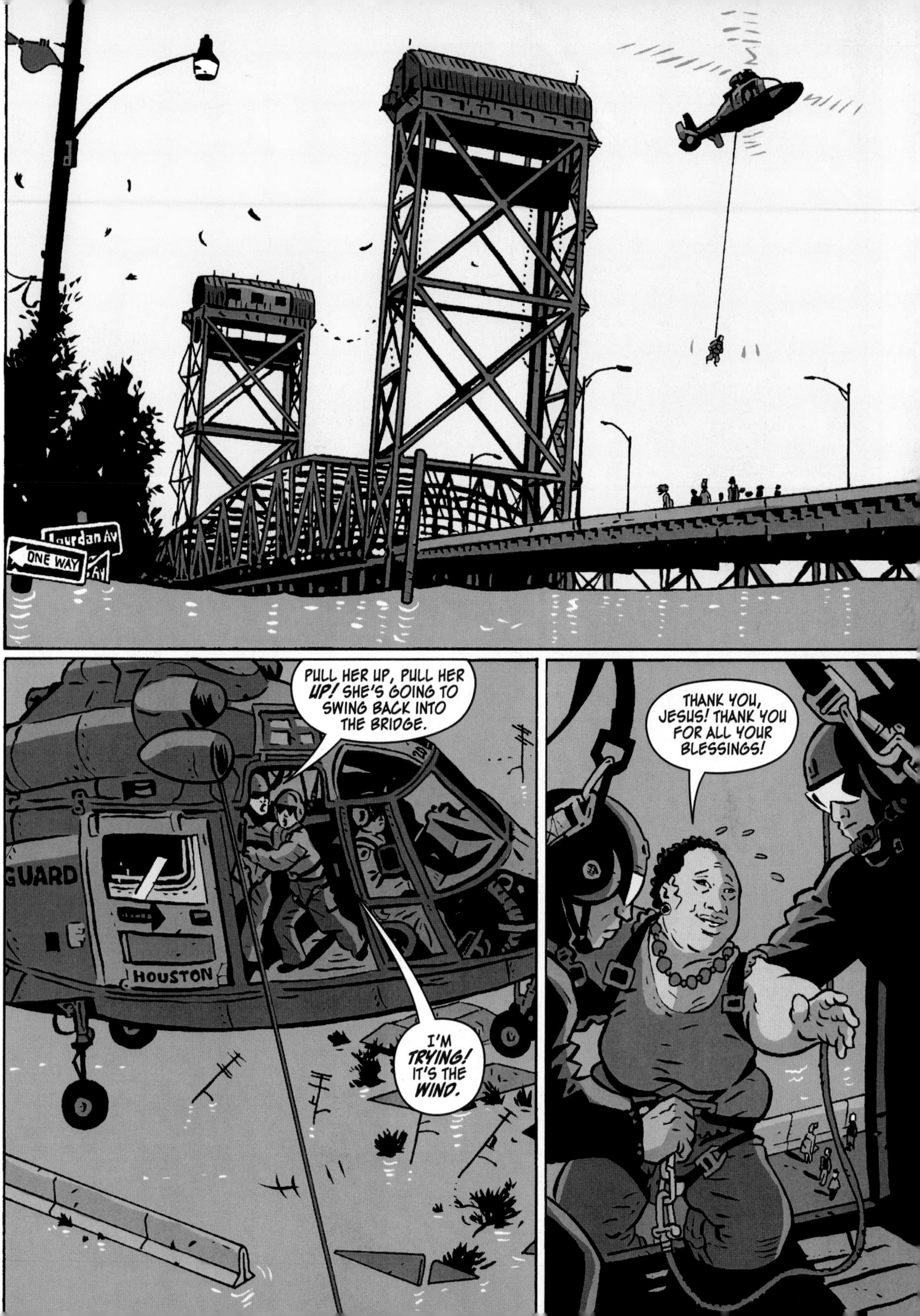
Jourdan Av
ONE WAY
PULL HER UP, PULL HER UP! SHE'S GOING TO SWING BACK INTO THE BRIDGE.
I'M TRYING! IT'S THE WIND.
GUARD
HOUSTON
THANK YOU, JESUS! THANK YOU FOR ALL YOUR BLESSINGS!

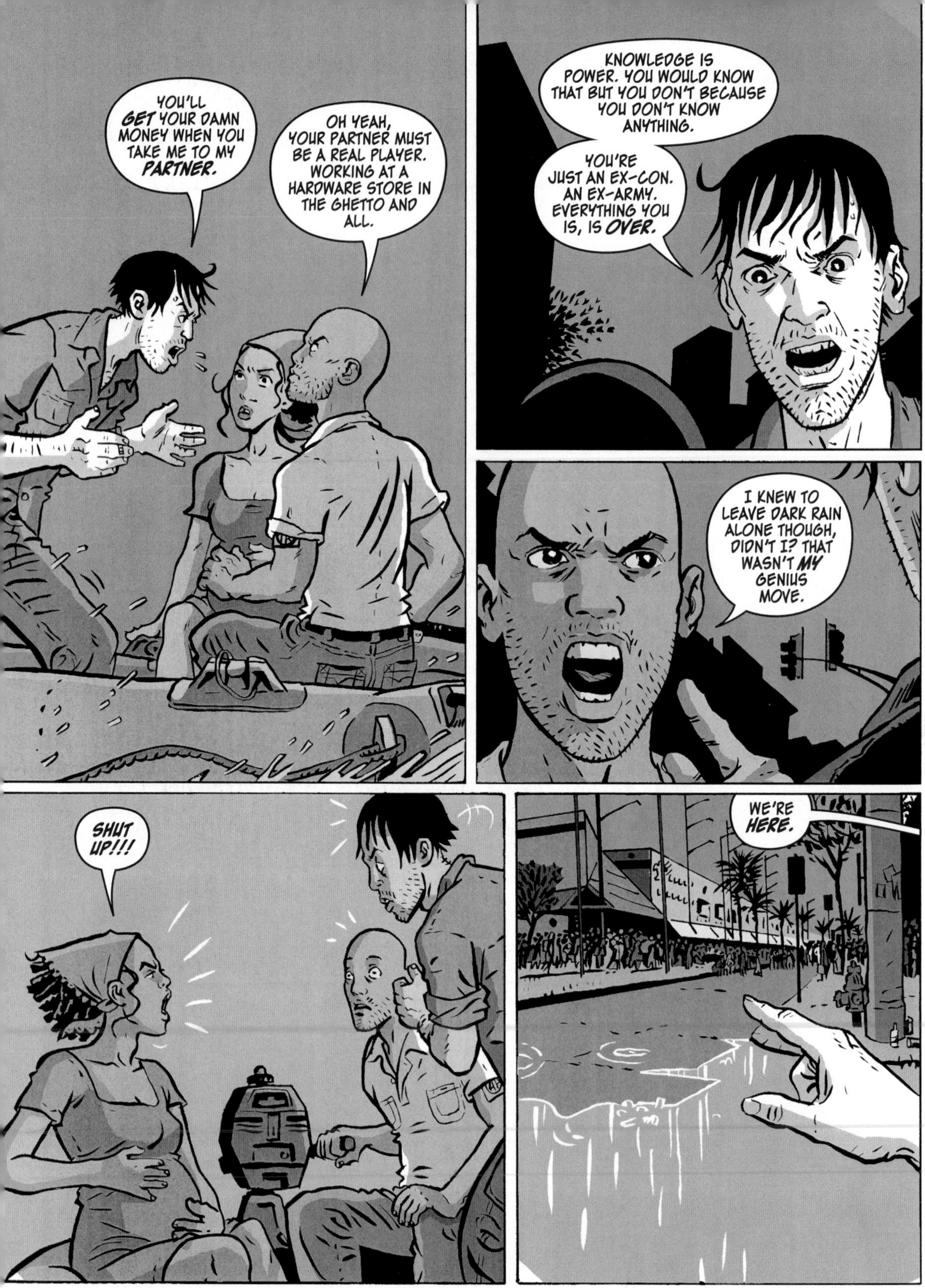
YOU'LL GET YOUR DAMN MONEY WHEN YOU TAKE ME TO MY PARTNER.
OH YEAH, YOUR PARTNER MUST BE A REAL PLAYER. WORKING AT A HARDWARE STORE IN THE GHETTO AND ALL.
KNOWLEDGE IS POWER. YOU WOULD KNOW THAT BUT YOU DON'T BECAUSE YOU DON'T KNOW ANYTHING.
YOU'RE JUST AN EX-CON. AN EX-ARMY. EVERYTHING YOU IS, IS OVER.
I KNEW TO LEAVE DARK RAIN ALONE THOUGH, DIDN'T I? THAT WASN'T MY GENIUS MOVE.
SHUT UP!!!
WE'RE HERE.

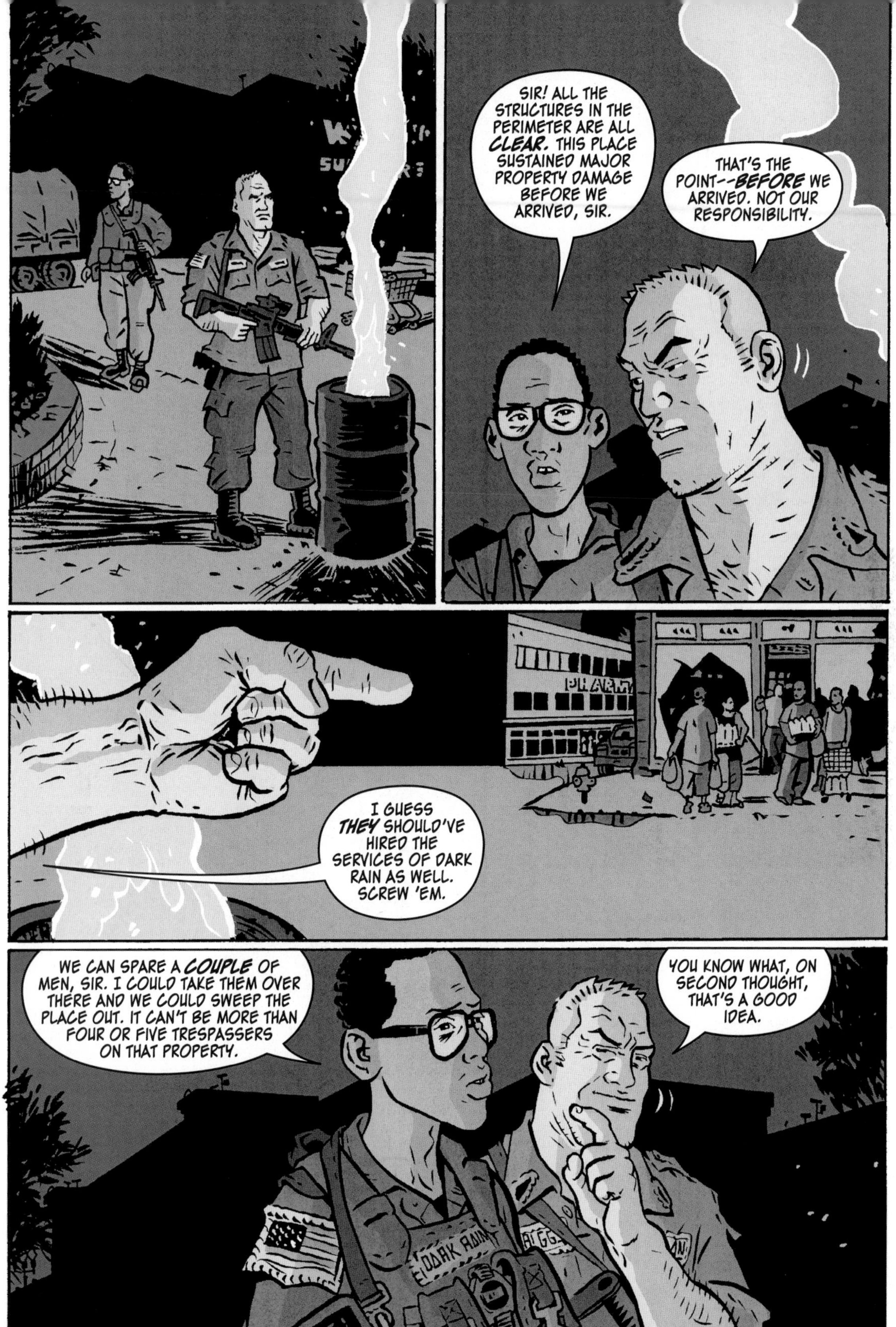
SIR! ALL THE STRUCTURES IN THE PERIMETER ARE ALL CLEAR. THIS PLACE SUSTAINED MAJOR PROPERTY DAMAGE BEFORE WE ARRIVED, SIR.
THAT'S THE POINT--BEFORE WE ARRIVED. NOT OUR RESPONSIBILITY.
PHARM
I GUESS THEY SHOULD'VE HIRED THE SERVICES OF DARK RAIN AS WELL. SCREW 'EM.
WE CAN SPARE A COUPLE OF MEN, SIR. I COULD TAKE THEM OVER THERE AND WE COULD SWEEP THE PLACE OUT. IT CAN'T BE MORE THAN FOUR OR FIVE TRESPASSERS ON THAT PROPERTY.
YOU KNOW WHAT, ON SECOND THOUGHT, THAT'S A GOOD IDEA.
DARK RAIN

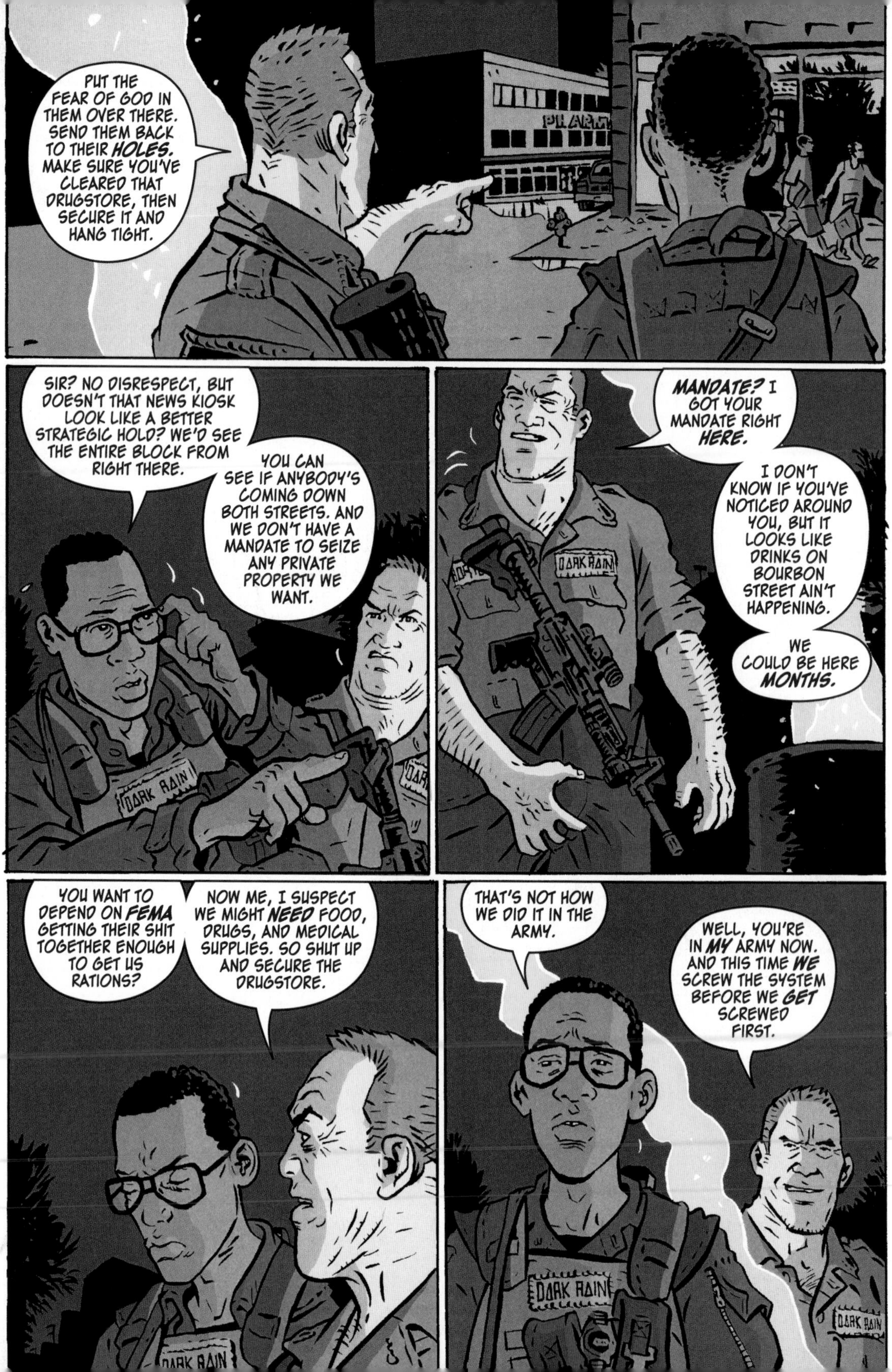
PUT THE FEAR OF GOD IN THEM OVER THERE. SEND THEM BACK TO THEIR HOLES. MAKE SURE YOU'VE CLEARED THAT DRUGSTORE, THEN SECURE IT AND HANG TIGHT.
PHARM
SIR? NO DISRESPECT, BUT DOESN'T THAT NEWS KIOSK LOOK LIKE A BETTER STRATEGIC HOLD? WE'D SEE THE ENTIRE BLOCK FROM RIGHT THERE.
YOU CAN SEE IF ANYBODY'S COMING DOWN BOTH STREETS. AND WE DON'T HAVE A MANDATE TO SEIZE ANY PRIVATE PROPERTY WE WANT.
DARK RAIN
MANDATE? I GOT YOUR MANDATE RIGHT HERE.
I DON'T KNOW IF YOU'VE NOTICED AROUND YOU, BUT IT LOOKS LIKE DRINKS ON BOURBON STREET AIN'T HAPPENING.
WE COULD BE HERE MONTHS.
DARK RAIN
YOU WANT TO DEPEND ON FEMA GETTING THEIR SHIT TOGETHER ENOUGH TO GET US RATIONS?
NOW ME, I SUSPECT WE MIGHT NEED FOOD, DRUGS, AND MEDICAL SUPPLIES. SO SHUT UP AND SECURE THE DRUGSTORE.
DARK RAIN
THAT'S NOT HOW WE DID IT IN THE ARMY.
WELL, YOU'RE IN MY ARMY NOW. AND THIS TIME WE SCREW THE SYSTEM BEFORE WE GET SCREWED FIRST.
DARK RAIN
DARK RAIN

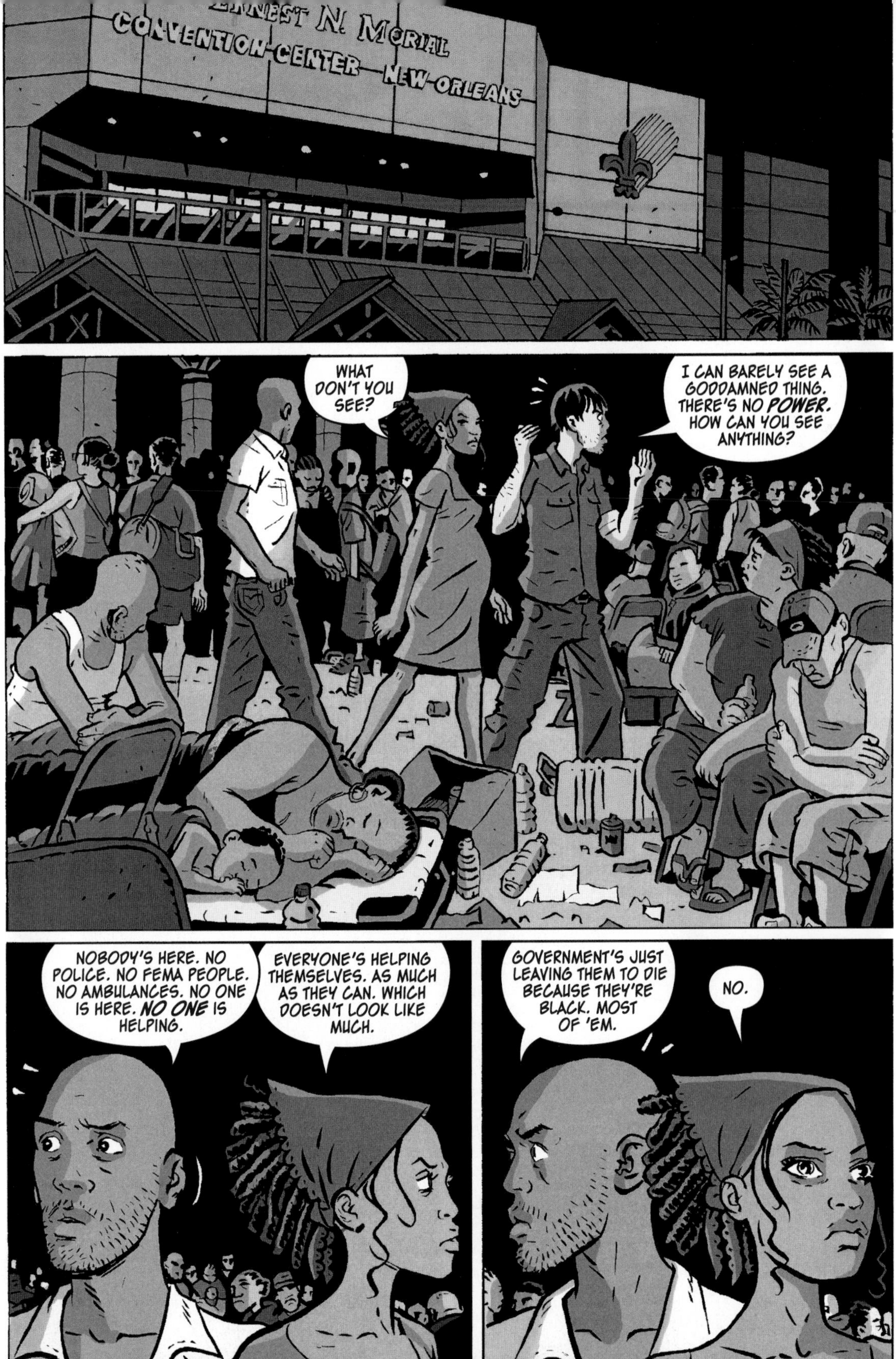
ERNEST N. MORIAL
CONVENTION CENTER NEW ORLEANS
WHAT DON'T YOU SEE?
I CAN BARELY SEE A GODDAMNED THING. THERE'S NO POWER. HOW CAN YOU SEE ANYTHING?
NOBODY'S HERE. NO POLICE. NO FEMA PEOPLE. NO AMBULANCES. NO ONE IS HERE. NO ONE IS HELPING.
EVERYONE'S HELPING THEMSELVES. AS MUCH AS THEY CAN. WHICH DOESN'T LOOK LIKE MUCH.
GOVERNMENT'S JUST LEAVING THEM TO DIE BECAUSE THEY'RE BLACK. MOST OF 'EM.
NO.

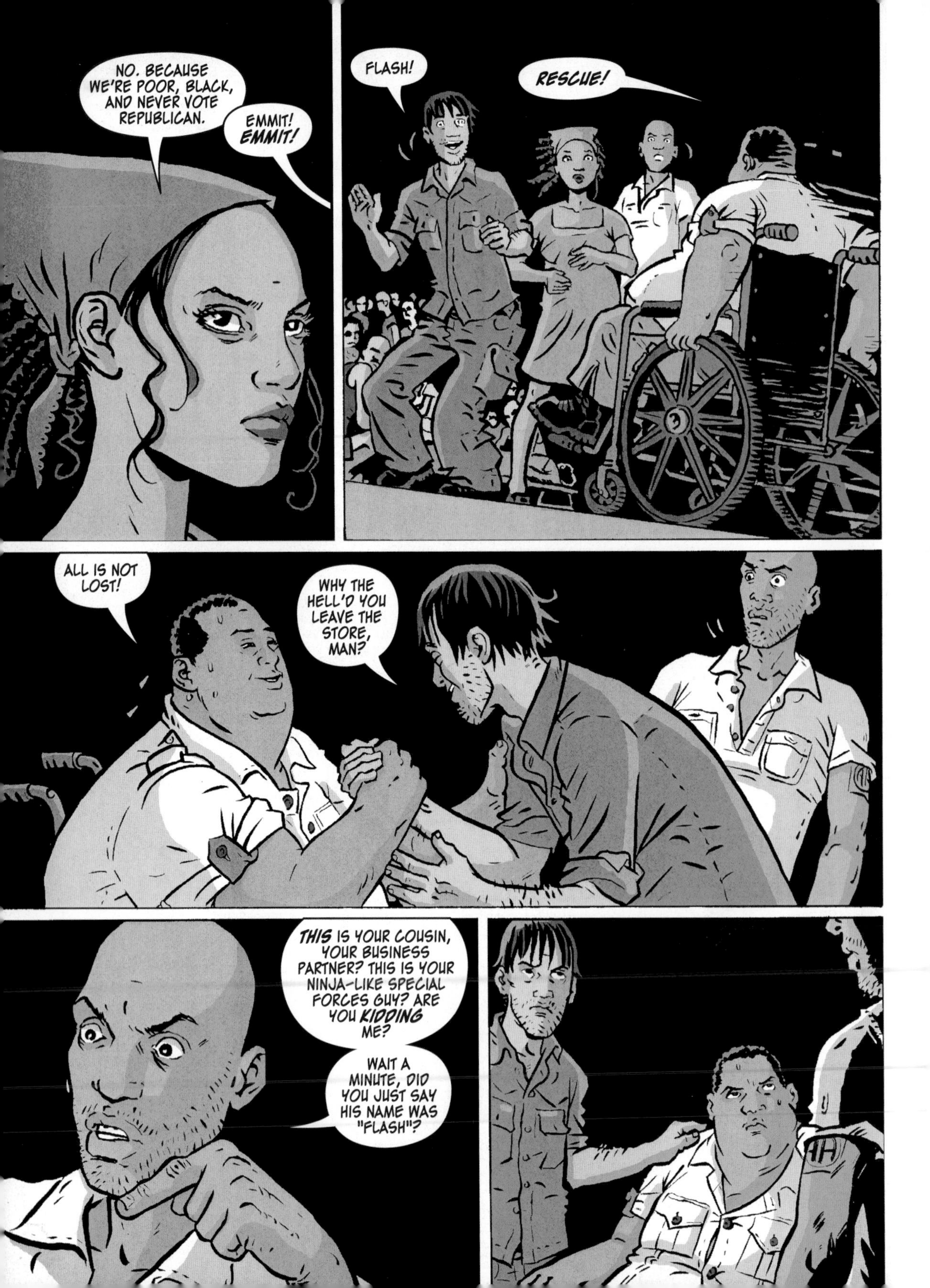
NO. BECAUSE WE'RE POOR, BLACK, AND NEVER VOTE REPUBLICAN.
EMMIT! EMMIT!
FLASH!
RESCUE!
ALL IS NOT LOST!
WHY THE HELL'D YOU LEAVE THE STORE, MAN?
THIS IS YOUR COUSIN, YOUR BUSINESS PARTNER? THIS IS YOUR NINJA-LIKE SPECIAL FORCES GUY? ARE YOU KIDDING ME?
WAIT A MINUTE, DID YOU JUST SAY HIS NAME WAS "FLASH"?

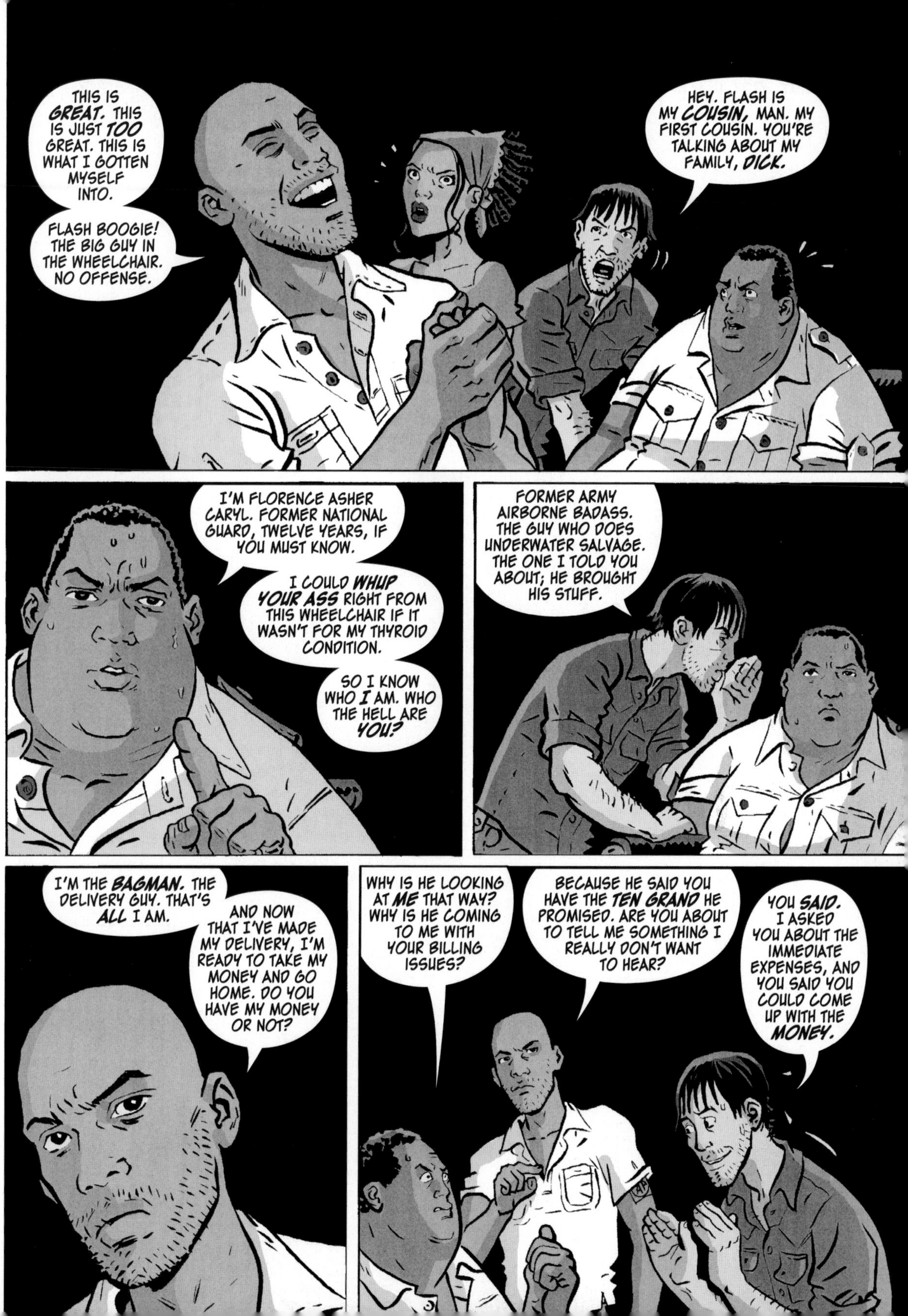
THIS IS GREAT. THIS IS JUST TOO GREAT. THIS IS WHAT I GOTTEN MYSELF INTO.
FLASH BOOGIE! THE BIG GUY IN THE WHEELCHAIR. NO OFFENSE.
HEY. FLASH IS MY COUSIN, MAN. MY FIRST COUSIN. YOU'RE TALKING ABOUT MY FAMILY, DICK.
I'M FLORENCE ASHER CARYL. FORMER NATIONAL GUARD, TWELVE YEARS, IF YOU MUST KNOW.
I COULD WHUP YOUR ASS RIGHT FROM THIS WHEELCHAIR IF IT WASN'T FOR MY THYROID CONDITION.
SO I KNOW WHO I AM. WHO THE HELL ARE YOU?
FORMER ARMY AIRBORNE BADASS. THE GUY WHO DOES UNDERWATER SALVAGE. THE ONE I TOLD YOU ABOUT; HE BROUGHT HIS STUFF.
I'M THE BAGMAN. THE DELIVERY GUY. THAT'S ALL I AM.
AND NOW THAT I'VE MADE MY DELIVERY, I'M READY TO TAKE MY MONEY AND GO HOME. DO YOU HAVE MY MONEY OR NOT?
WHY IS HE LOOKING AT ME THAT WAY? WHY IS HE COMING TO ME WITH YOUR BILLING ISSUES?
BECAUSE HE SAID YOU HAVE THE TEN GRAND HE PROMISED. ARE YOU ABOUT TO TELL ME SOMETHING I REALLY DON'T WANT TO HEAR?
YOU SAID. I ASKED YOU ABOUT THE IMMEDIATE EXPENSES, AND YOU SAID YOU COULD COME UP WITH THE MONEY.

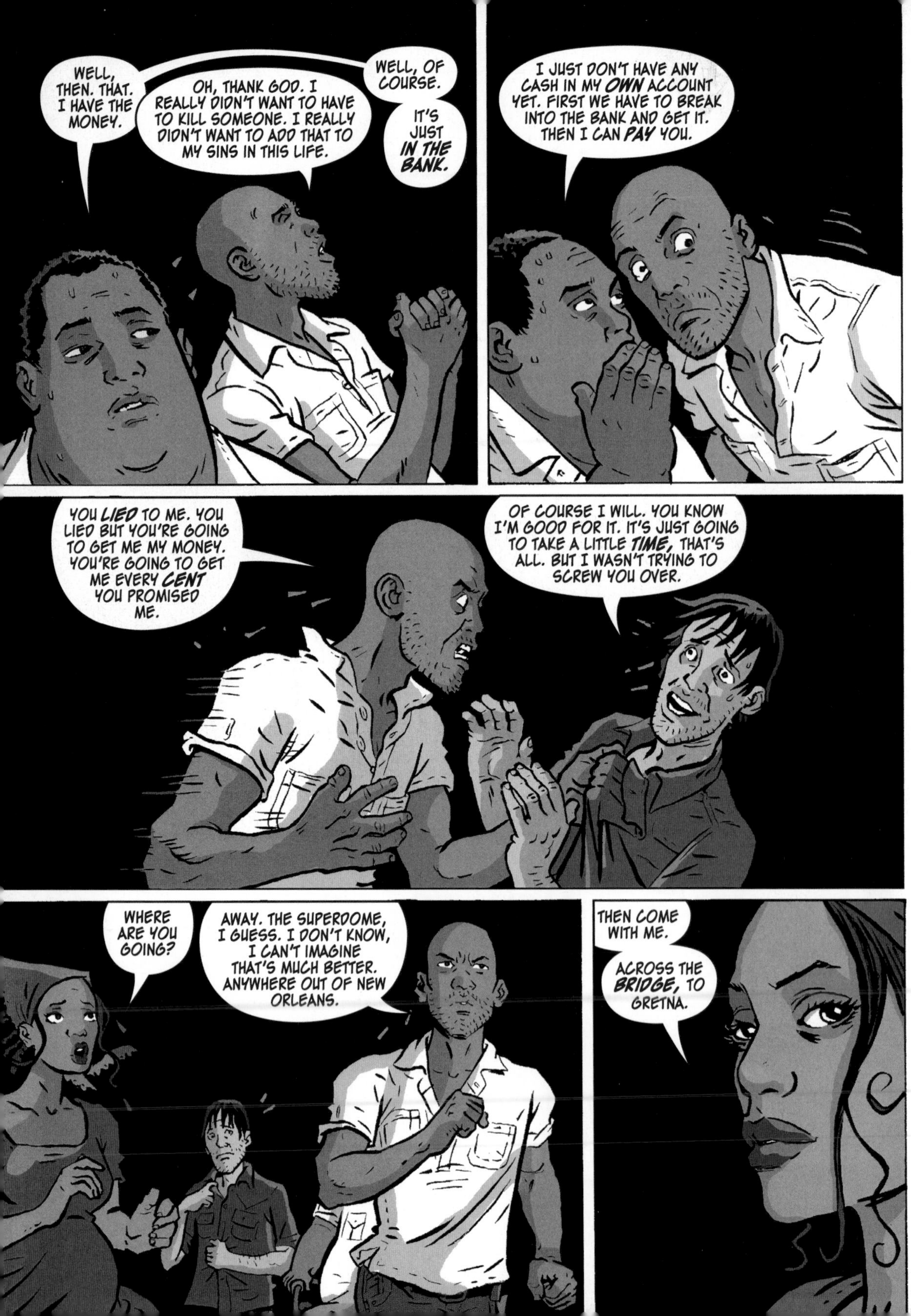
WELL, THEN. THAT. I HAVE THE MONEY.
OH, THANK GOD. I REALLY DIDN'T WANT TO HAVE TO KILL SOMEONE. I REALLY DIDN'T WANT TO ADD THAT TO MY SINS IN THIS LIFE.
WELL, OF COURSE.
IT'S JUST IN THE BANK.
I JUST DON'T HAVE ANY CASH IN MY OWN ACCOUNT YET. FIRST WE HAVE TO BREAK INTO THE BANK AND GET IT. THEN I CAN PAY YOU.
YOU LIED TO ME. YOU LIED BUT YOU'RE GOING TO GET ME MY MONEY. YOU'RE GOING TO GET ME EVERY CENT YOU PROMISED ME.
OF COURSE I WILL. YOU KNOW I'M GOOD FOR IT. IT'S JUST GOING TO TAKE A LITTLE TIME, THAT'S ALL. BUT I WASN'T TRYING TO SCREW YOU OVER.
WHERE ARE YOU GOING?
AWAY. THE SUPERDOME, I GUESS. I DON'T KNOW, I CAN'T IMAGINE THAT'S MUCH BETTER. ANYWHERE OUT OF NEW ORLEANS.
THEN COME WITH ME.
ACROSS THE BRIDGE, TO GRETNA.

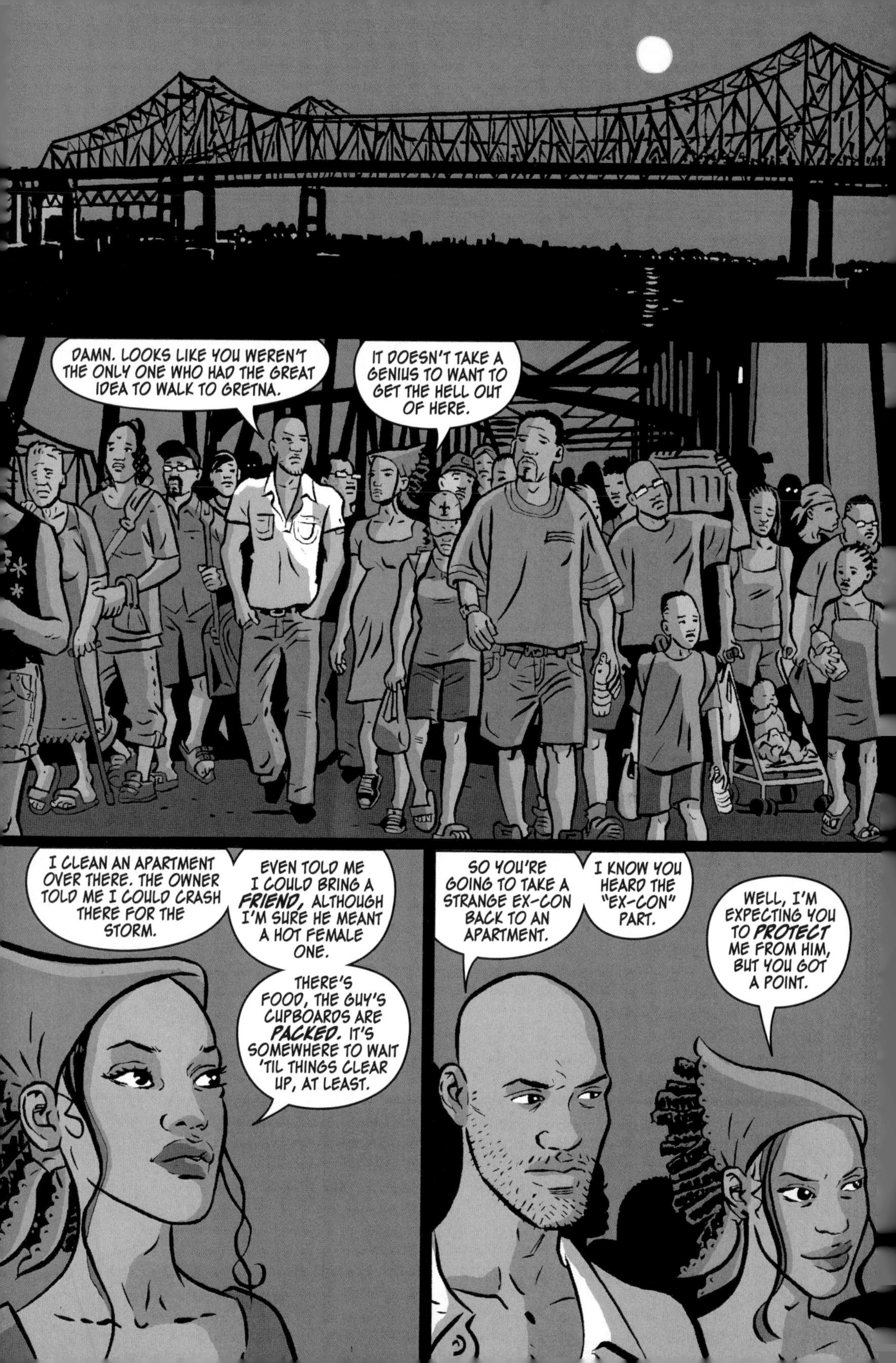
DAMN. LOOKS LIKE YOU WEREN'T THE ONLY ONE WHO HAD THE GREAT IDEA TO WALK TO GRETNA.
IT DOESN'T TAKE A GENIUS TO WANT TO GET THE HELL OUT OF HERE.
I CLEAN AN APARTMENT OVER THERE. THE OWNER TOLD ME I COULD CRASH THERE FOR THE STORM.
EVEN TOLD ME I COULD BRING A FRIEND, ALTHOUGH I'M SURE HE MEANT A HOT FEMALE ONE.
THERE'S FOOD, THE GUY'S CUPBOARDS ARE PACKED. IT'S SOMEWHERE TO WAIT 'TIL THINGS CLEAR UP, AT LEAST.
SO YOU'RE GOING TO TAKE A STRANGE EX-CON BACK TO AN APARTMENT.
I KNOW YOU HEARD THE "EX-CON" PART.
WELL, I'M EXPECTING YOU TO PROTECT ME FROM HIM, BUT YOU GOT A POINT.

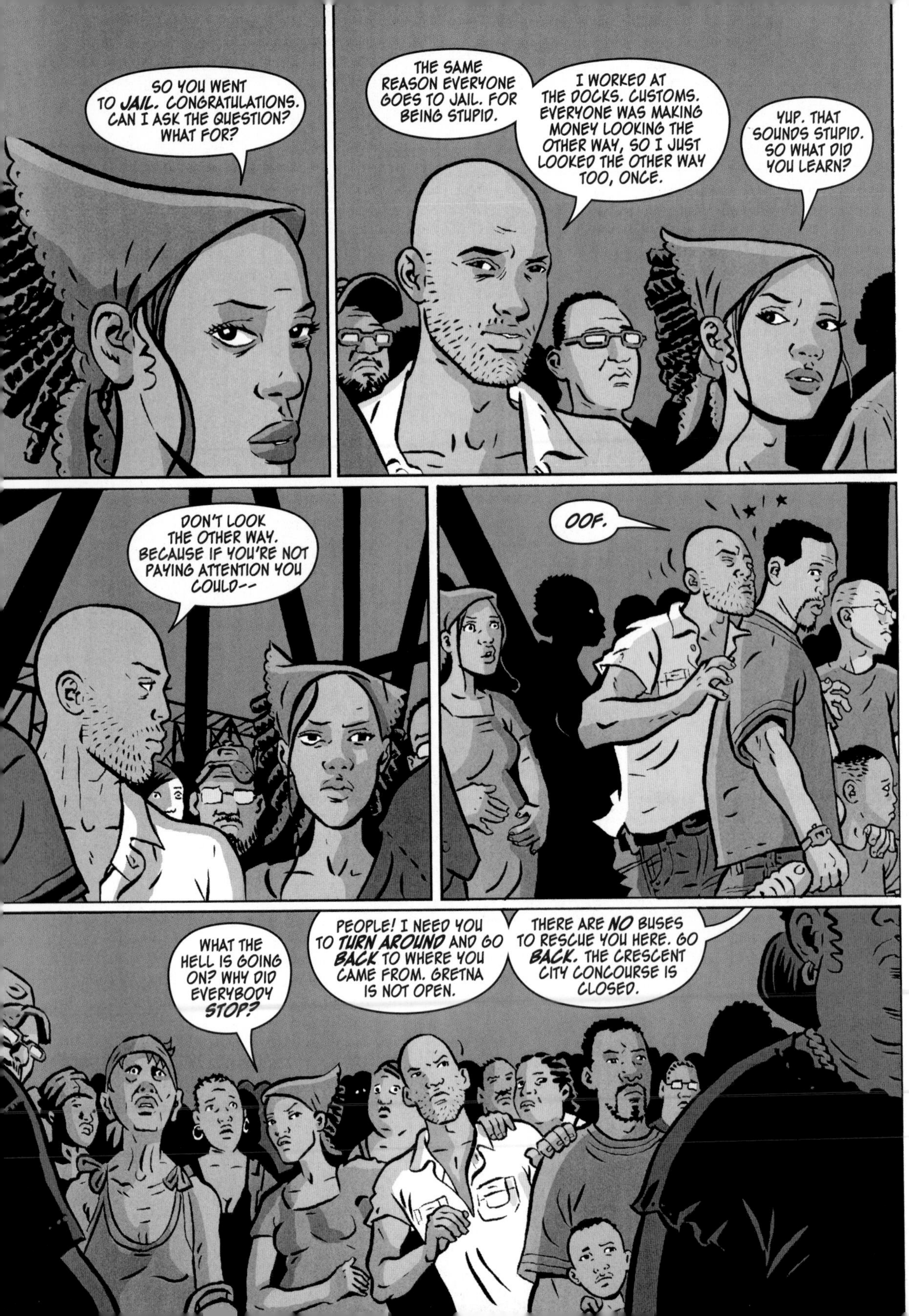
SO YOU WENT TO JAIL. CONGRATULATIONS. CAN I ASK THE QUESTION? WHAT FOR?
THE SAME REASON EVERYONE GOES TO JAIL. FOR BEING STUPID.
I WORKED AT THE DOCKS. CUSTOMS. EVERYONE WAS MAKING MONEY LOOKING THE OTHER WAY, SO I JUST LOOKED THE OTHER WAY TOO, ONCE.
YUP. THAT SOUNDS STUPID. SO WHAT DID YOU LEARN?
DON'T LOOK THE OTHER WAY. BECAUSE IF YOU'RE NOT PAYING ATTENTION YOU COULD--
OOF.
WHAT THE HELL IS GOING ON? WHY DID EVERYBODY STOP?
PEOPLE! I NEED YOU TO TURN AROUND AND GO BACK TO WHERE YOU CAME FROM. GRETNA IS NOT OPEN.
THERE ARE NO BUSES TO RESCUE YOU HERE. GO BACK. THE CRESCENT CITY CONCOURSE IS CLOSED.

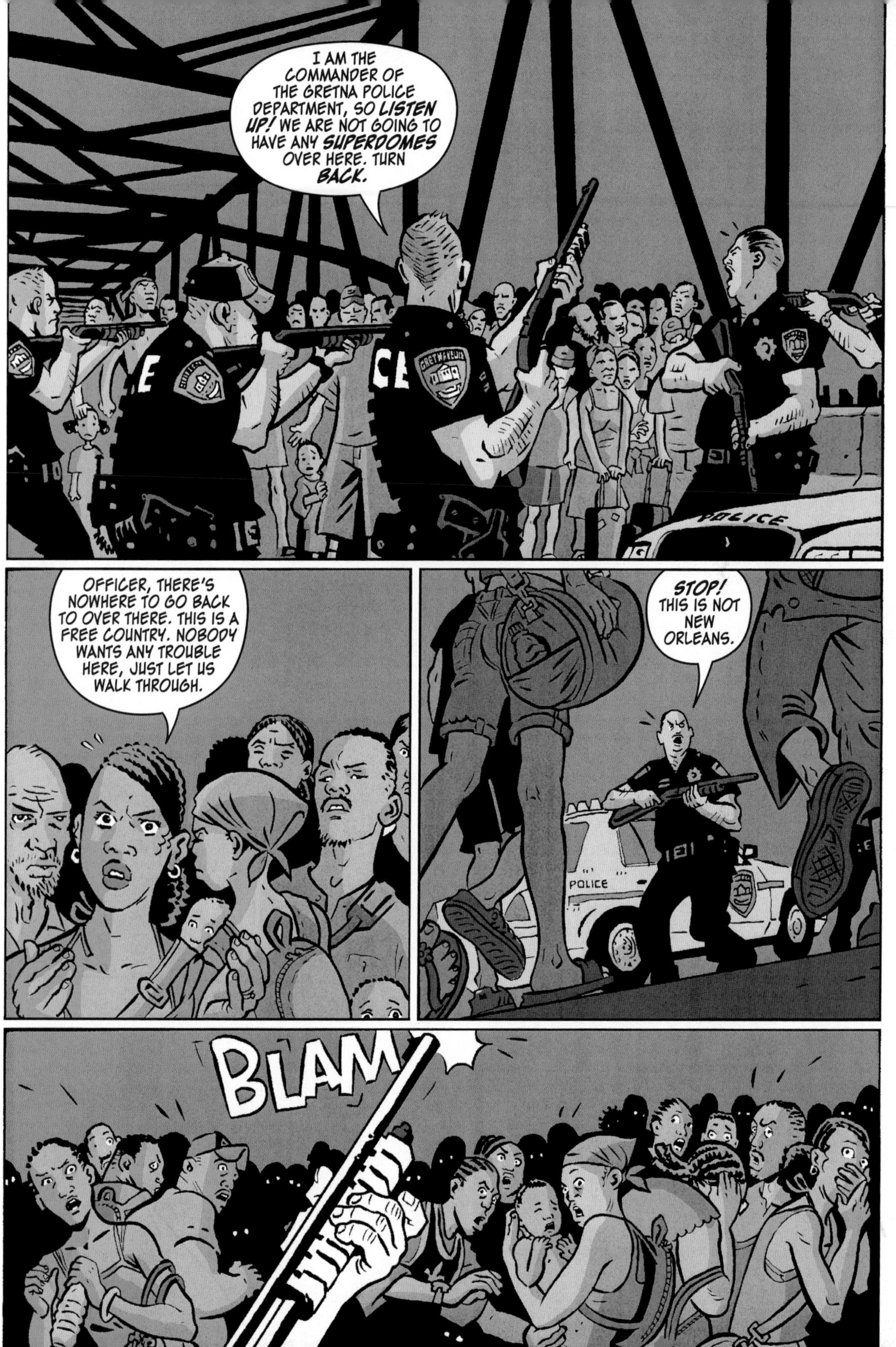
I AM THE COMMANDER OF THE GRETNA POLICE DEPARTMENT, SO LISTEN UP! WE ARE NOT GOING TO HAVE ANY SUPERDOMES OVER HERE. TURN BACK.
POLICE
OFFICER, THERE'S NOWHERE TO GO BACK TO OVER THERE. THIS IS A FREE COUNTRY. NOBODY WANTS ANY TROUBLE HERE, JUST LET US WALK THROUGH.
STOP! THIS IS NOT NEW ORLEANS.
POLICE
BLAM

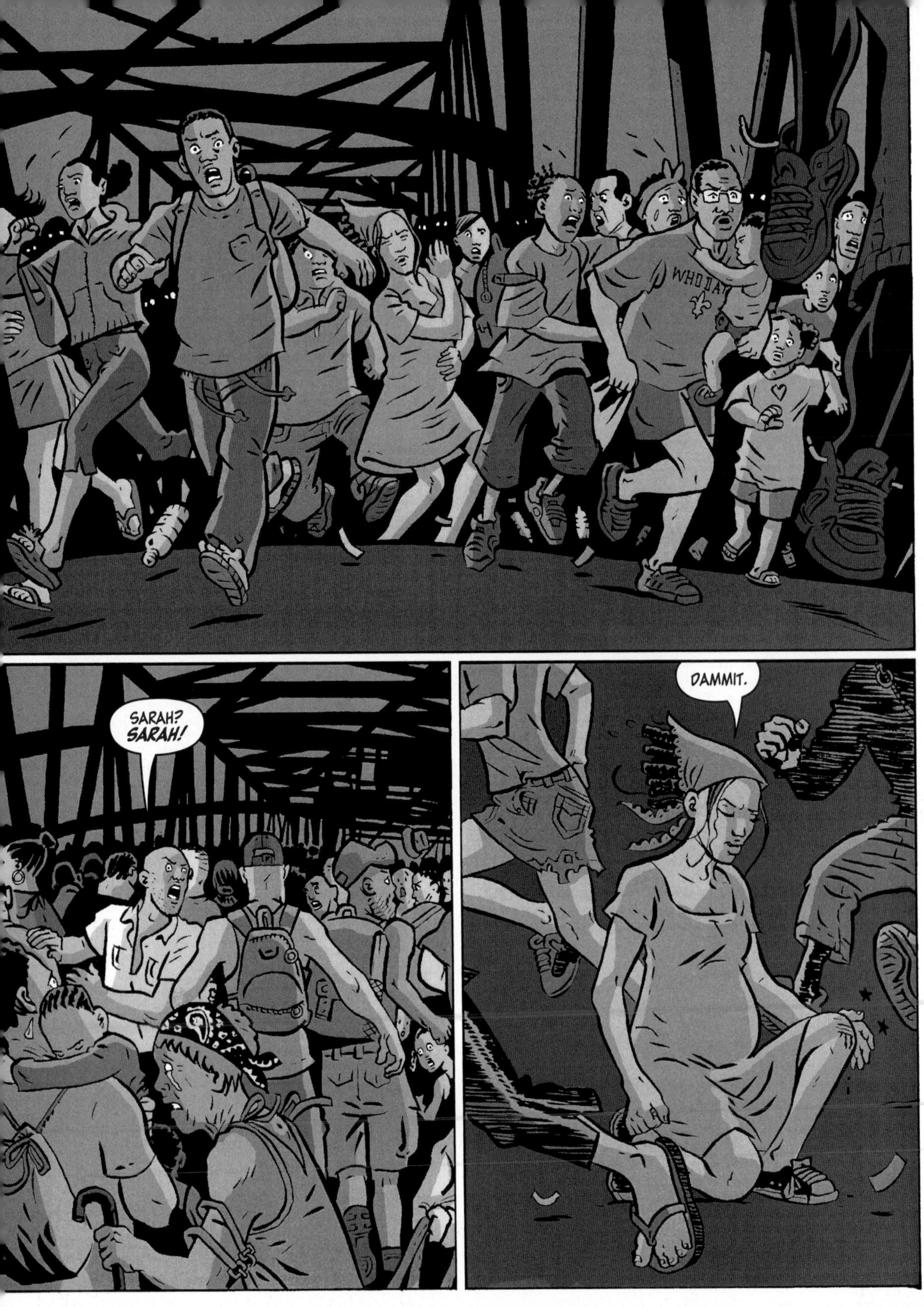
WHO DAT
SARAH? SARAH!
DAMMIT.

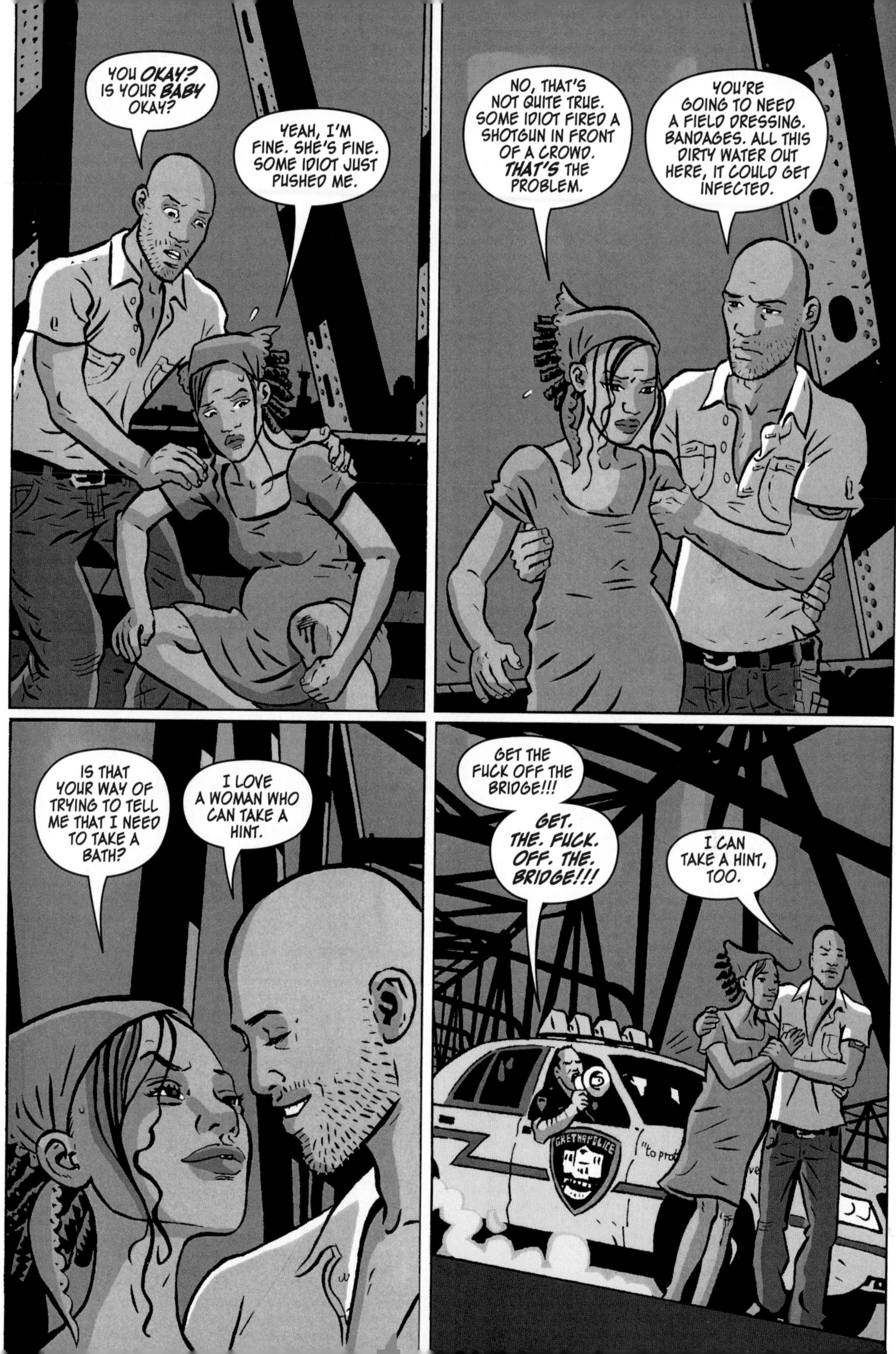
YOU OKAY? IS YOUR BABY OKAY?
YEAH, I'M FINE. SHE'S FINE. SOME IDIOT JUST PUSHED ME.
NO, THAT'S NOT QUITE TRUE. SOME IDIOT FIRED A SHOTGUN IN FRONT OF A CROWD. THAT'S THE PROBLEM.
YOU'RE GOING TO NEED A FIELD DRESSING. BANDAGES. ALL THIS DIRTY WATER OUT HERE, IT COULD GET INFECTED.
IS THAT YOUR WAY OF TRYING TO TELL ME THAT I NEED TO TAKE A BATH?
I LOVE A WOMAN WHO CAN TAKE A HINT.
GET THE FUCK OFF THE BRIDGE!!!
GET. THE. FUCK. OFF. THE. BRIDGE!!!
I CAN TAKE A HINT, TOO.
GRETNA POLICE

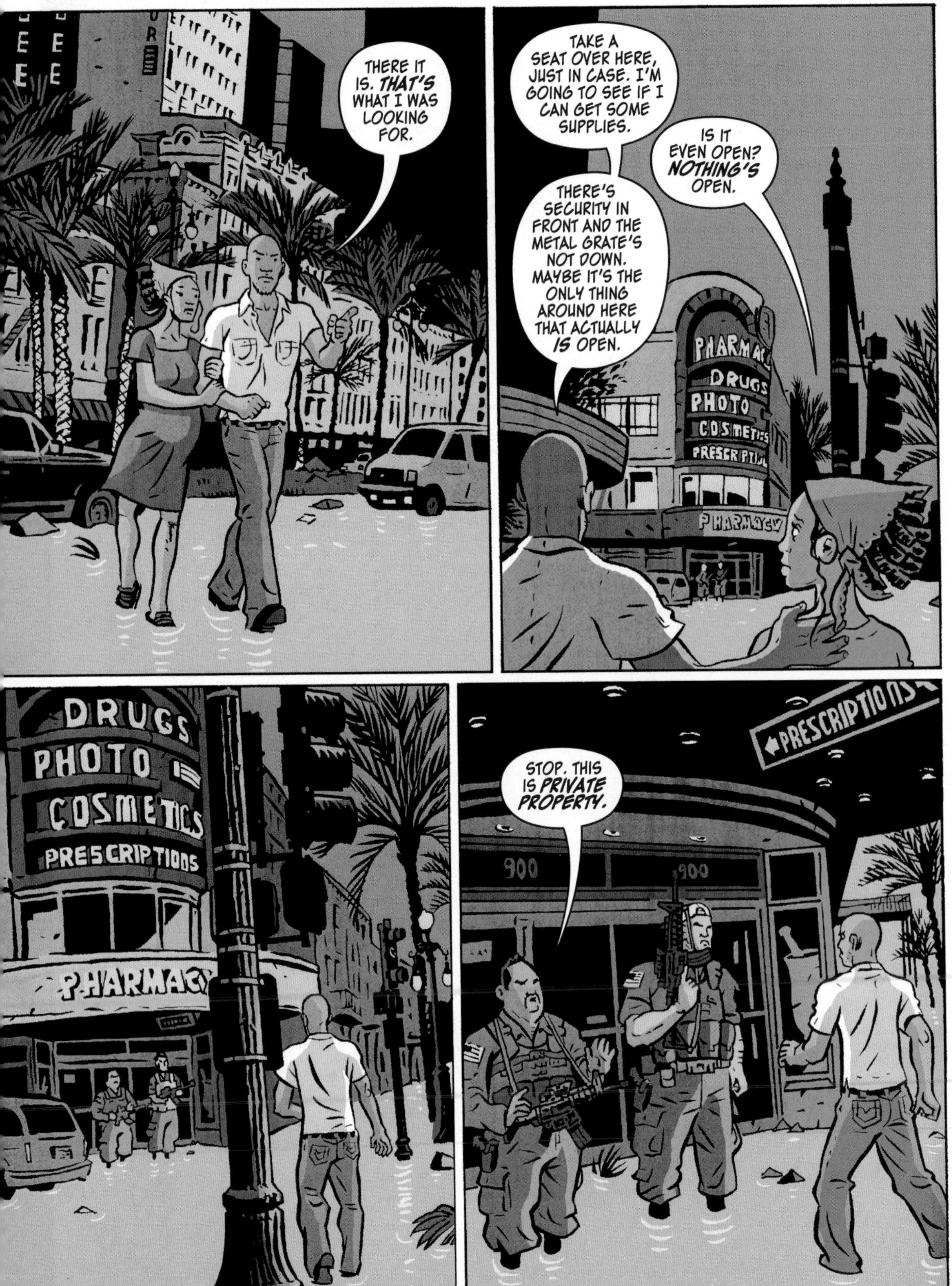
THERE IT IS. ***THAT'S*** WHAT I WAS LOOKING FOR.
TAKE A SEAT OVER HERE, JUST IN CASE. I'M GOING TO SEE IF I CAN GET SOME SUPPLIES.
IS IT EVEN OPEN? ***NOTHING'S*** OPEN.
THERE'S SECURITY IN FRONT AND THE METAL GRATE'S NOT DOWN. MAYBE IT'S THE ONLY THING AROUND HERE THAT ACTUALLY ***IS*** OPEN.
DRUGS
PHOTO
COSMETICS
PRESCRIPTIONS
PRESCRIPTIONS
900
STOP. THIS IS ***PRIVATE PROPERTY.***

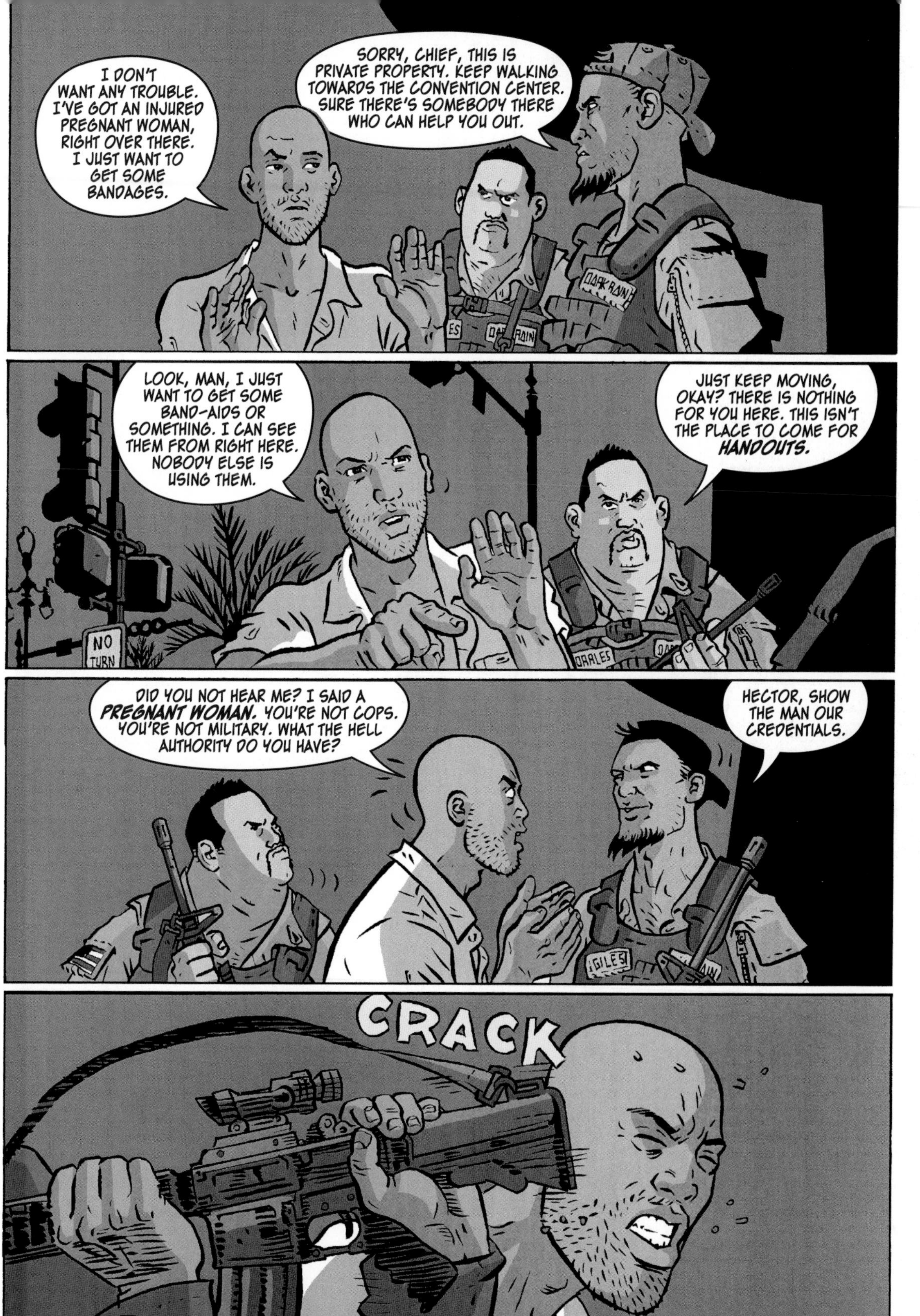
I DON'T WANT ANY TROUBLE. I'VE GOT AN INJURED PREGNANT WOMAN, RIGHT OVER THERE. I JUST WANT TO GET SOME BANDAGES.
SORRY, CHIEF, THIS IS PRIVATE PROPERTY. KEEP WALKING TOWARDS THE CONVENTION CENTER. SURE THERE'S SOMEBODY THERE WHO CAN HELP YOU OUT.
LOOK, MAN, I JUST WANT TO GET SOME BAND-AIDS OR SOMETHING. I CAN SEE THEM FROM RIGHT HERE. NOBODY ELSE IS USING THEM.
JUST KEEP MOVING, OKAY? THERE IS NOTHING FOR YOU HERE. THIS ISN'T THE PLACE TO COME FOR *HANDOUTS.*
NO TURN
DID YOU NOT HEAR ME? I SAID A *PREGNANT WOMAN.* YOU'RE NOT COPS. YOU'RE NOT MILITARY. WHAT THE HELL AUTHORITY DO YOU HAVE?
HECTOR, SHOW THE MAN OUR CREDENTIALS.
GILES
CRACK

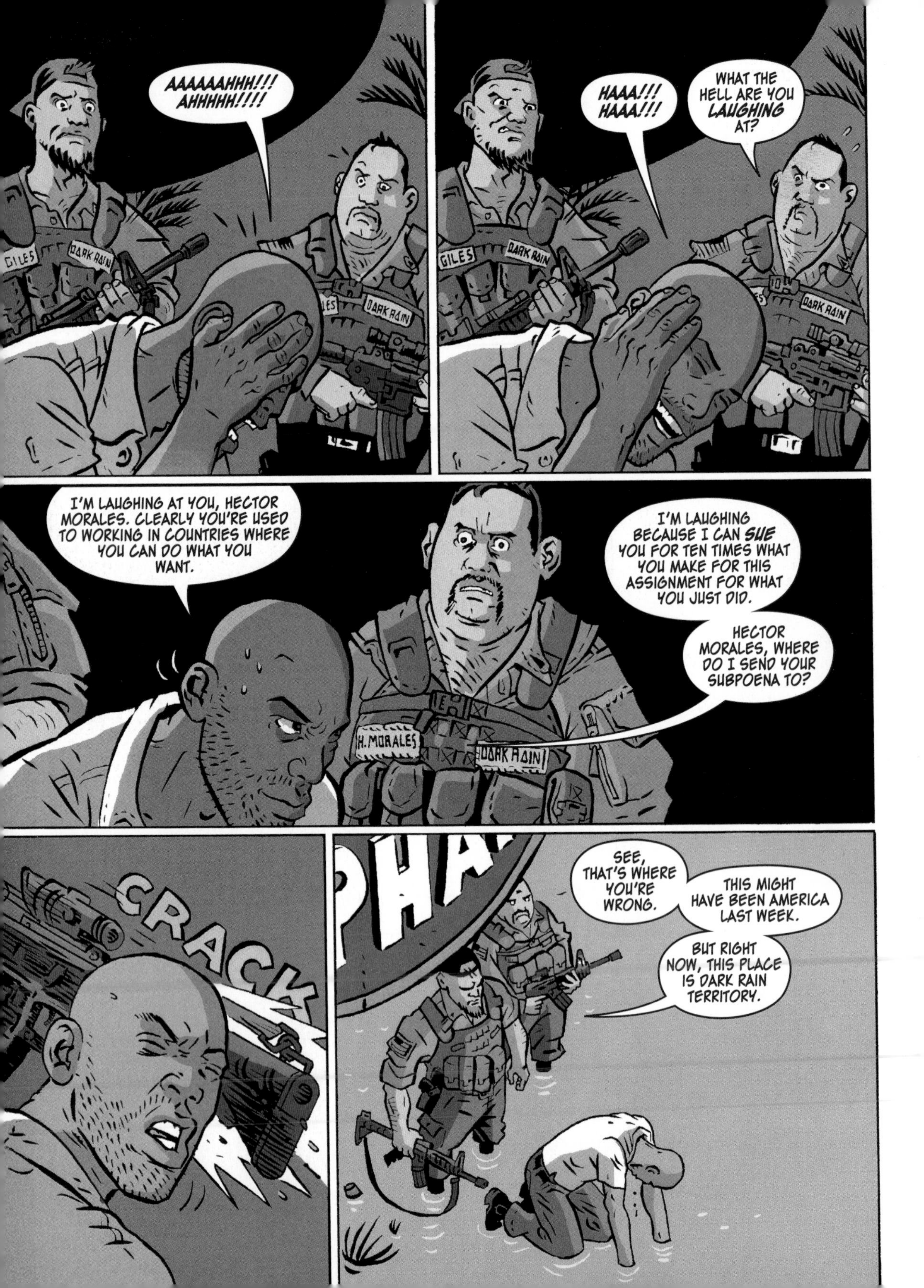
AAAAAAHHH!!!
AHHHHH!!!!
GILES
DARK RAIN
HAAA!!!
HAAA!!!
WHAT THE HELL ARE YOU LAUGHING AT?
GILES
DARK RAIN
I'M LAUGHING AT YOU, HECTOR MORALES. CLEARLY YOU'RE USED TO WORKING IN COUNTRIES WHERE YOU CAN DO WHAT YOU WANT.
I'M LAUGHING BECAUSE I CAN SUE YOU FOR TEN TIMES WHAT YOU MAKE FOR THIS ASSIGNMENT FOR WHAT YOU JUST DID.
HECTOR MORALES, WHERE DO I SEND YOUR SUBPOENA TO?
H. MORALES
DARK RAIN
CRACK
SEE, THAT'S WHERE YOU'RE WRONG.
THIS MIGHT HAVE BEEN AMERICA LAST WEEK.
BUT RIGHT NOW, THIS PLACE IS DARK RAIN TERRITORY.

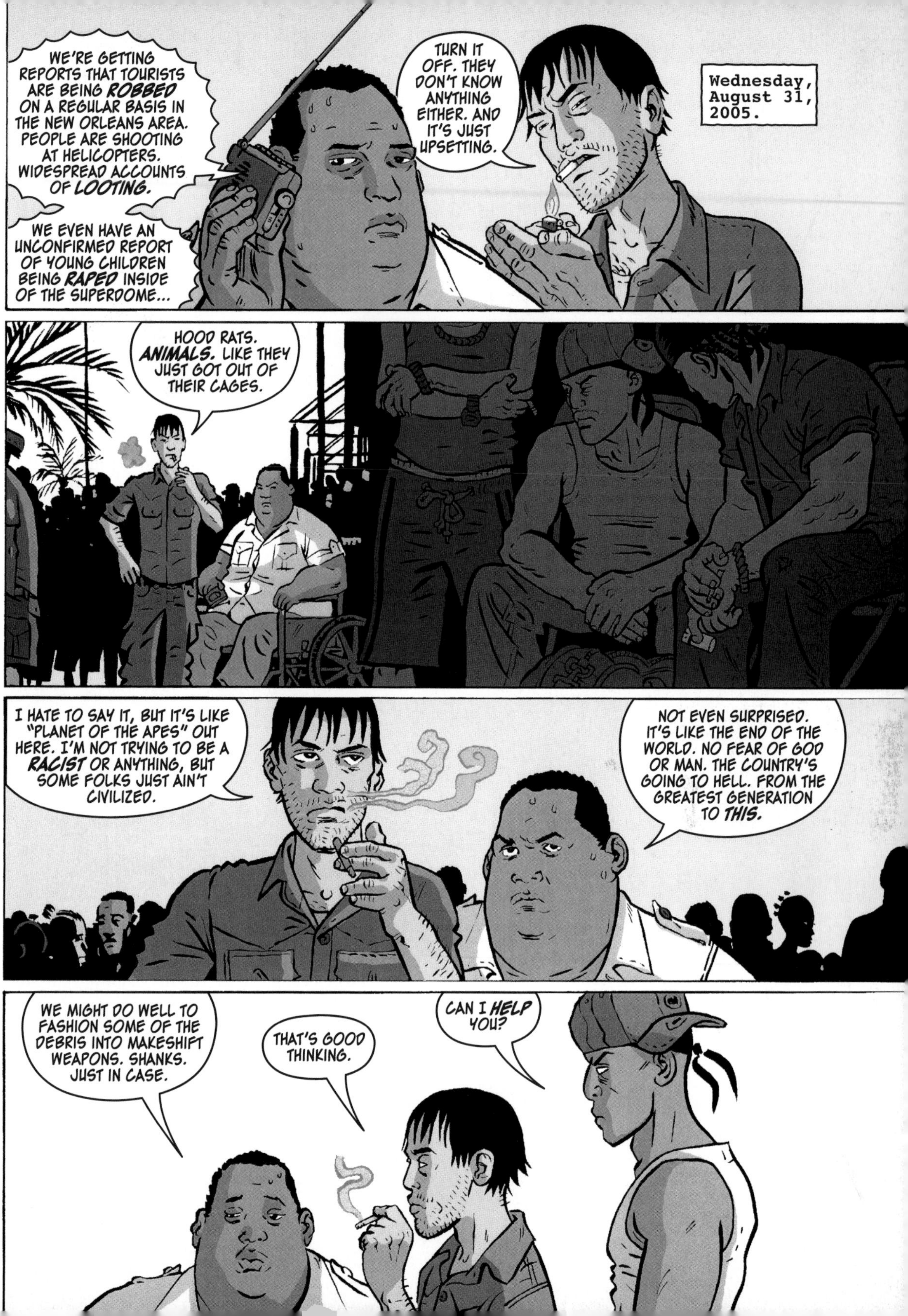
WE'RE GETTING REPORTS THAT TOURISTS ARE BEING ROBBED ON A REGULAR BASIS IN THE NEW ORLEANS AREA. PEOPLE ARE SHOOTING AT HELICOPTERS. WIDESPREAD ACCOUNTS OF LOOTING.
WE EVEN HAVE AN UNCONFIRMED REPORT OF YOUNG CHILDREN BEING RAPED INSIDE OF THE SUPERDOME...
TURN IT OFF. THEY DON'T KNOW ANYTHING EITHER. AND IT'S JUST UPSETTING.
Wednesday, August 31, 2005.
HOOD RATS. ANIMALS. LIKE THEY JUST GOT OUT OF THEIR CAGES.
I HATE TO SAY IT, BUT IT'S LIKE "PLANET OF THE APES" OUT HERE. I'M NOT TRYING TO BE A RACIST OR ANYTHING, BUT SOME FOLKS JUST AIN'T CIVILIZED.
NOT EVEN SURPRISED. IT'S LIKE THE END OF THE WORLD. NO FEAR OF GOD OR MAN. THE COUNTRY'S GOING TO HELL. FROM THE GREATEST GENERATION TO THIS.
WE MIGHT DO WELL TO FASHION SOME OF THE DEBRIS INTO MAKESHIFT WEAPONS. SHANKS. JUST IN CASE.
THAT'S GOOD THINKING.
CAN I HELP YOU?

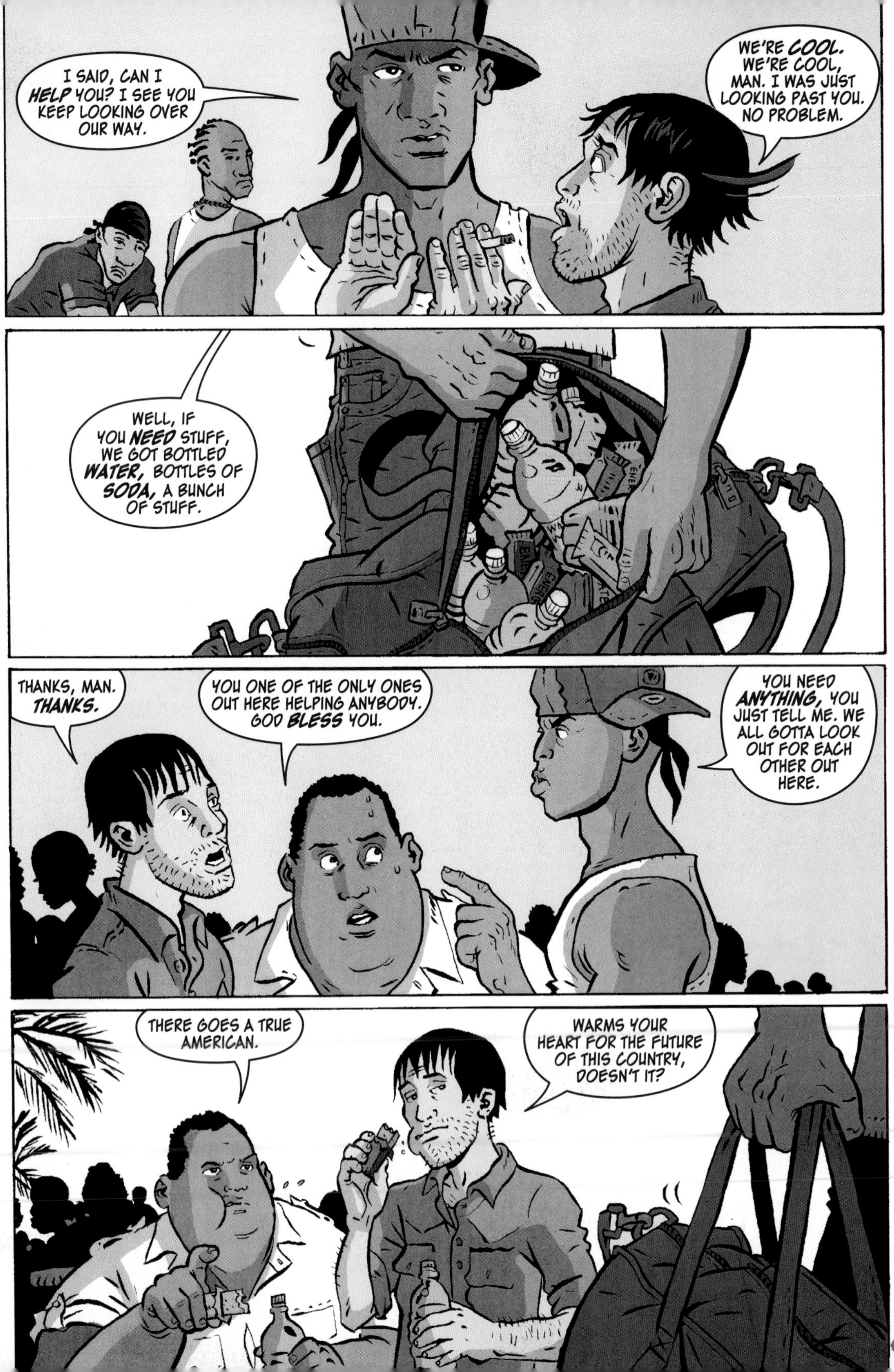
I SAID, CAN I HELP YOU? I SEE YOU KEEP LOOKING OVER OUR WAY.
WE'RE COOL. WE'RE COOL, MAN. I WAS JUST LOOKING PAST YOU. NO PROBLEM.
WELL, IF YOU NEED STUFF, WE GOT BOTTLED WATER, BOTTLES OF SODA, A BUNCH OF STUFF.
THANKS, MAN. THANKS.
YOU ONE OF THE ONLY ONES OUT HERE HELPING ANYBODY. GOD BLESS YOU.
YOU NEED ANYTHING, YOU JUST TELL ME. WE ALL GOTTA LOOK OUT FOR EACH OTHER OUT HERE.
THERE GOES A TRUE AMERICAN.
WARMS YOUR HEART FOR THE FUTURE OF THIS COUNTRY, DOESN'T IT?

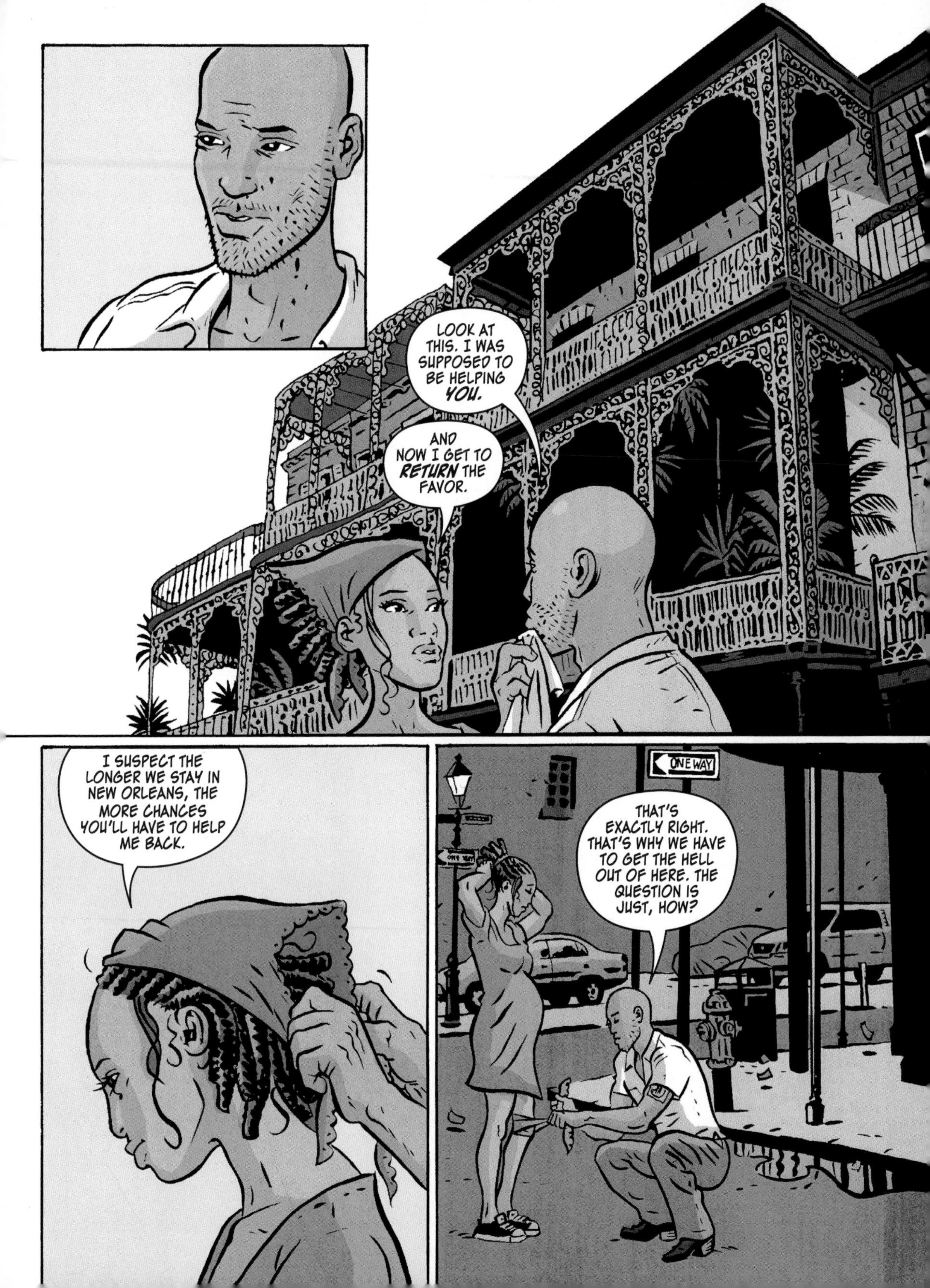
LOOK AT THIS. I WAS SUPPOSED TO BE HELPING *YOU.*
AND NOW I GET TO *RETURN* THE FAVOR.
I SUSPECT THE LONGER WE STAY IN NEW ORLEANS, THE MORE CHANCES YOU'LL HAVE TO HELP ME BACK.
ONE WAY
THAT'S EXACTLY RIGHT. THAT'S WHY WE HAVE TO GET THE HELL OUT OF HERE. THE QUESTION IS JUST, HOW?

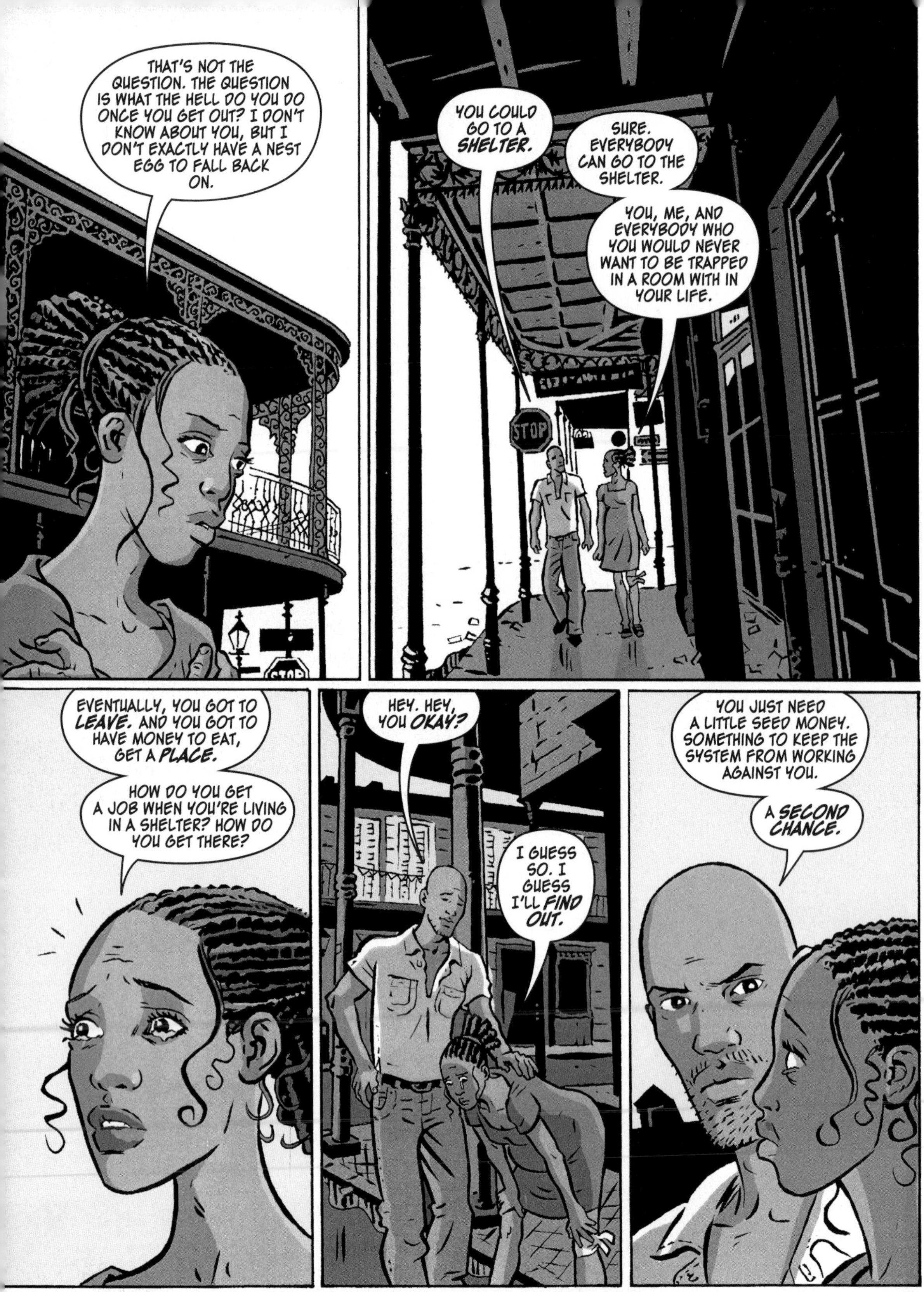
THAT'S NOT THE QUESTION. THE QUESTION IS WHAT THE HELL DO YOU DO ONCE YOU GET OUT? I DON'T KNOW ABOUT YOU, BUT I DON'T EXACTLY HAVE A NEST EGG TO FALL BACK ON.
YOU COULD GO TO A SHELTER.
SURE. EVERYBODY CAN GO TO THE SHELTER.
YOU, ME, AND EVERYBODY WHO YOU WOULD NEVER WANT TO BE TRAPPED IN A ROOM WITH IN YOUR LIFE.
STOP
EVENTUALLY, YOU GOT TO LEAVE. AND YOU GOT TO HAVE MONEY TO EAT, GET A PLACE.
HOW DO YOU GET A JOB WHEN YOU'RE LIVING IN A SHELTER? HOW DO YOU GET THERE?
HEY. HEY, YOU OKAY?
I GUESS SO. I GUESS I'LL FIND OUT.
YOU JUST NEED A LITTLE SEED MONEY. SOMETHING TO KEEP THE SYSTEM FROM WORKING AGAINST YOU.
A SECOND CHANCE.

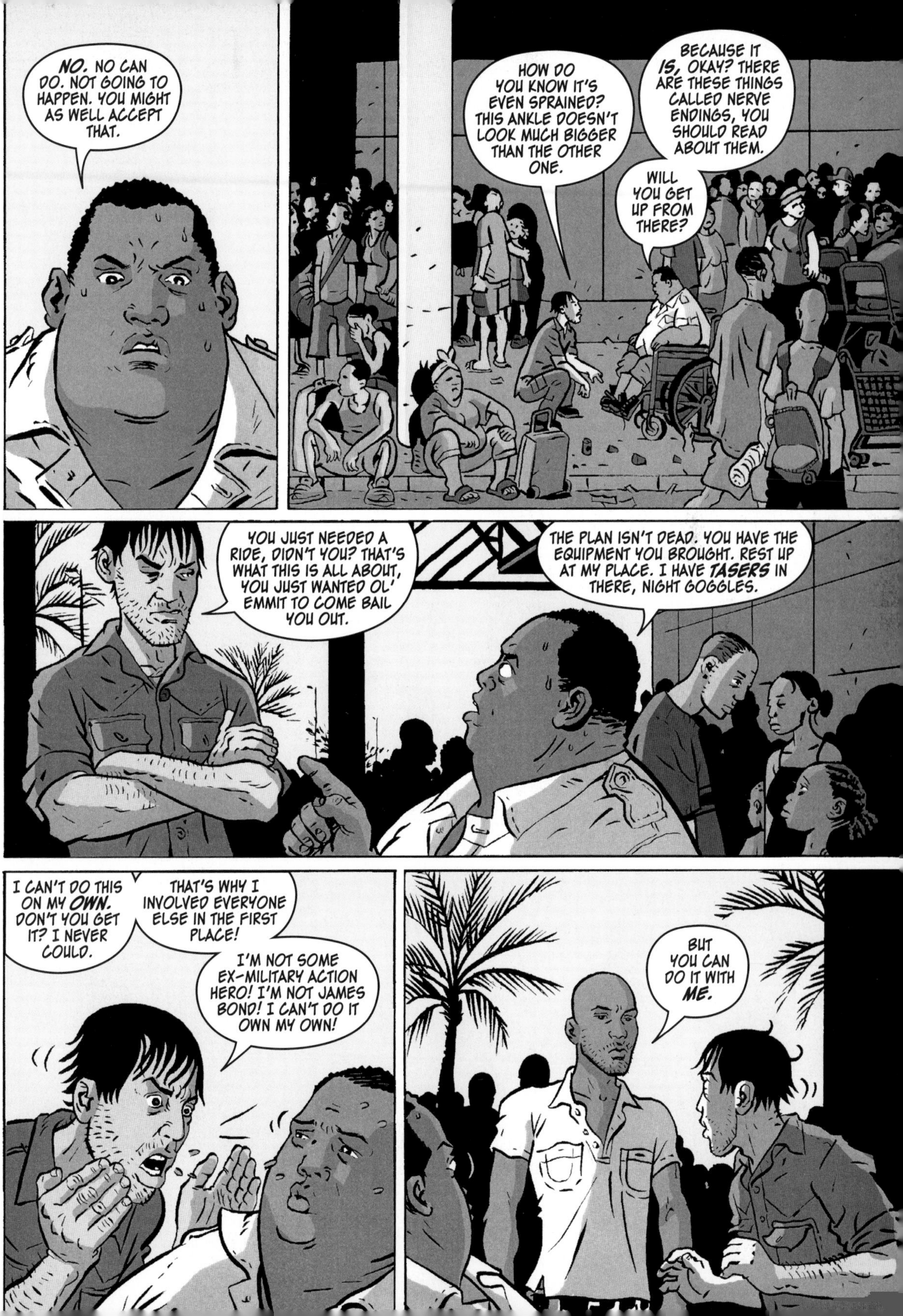
NO. NO CAN DO. NOT GOING TO HAPPEN. YOU MIGHT AS WELL ACCEPT THAT.
HOW DO YOU KNOW IT'S EVEN SPRAINED? THIS ANKLE DOESN'T LOOK MUCH BIGGER THAN THE OTHER ONE.
BECAUSE IT IS, OKAY? THERE ARE THESE THINGS CALLED NERVE ENDINGS, YOU SHOULD READ ABOUT THEM.
WILL YOU GET UP FROM THERE?
YOU JUST NEEDED A RIDE, DIDN'T YOU? THAT'S WHAT THIS IS ALL ABOUT, YOU JUST WANTED OL' EMMIT TO COME BAIL YOU OUT.
THE PLAN ISN'T DEAD. YOU HAVE THE EQUIPMENT YOU BROUGHT. REST UP AT MY PLACE. I HAVE TASERS IN THERE, NIGHT GOGGLES.
I CAN'T DO THIS ON MY OWN. DON'T YOU GET IT? I NEVER COULD.
THAT'S WHY I INVOLVED EVERYONE ELSE IN THE FIRST PLACE!
I'M NOT SOME EX-MILITARY ACTION HERO! I'M NOT JAMES BOND! I CAN'T DO IT OWN MY OWN!
BUT YOU CAN DO IT WITH ME.

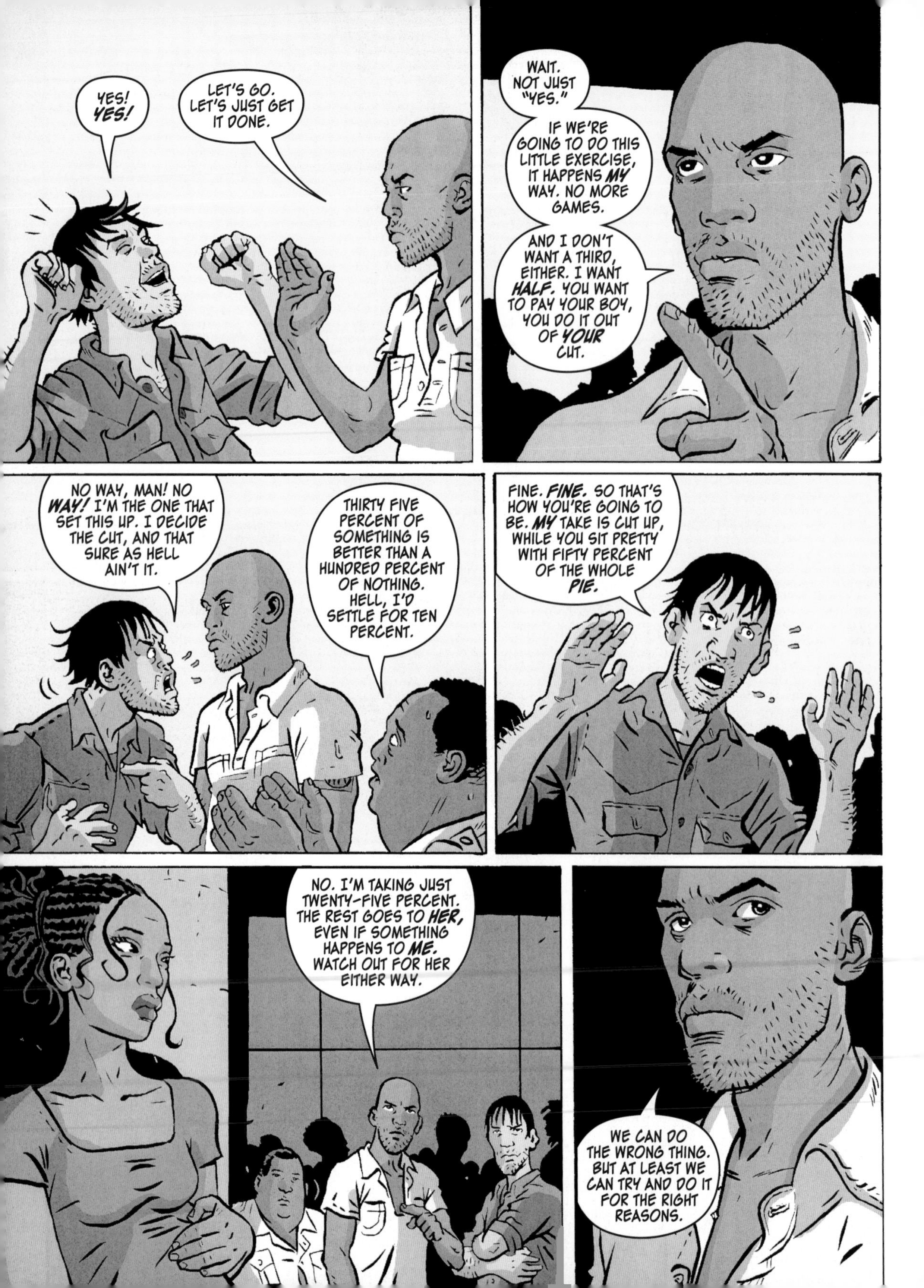
YES! YES!
LET'S GO. LET'S JUST GET IT DONE.
WAIT. NOT JUST "YES."
IF WE'RE GOING TO DO THIS LITTLE EXERCISE, IT HAPPENS MY WAY. NO MORE GAMES.
AND I DON'T WANT A THIRD, EITHER. I WANT HALF. YOU WANT TO PAY YOUR BOY, YOU DO IT OUT OF YOUR CUT.
NO WAY, MAN! NO WAY! I'M THE ONE THAT SET THIS UP. I DECIDE THE CUT, AND THAT SURE AS HELL AIN'T IT.
THIRTY FIVE PERCENT OF SOMETHING IS BETTER THAN A HUNDRED PERCENT OF NOTHING. HELL, I'D SETTLE FOR TEN PERCENT.
FINE. FINE. SO THAT'S HOW YOU'RE GOING TO BE. MY TAKE IS CUT UP, WHILE YOU SIT PRETTY WITH FIFTY PERCENT OF THE WHOLE PIE.
NO. I'M TAKING JUST TWENTY-FIVE PERCENT. THE REST GOES TO HER, EVEN IF SOMETHING HAPPENS TO ME. WATCH OUT FOR HER EITHER WAY.
WE CAN DO THE WRONG THING. BUT AT LEAST WE CAN TRY AND DO IT FOR THE RIGHT REASONS.

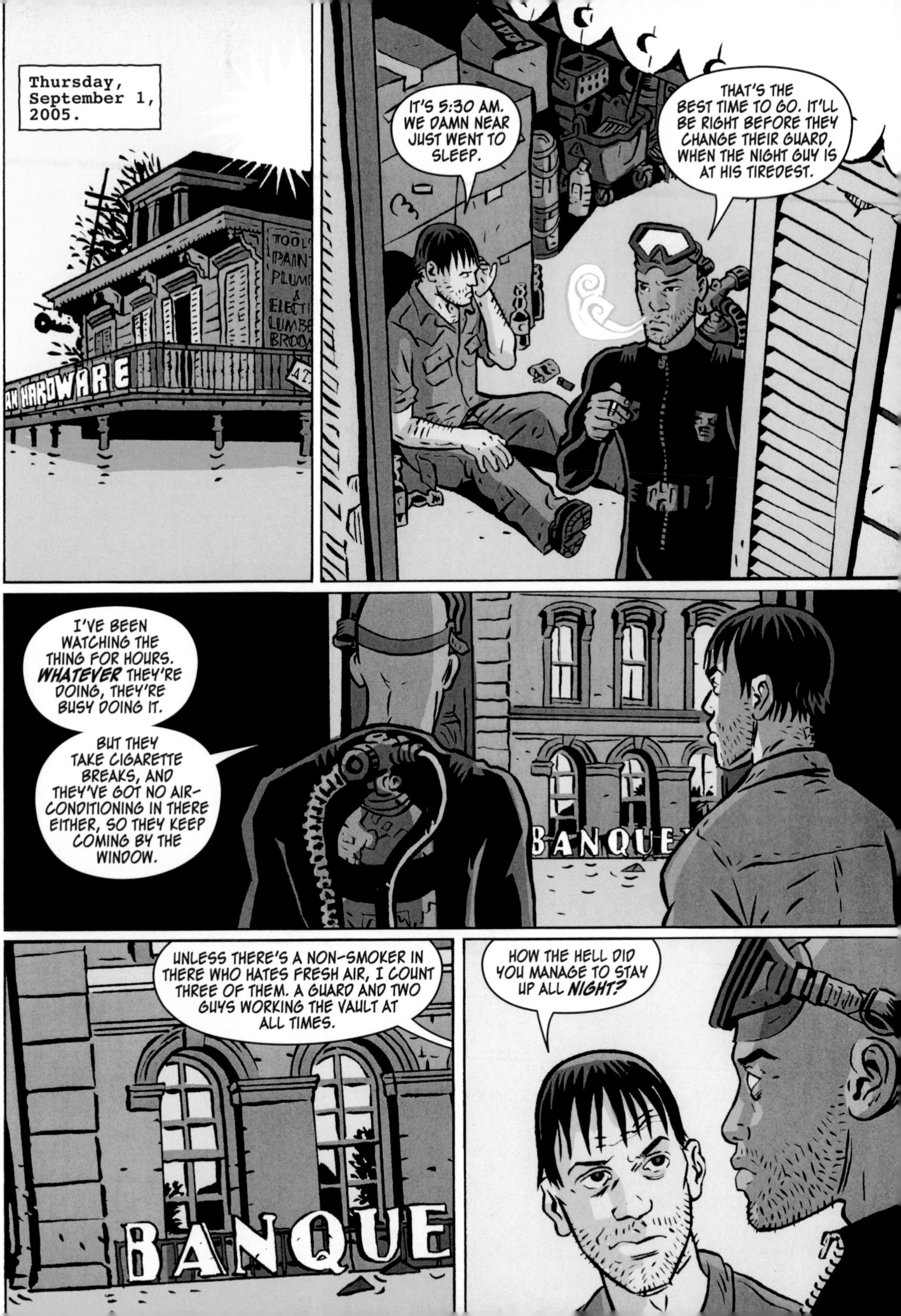
Thursday, September 1, 2005.
HARDWARE
TOOLS PAINT PLUMB & ELECTI LUMBE BROO
IT'S 5:30 AM. WE DAMN NEAR JUST WENT TO SLEEP.
THAT'S THE BEST TIME TO GO. IT'LL BE RIGHT BEFORE THEY CHANGE THEIR GUARD, WHEN THE NIGHT GUY IS AT HIS TIREDEST.
I'VE BEEN WATCHING THE THING FOR HOURS. *WHATEVER* THEY'RE DOING, THEY'RE BUSY DOING IT.
BUT THEY TAKE CIGARETTE BREAKS, AND THEY'VE GOT NO AIR-CONDITIONING IN THERE EITHER, SO THEY KEEP COMING BY THE WINDOW.
BANQUE
UNLESS THERE'S A NON-SMOKER IN THERE WHO HATES FRESH AIR, I COUNT THREE OF THEM. A GUARD AND TWO GUYS WORKING THE VAULT AT ALL TIMES.
BANQUE
HOW THE HELL DID YOU MANAGE TO STAY UP ALL *NIGHT?*

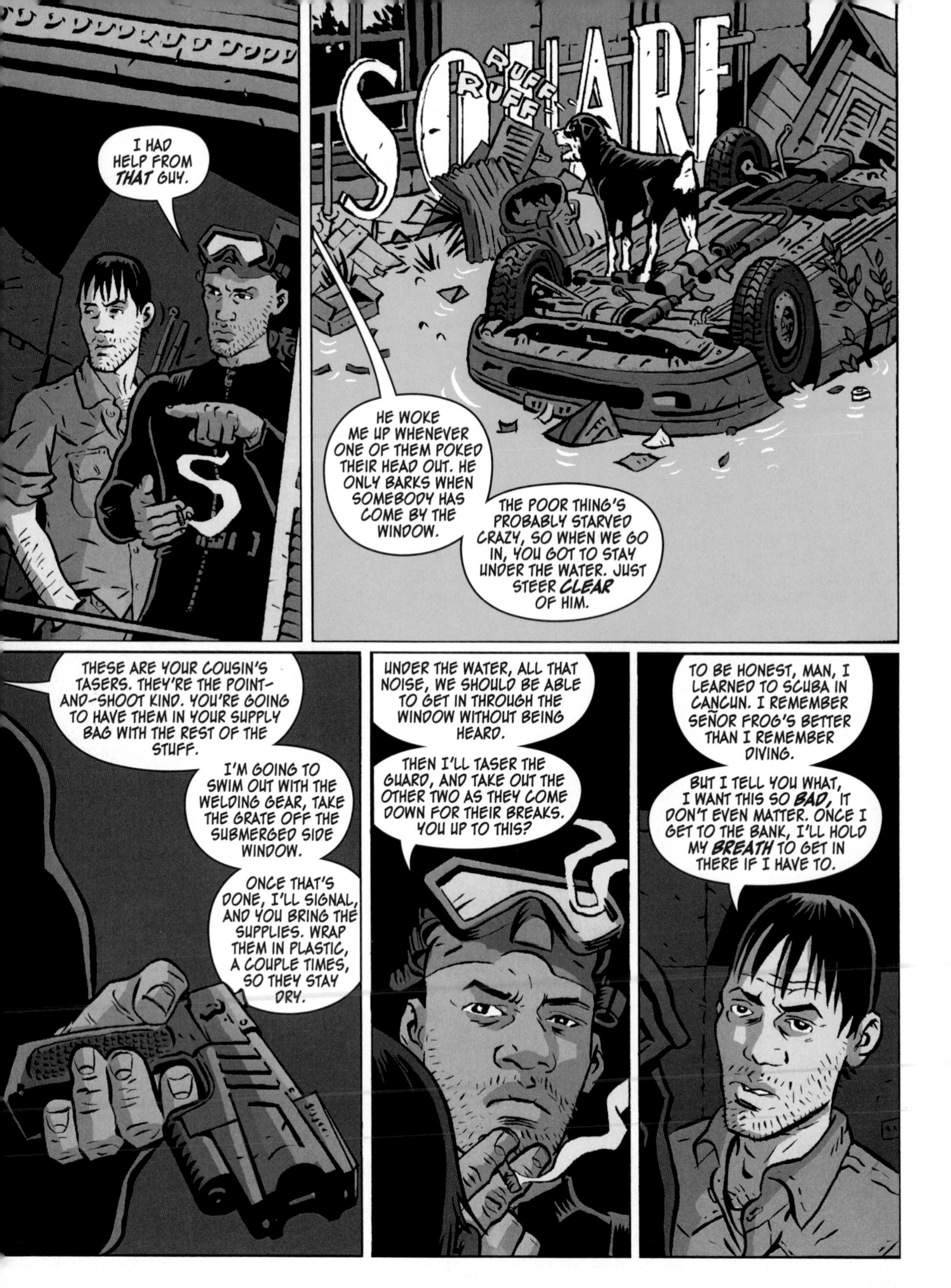

I HAD HELP FROM THAT GUY.
RUFF RUFF
HE WOKE ME UP WHENEVER ONE OF THEM POKED THEIR HEAD OUT. HE ONLY BARKS WHEN SOMEBODY HAS COME BY THE WINDOW.
THE POOR THING'S PROBABLY STARVED CRAZY, SO WHEN WE GO IN, YOU GOT TO STAY UNDER THE WATER. JUST STEER CLEAR OF HIM.
THESE ARE YOUR COUSIN'S TASERS. THEY'RE THE POINT-AND-SHOOT KIND. YOU'RE GOING TO HAVE THEM IN YOUR SUPPLY BAG WITH THE REST OF THE STUFF.
I'M GOING TO SWIM OUT WITH THE WELDING GEAR, TAKE THE GRATE OFF THE SUBMERGED SIDE WINDOW.
ONCE THAT'S DONE, I'LL SIGNAL, AND YOU BRING THE SUPPLIES. WRAP THEM IN PLASTIC, A COUPLE TIMES, SO THEY STAY DRY.
UNDER THE WATER, ALL THAT NOISE, WE SHOULD BE ABLE TO GET IN THROUGH THE WINDOW WITHOUT BEING HEARD.
THEN I'LL TASER THE GUARD, AND TAKE OUT THE OTHER TWO AS THEY COME DOWN FOR THEIR BREAKS. YOU UP TO THIS?
TO BE HONEST, MAN, I LEARNED TO SCUBA IN CANCUN. I REMEMBER SEÑOR FROG'S BETTER THAN I REMEMBER DIVING.
BUT I TELL YOU WHAT, I WANT THIS SO BAD, IT DON'T EVEN MATTER. ONCE I GET TO THE BANK, I'LL HOLD MY BREATH TO GET IN THERE IF I HAVE TO.

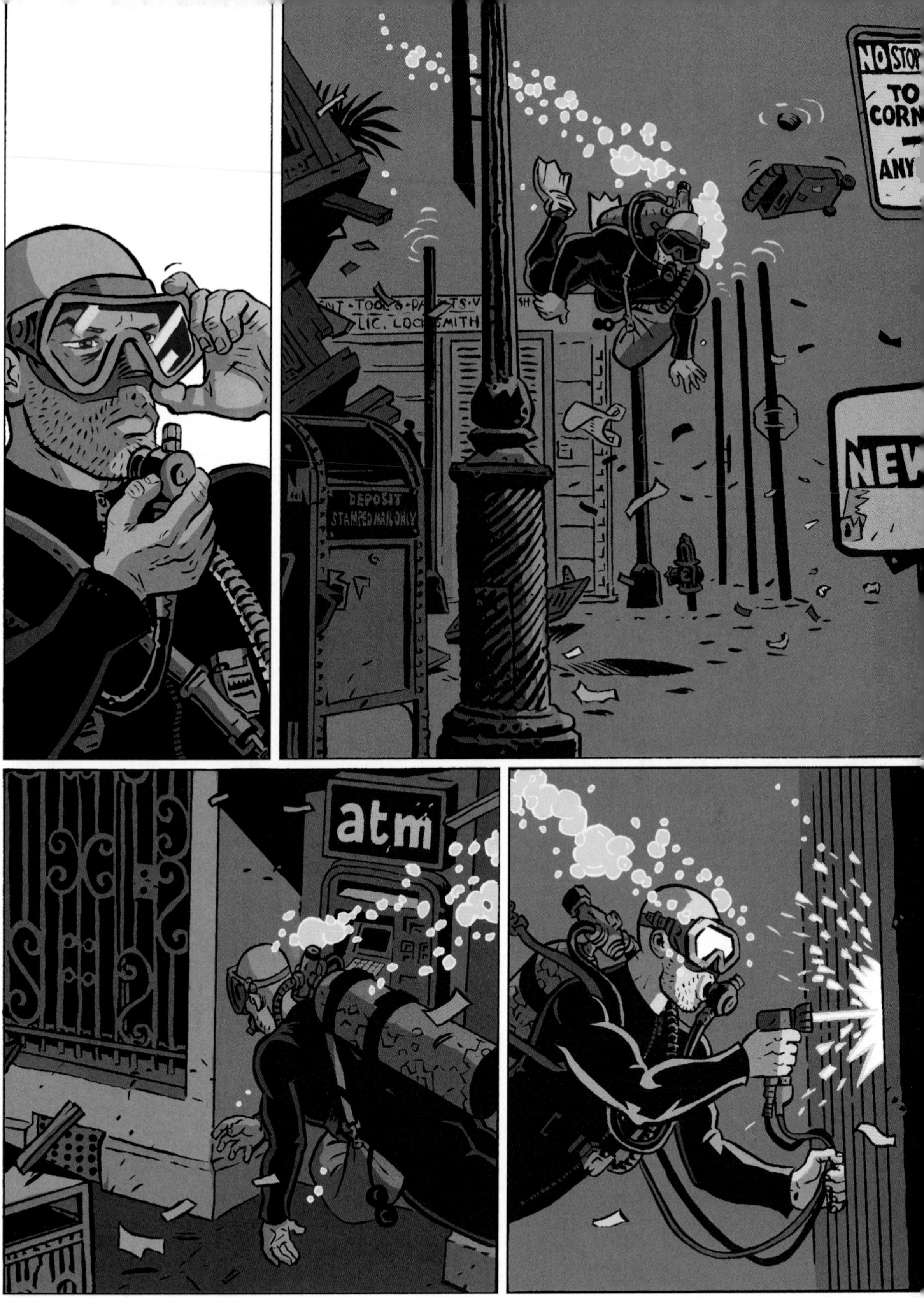
LIC. LOCKSMITH
DEPOSIT
STAMPED MAIL ONLY
atm

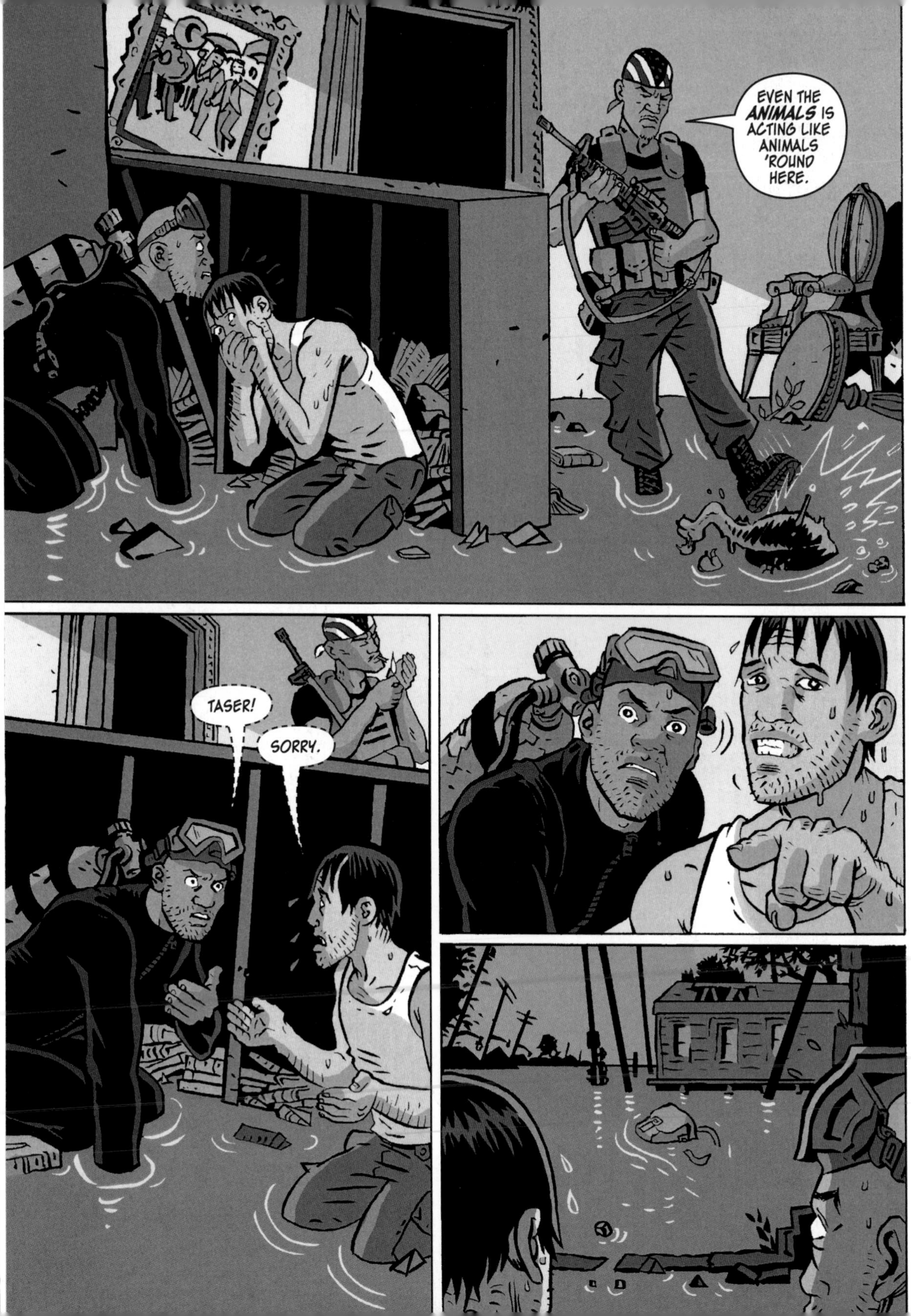
EVEN THE ANIMALS IS ACTING LIKE ANIMALS 'ROUND HERE.
TASER!
SORRY.

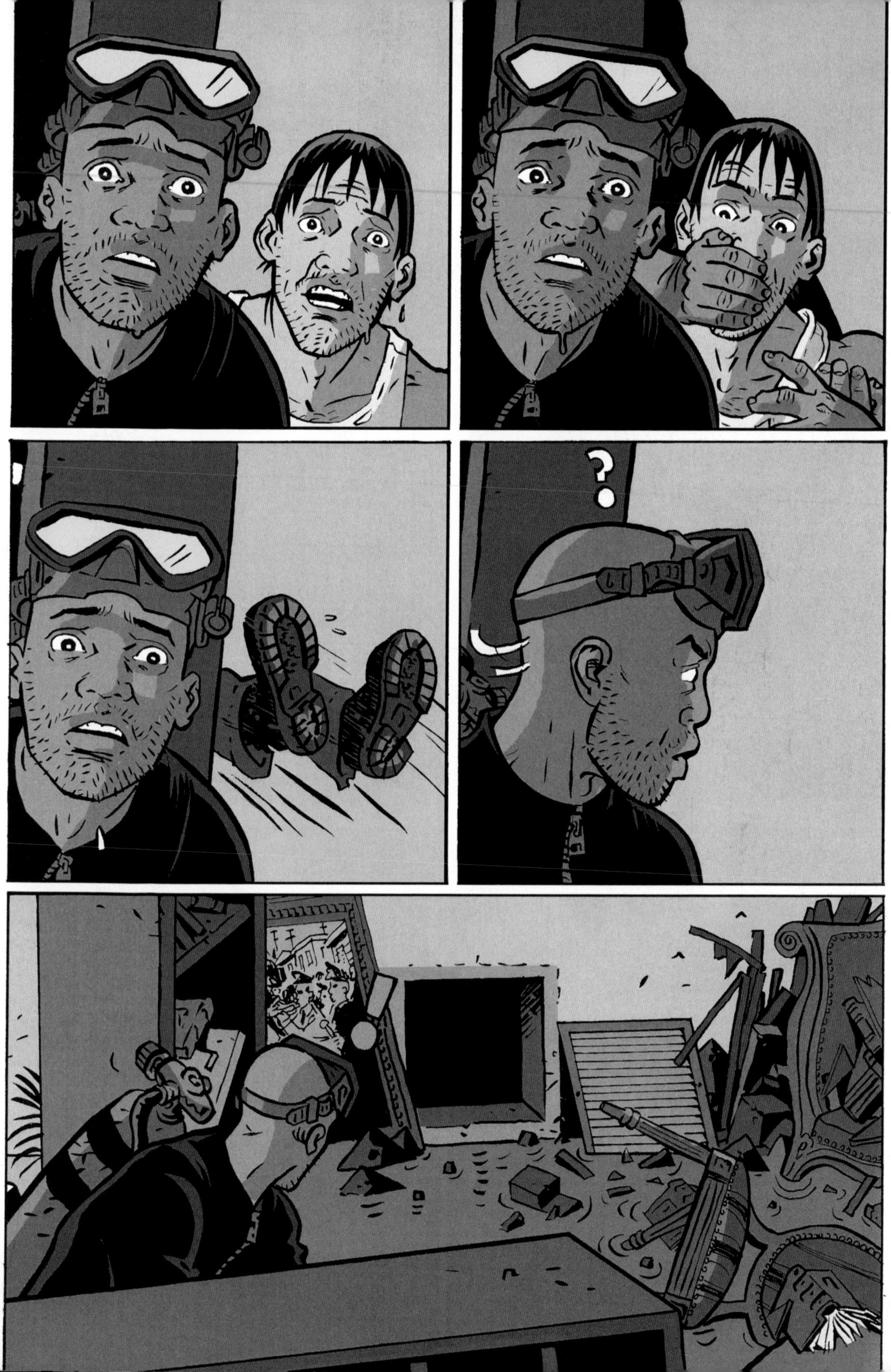
?

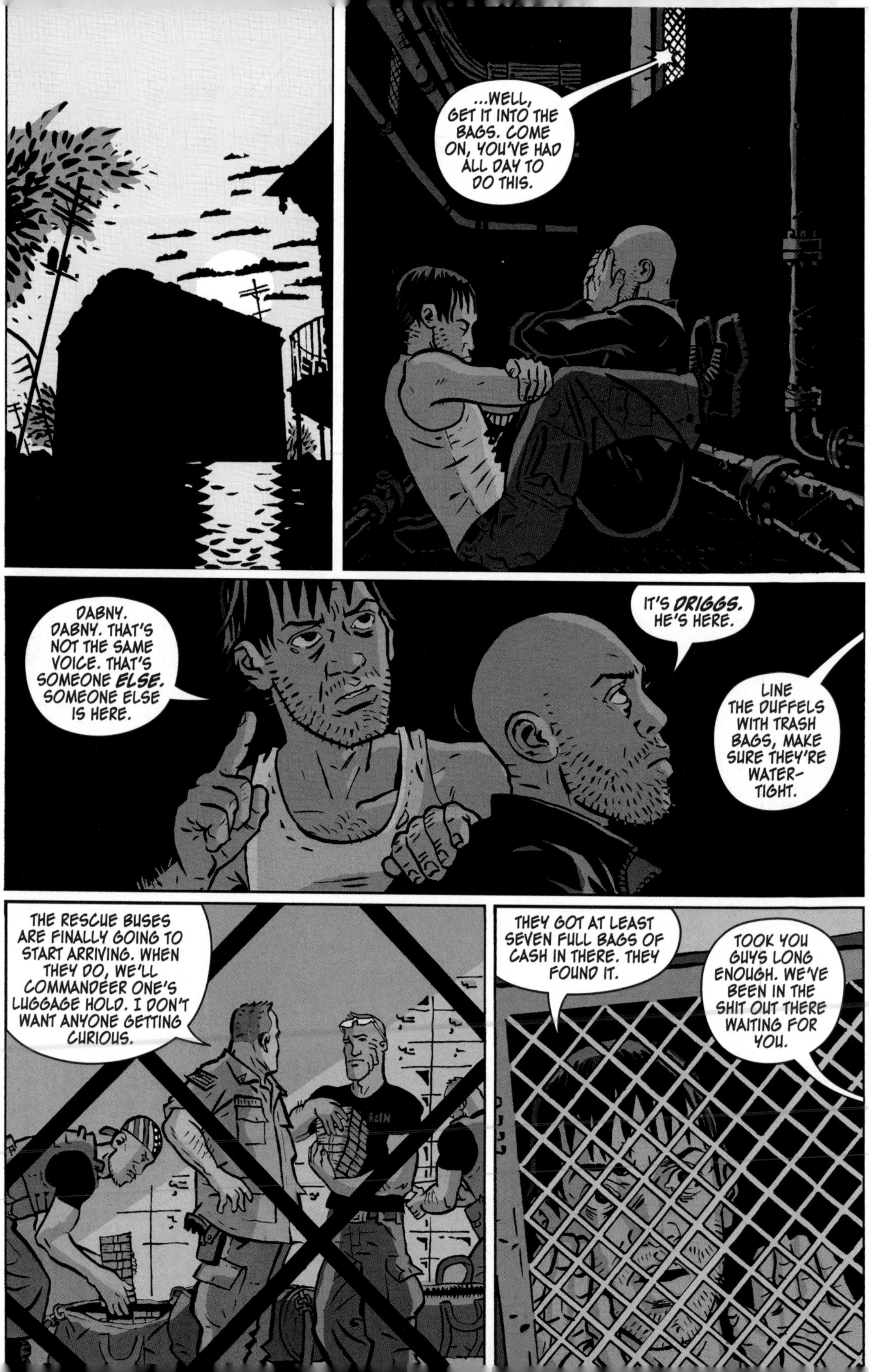
...WELL, GET IT INTO THE BAGS. COME ON, YOU'VE HAD ALL DAY TO DO THIS.
DABNY. DABNY. THAT'S NOT THE SAME VOICE. THAT'S SOMEONE *ELSE*. SOMEONE ELSE IS HERE.
IT'S *DRIGGS*. HE'S HERE.
LINE THE DUFFELS WITH TRASH BAGS, MAKE SURE THEY'RE WATER-TIGHT.
THE RESCUE BUSES ARE FINALLY GOING TO START ARRIVING. WHEN THEY DO, WE'LL COMMANDEER ONE'S LUGGAGE HOLD. I DON'T WANT ANYONE GETTING CURIOUS.
THEY GOT AT LEAST SEVEN FULL BAGS OF CASH IN THERE. THEY FOUND IT.
TOOK YOU GUYS LONG ENOUGH. WE'VE BEEN IN THE SHIT OUT THERE WAITING FOR YOU.

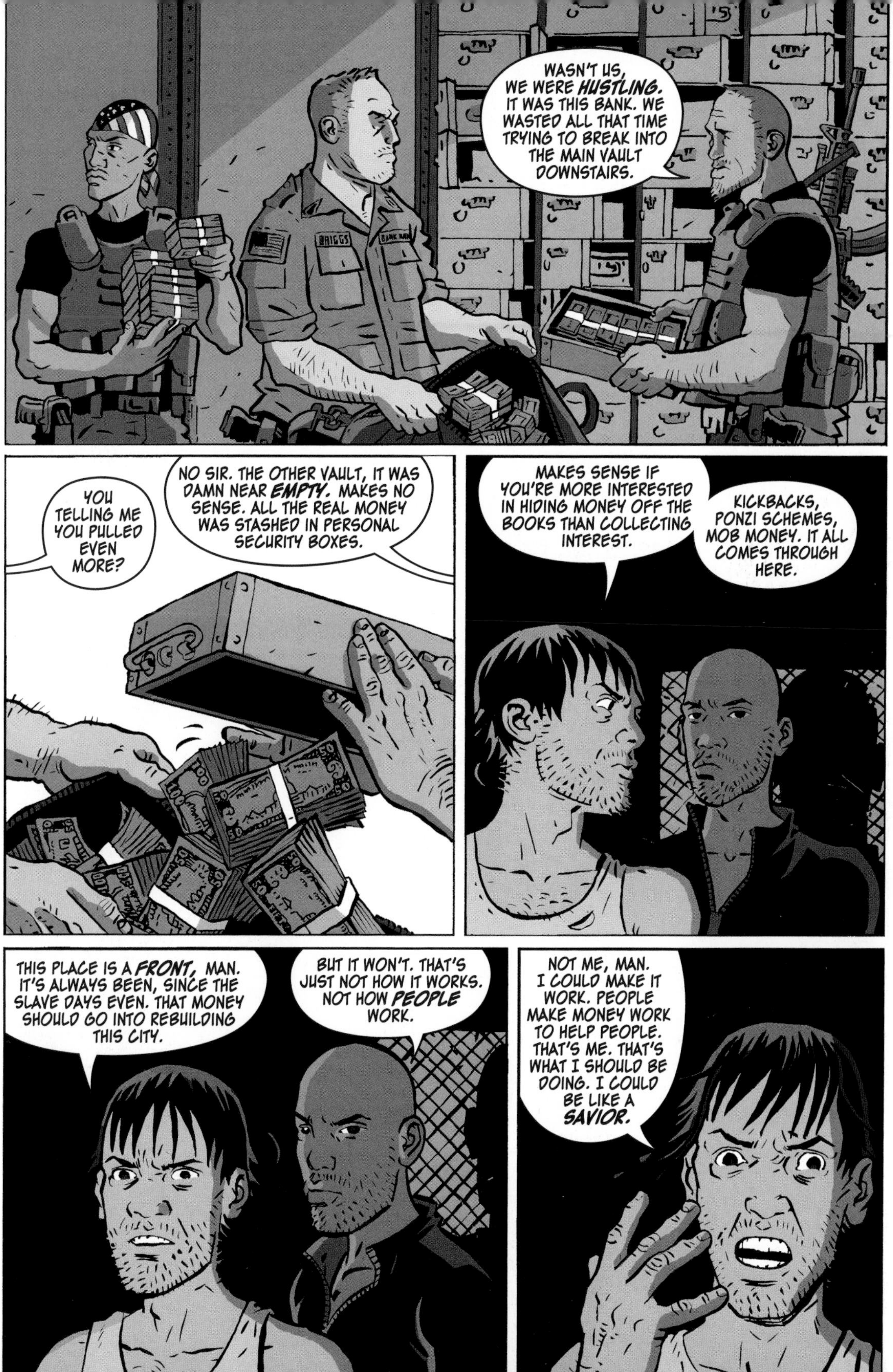
WASN'T US, WE WERE HUSTLING. IT WAS THIS BANK. WE WASTED ALL THAT TIME TRYING TO BREAK INTO THE MAIN VAULT DOWNSTAIRS.
BRIGGS
YOU TELLING ME YOU PULLED EVEN MORE?
NO SIR. THE OTHER VAULT, IT WAS DAMN NEAR EMPTY. MAKES NO SENSE. ALL THE REAL MONEY WAS STASHED IN PERSONAL SECURITY BOXES.
MAKES SENSE IF YOU'RE MORE INTERESTED IN HIDING MONEY OFF THE BOOKS THAN COLLECTING INTEREST.
KICKBACKS, PONZI SCHEMES, MOB MONEY. IT ALL COMES THROUGH HERE.
THIS PLACE IS A FRONT, MAN. IT'S ALWAYS BEEN, SINCE THE SLAVE DAYS EVEN. THAT MONEY SHOULD GO INTO REBUILDING THIS CITY.
BUT IT WON'T. THAT'S JUST NOT HOW IT WORKS. NOT HOW PEOPLE WORK.
NOT ME, MAN. I COULD MAKE IT WORK. PEOPLE MAKE MONEY WORK TO HELP PEOPLE. THAT'S ME. THAT'S WHAT I SHOULD BE DOING. I COULD BE LIKE A SAVIOR.

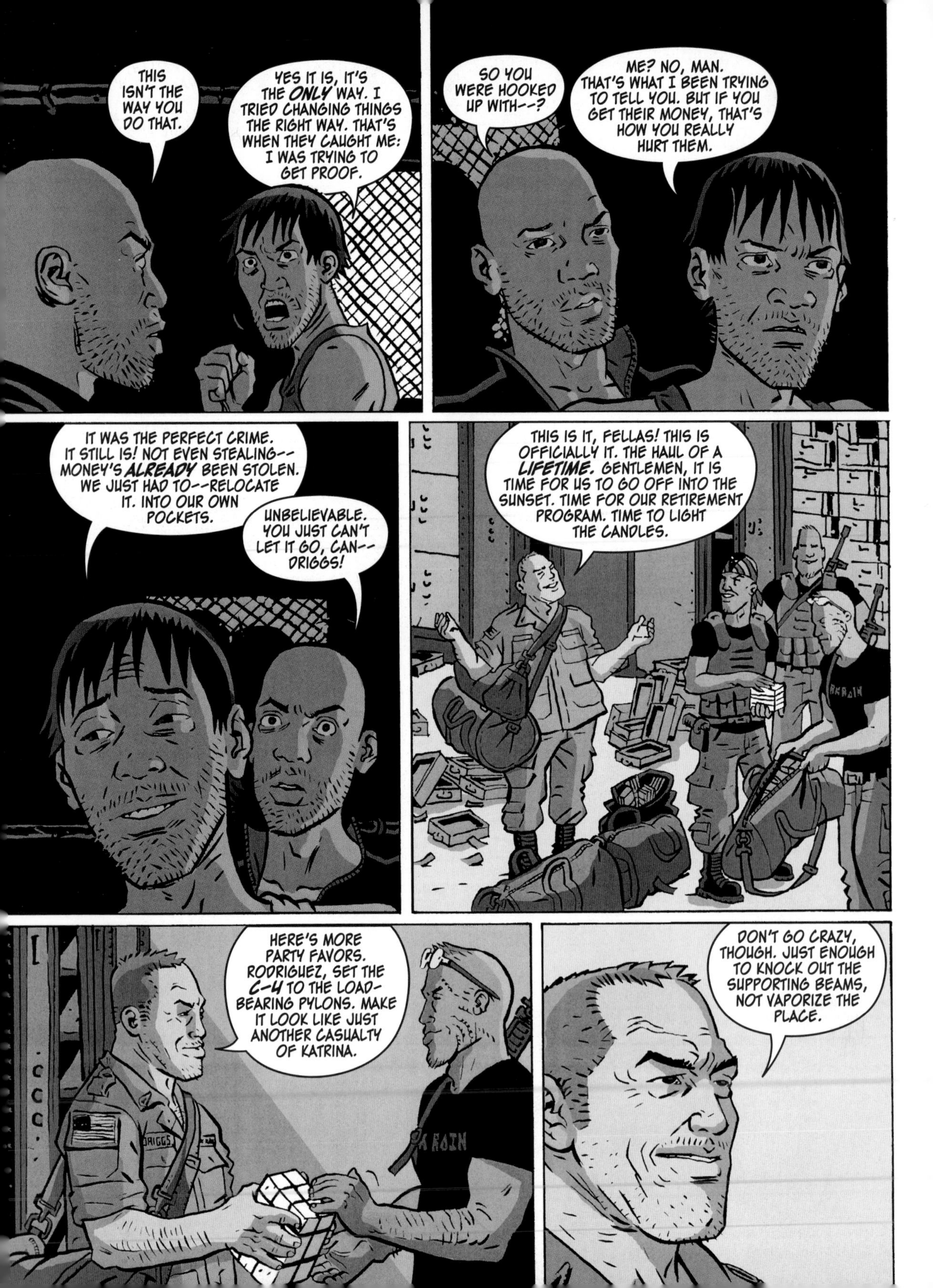
THIS ISN'T THE WAY YOU DO THAT.
YES IT IS, IT'S THE ONLY WAY. I TRIED CHANGING THINGS THE RIGHT WAY. THAT'S WHEN THEY CAUGHT ME: I WAS TRYING TO GET PROOF.
SO YOU WERE HOOKED UP WITH--?
ME? NO, MAN. THAT'S WHAT I BEEN TRYING TO TELL YOU. BUT IF YOU GET THEIR MONEY, THAT'S HOW YOU REALLY HURT THEM.
IT WAS THE PERFECT CRIME. IT STILL IS! NOT EVEN STEALING--MONEY'S ALREADY BEEN STOLEN. WE JUST HAD TO--RELOCATE IT. INTO OUR OWN POCKETS.
UNBELIEVABLE. YOU JUST CAN'T LET IT GO, CAN--DRIGGS!
THIS IS IT, FELLAS! THIS IS OFFICIALLY IT. THE HAUL OF A LIFETIME. GENTLEMEN, IT IS TIME FOR US TO GO OFF INTO THE SUNSET. TIME FOR OUR RETIREMENT PROGRAM. TIME TO LIGHT THE CANDLES.
HERE'S MORE PARTY FAVORS. RODRIGUEZ, SET THE C-4 TO THE LOAD-BEARING PYLONS. MAKE IT LOOK LIKE JUST ANOTHER CASUALTY OF KATRINA.
DRIGGS
DON'T GO CRAZY, THOUGH. JUST ENOUGH TO KNOCK OUT THE SUPPORTING BEAMS, NOT VAPORIZE THE PLACE.

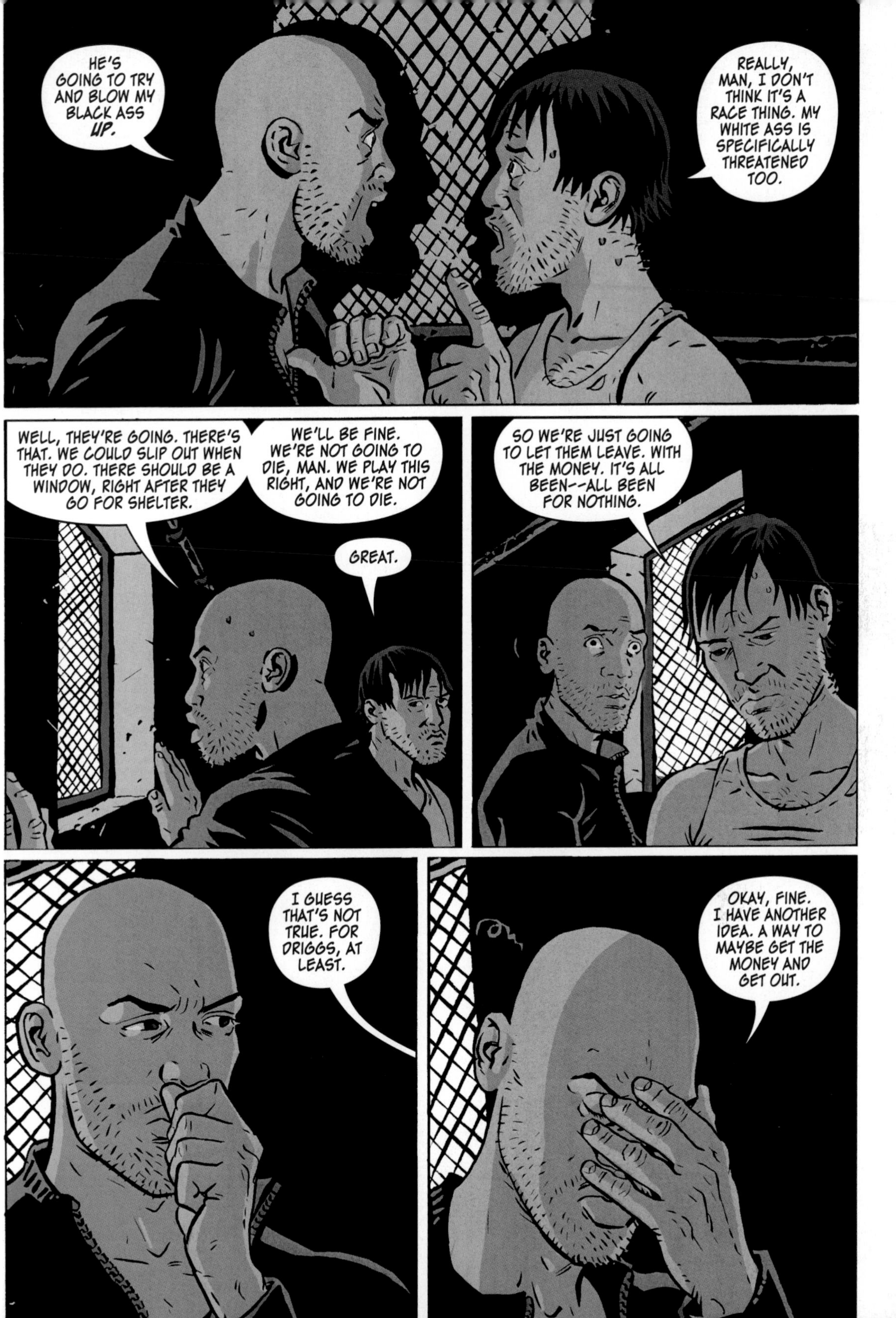
HE'S GOING TO TRY AND BLOW MY BLACK ASS UP.
REALLY, MAN, I DON'T THINK IT'S A RACE THING. MY WHITE ASS IS SPECIFICALLY THREATENED TOO.
WELL, THEY'RE GOING. THERE'S THAT. WE COULD SLIP OUT WHEN THEY DO. THERE SHOULD BE A WINDOW, RIGHT AFTER THEY GO FOR SHELTER.
WE'LL BE FINE. WE'RE NOT GOING TO DIE, MAN. WE PLAY THIS RIGHT, AND WE'RE NOT GOING TO DIE.
GREAT.
SO WE'RE JUST GOING TO LET THEM LEAVE. WITH THE MONEY. IT'S ALL BEEN--ALL BEEN FOR NOTHING.
I GUESS THAT'S NOT TRUE. FOR DRIGGS, AT LEAST.
OKAY, FINE. I HAVE ANOTHER IDEA. A WAY TO MAYBE GET THE MONEY AND GET OUT.

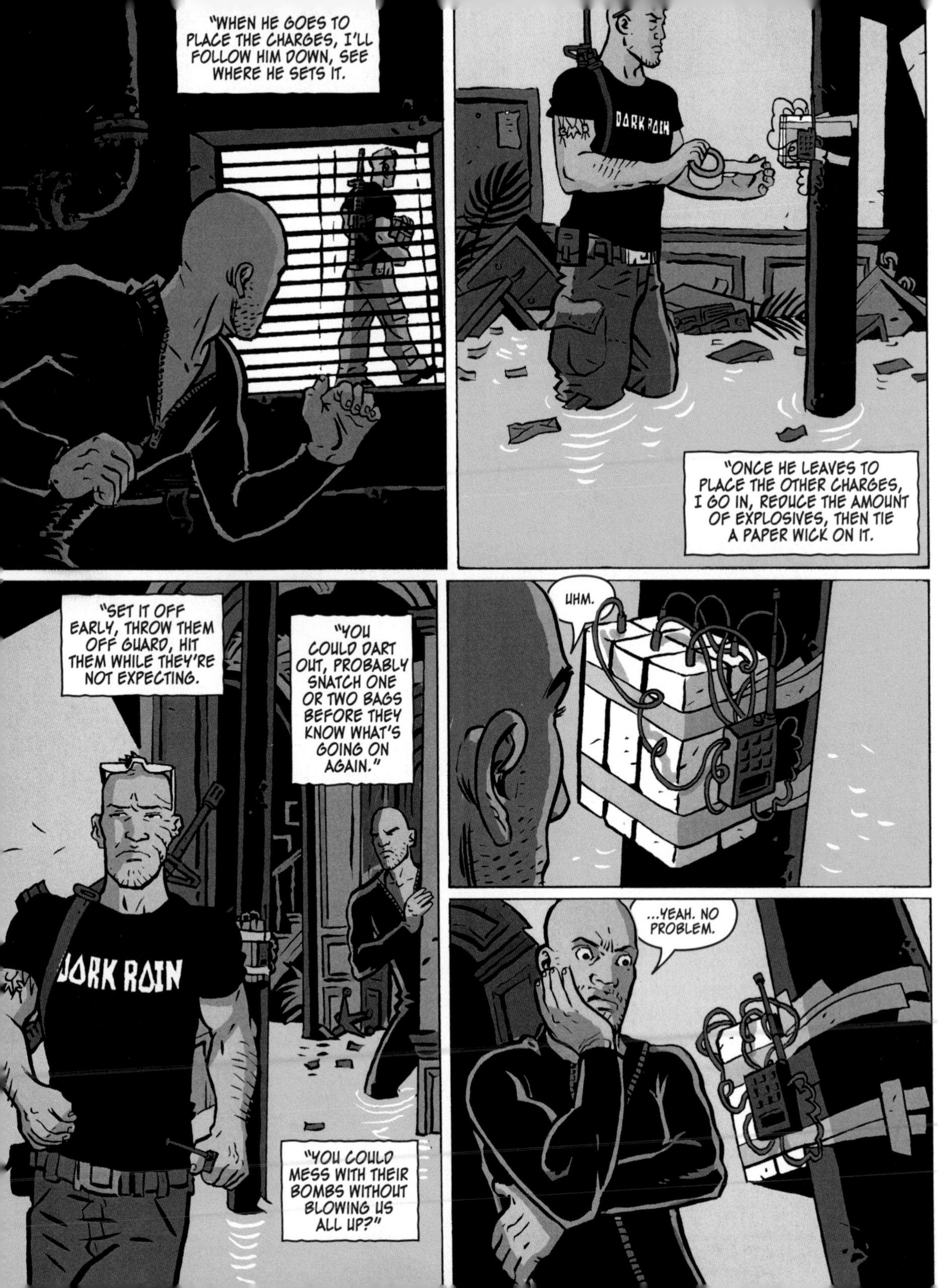
"WHEN HE GOES TO PLACE THE CHARGES, I'LL FOLLOW HIM DOWN, SEE WHERE HE SETS IT.
DARK RAIN
"ONCE HE LEAVES TO PLACE THE OTHER CHARGES, I GO IN, REDUCE THE AMOUNT OF EXPLOSIVES, THEN TIE A PAPER WICK ON IT.
"SET IT OFF EARLY, THROW THEM OFF GUARD, HIT THEM WHILE THEY'RE NOT EXPECTING.
"YOU COULD DART OUT, PROBABLY SNATCH ONE OR TWO BAGS BEFORE THEY KNOW WHAT'S GOING ON AGAIN."
DARK RAIN
"YOU COULD MESS WITH THEIR BOMBS WITHOUT BLOWING US ALL UP?"
UHM.
...YEAH. NO PROBLEM.

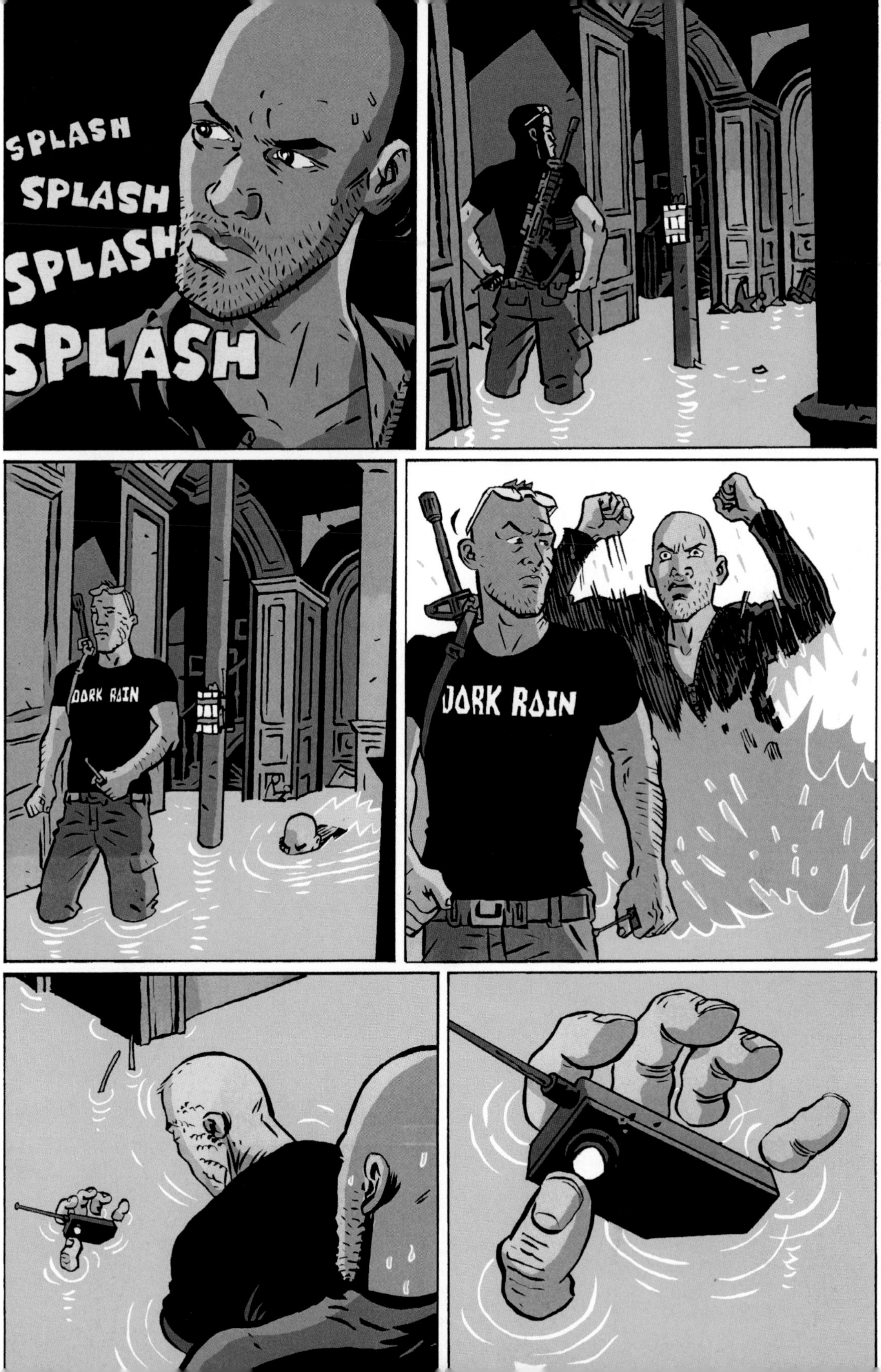
SPLASH
SPLASH
SPLASH
SPLASH
DORK RAIN
DORK RAIN

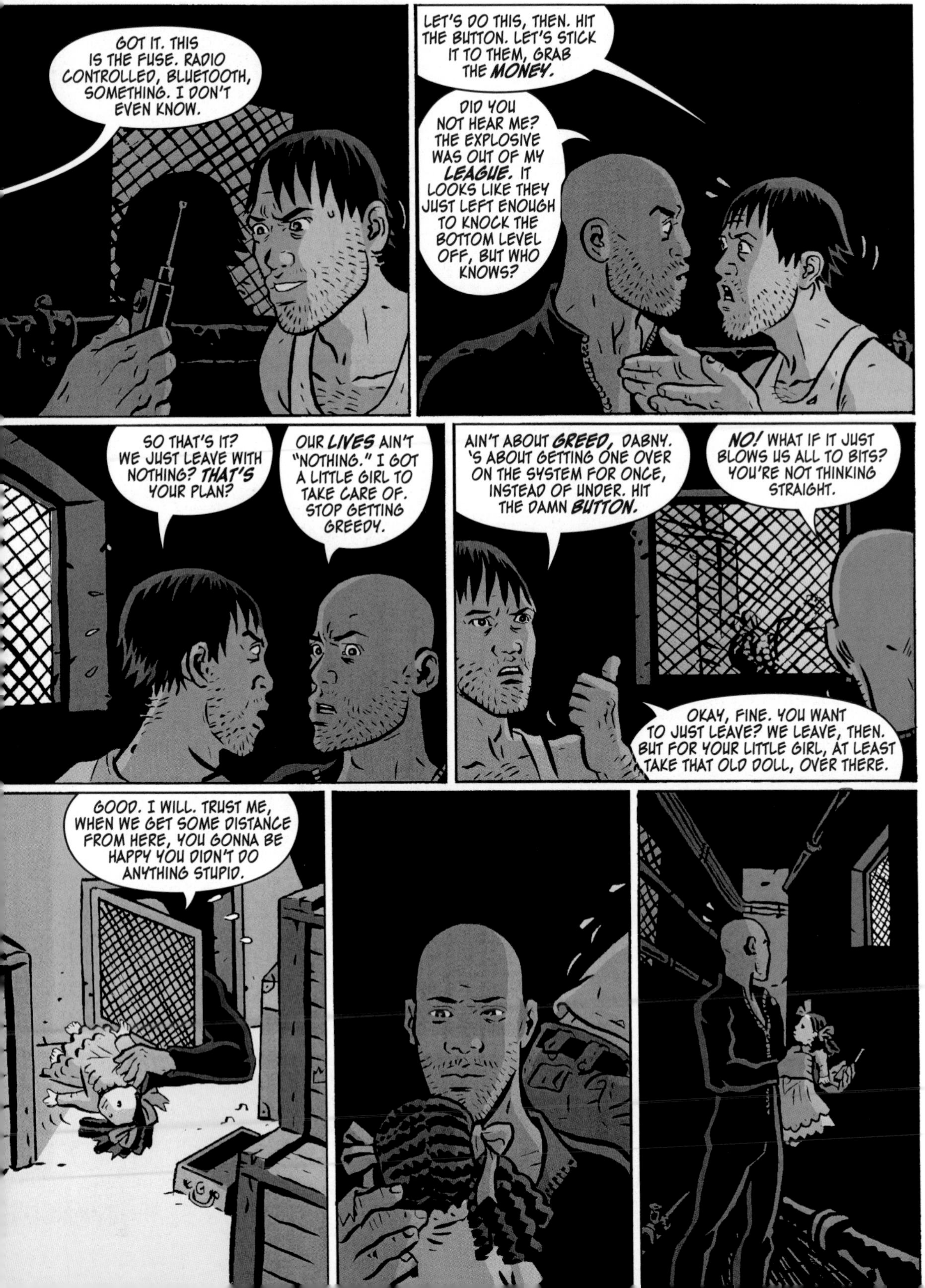
GOT IT. THIS IS THE FUSE. RADIO CONTROLLED, BLUETOOTH, SOMETHING. I DON'T EVEN KNOW.
LET'S DO THIS, THEN. HIT THE BUTTON. LET'S STICK IT TO THEM, GRAB THE MONEY.
DID YOU NOT HEAR ME? THE EXPLOSIVE WAS OUT OF MY LEAGUE. IT LOOKS LIKE THEY JUST LEFT ENOUGH TO KNOCK THE BOTTOM LEVEL OFF, BUT WHO KNOWS?
SO THAT'S IT? WE JUST LEAVE WITH NOTHING? THAT'S YOUR PLAN?
OUR LIVES AIN'T "NOTHING." I GOT A LITTLE GIRL TO TAKE CARE OF. STOP GETTING GREEDY.
AIN'T ABOUT GREED, DABNY. 'S ABOUT GETTING ONE OVER ON THE SYSTEM FOR ONCE, INSTEAD OF UNDER. HIT THE DAMN BUTTON.
NO! WHAT IF IT JUST BLOWS US ALL TO BITS? YOU'RE NOT THINKING STRAIGHT.
OKAY, FINE. YOU WANT TO JUST LEAVE? WE LEAVE, THEN. BUT FOR YOUR LITTLE GIRL, AT LEAST TAKE THAT OLD DOLL, OVER THERE.
GOOD. I WILL. TRUST ME, WHEN WE GET SOME DISTANCE FROM HERE, YOU GONNA BE HAPPY YOU DIDN'T DO ANYTHING STUPID.

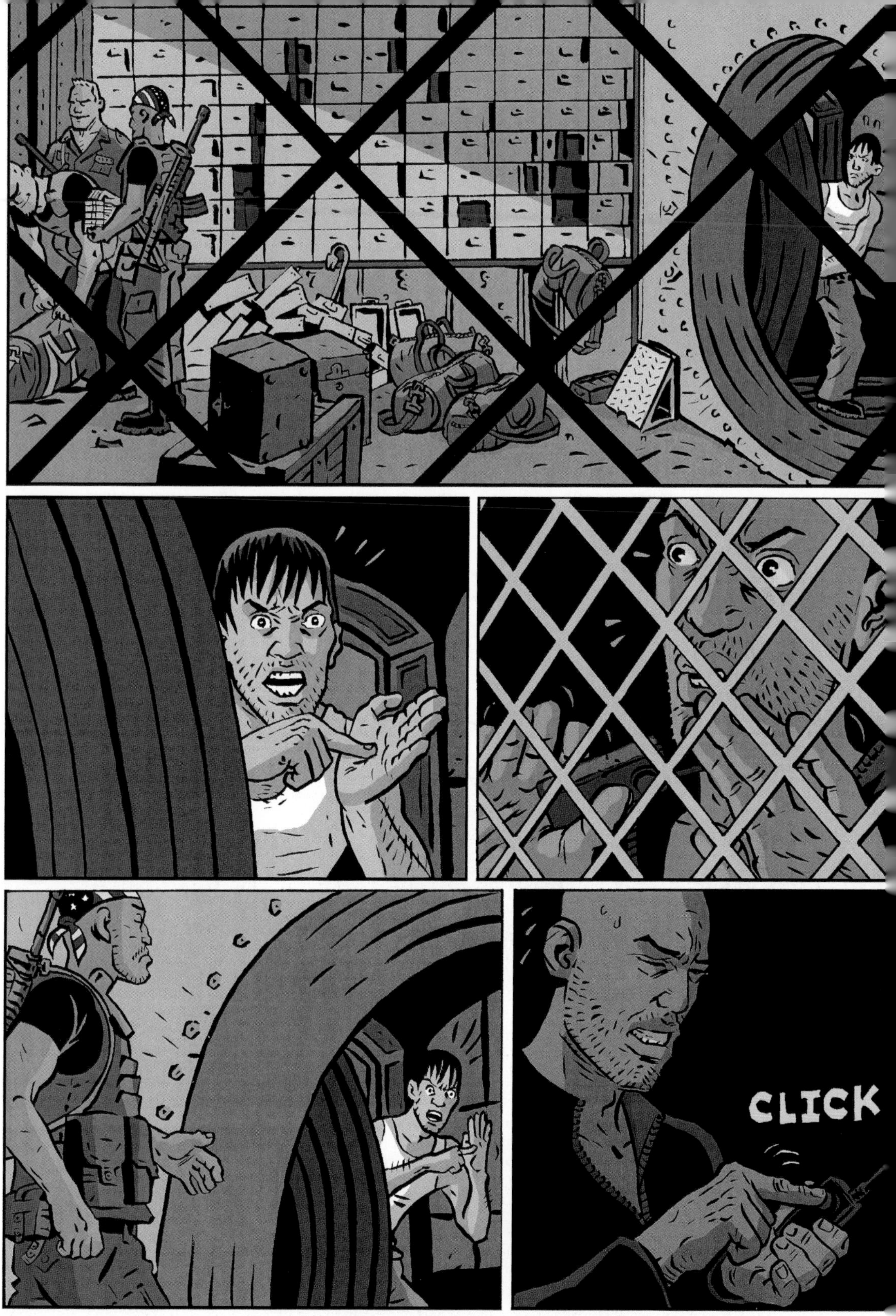
CLICK

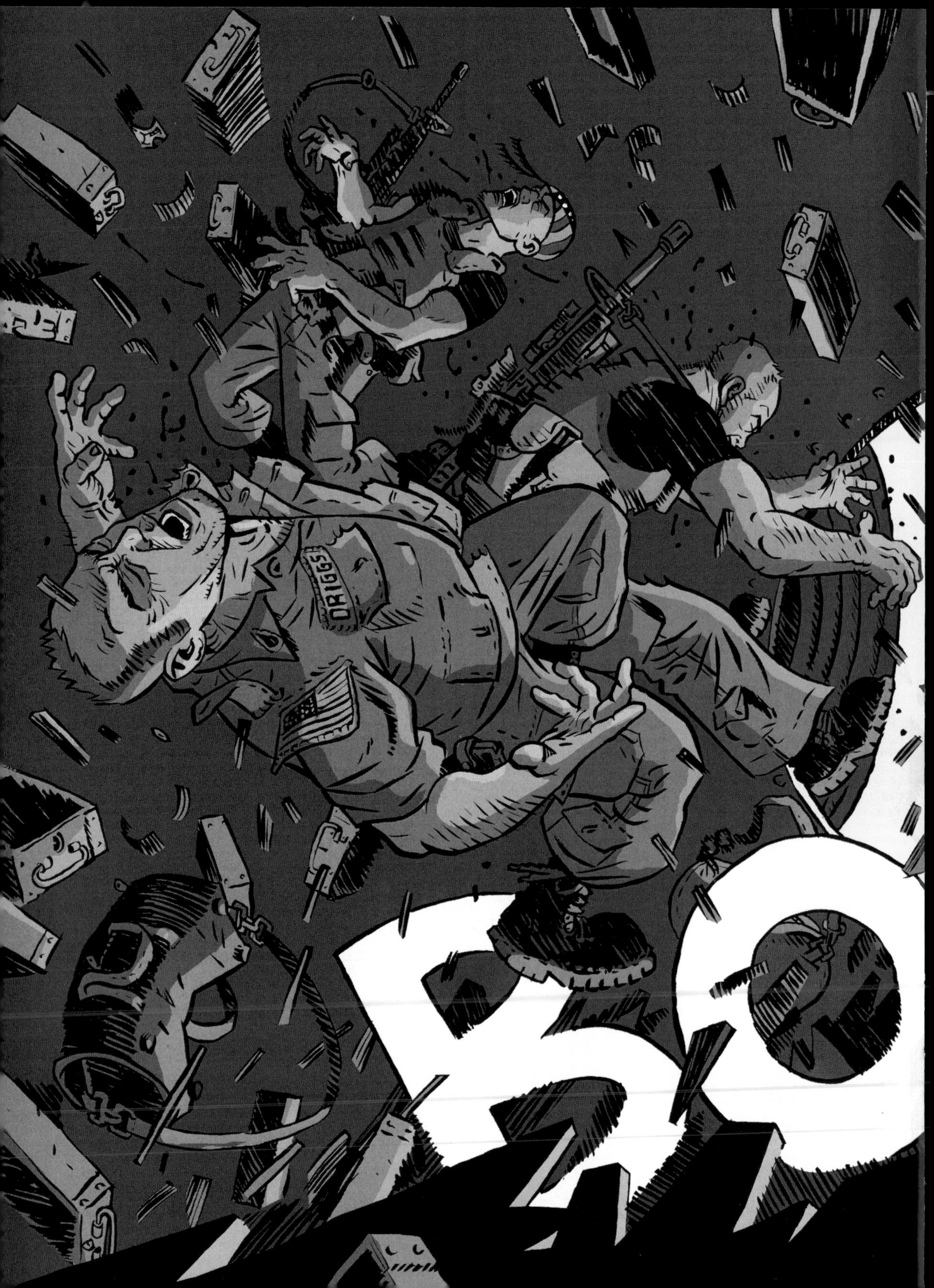
DRIGGS

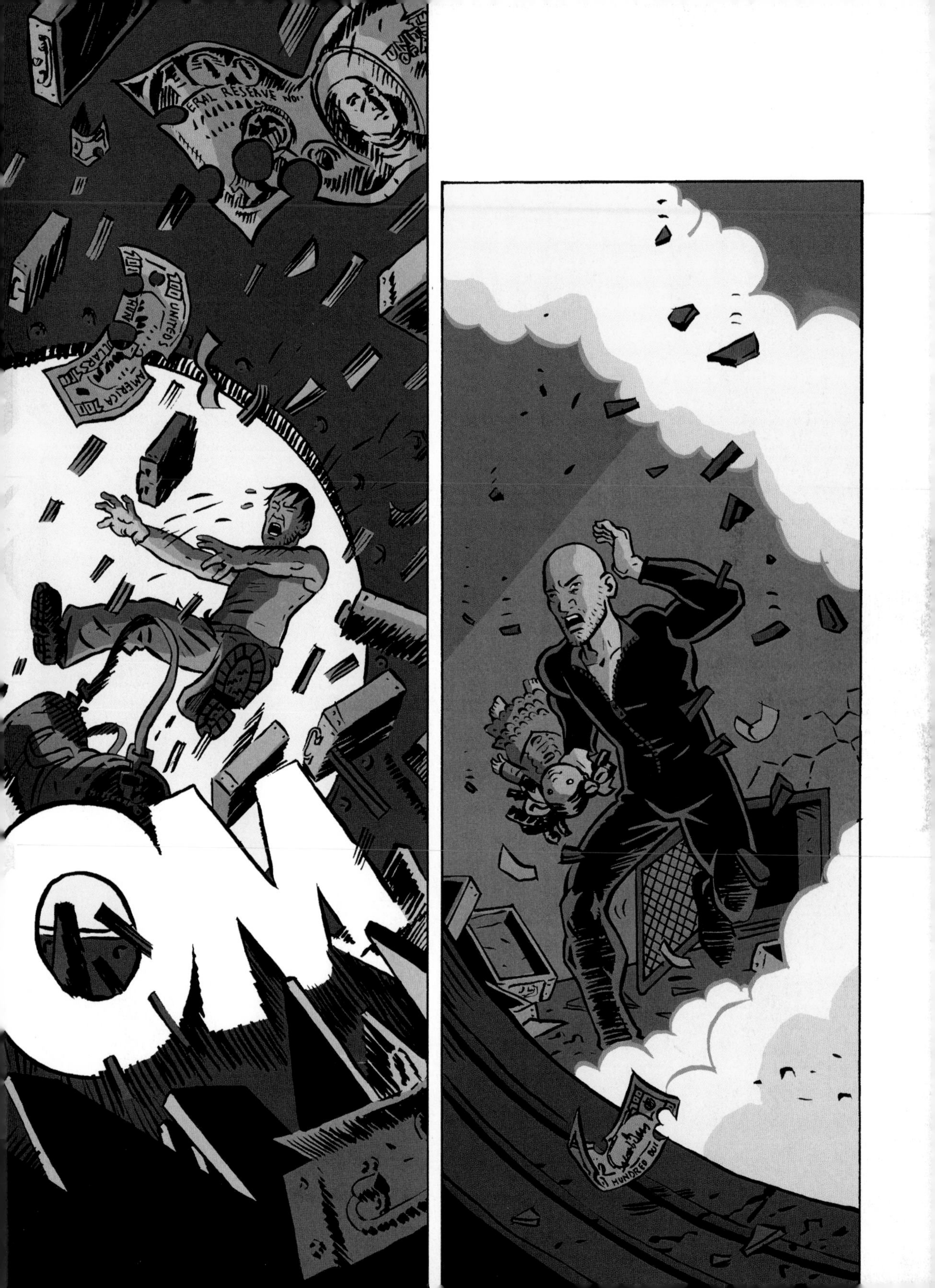
ERAL RESERVE NO
OM

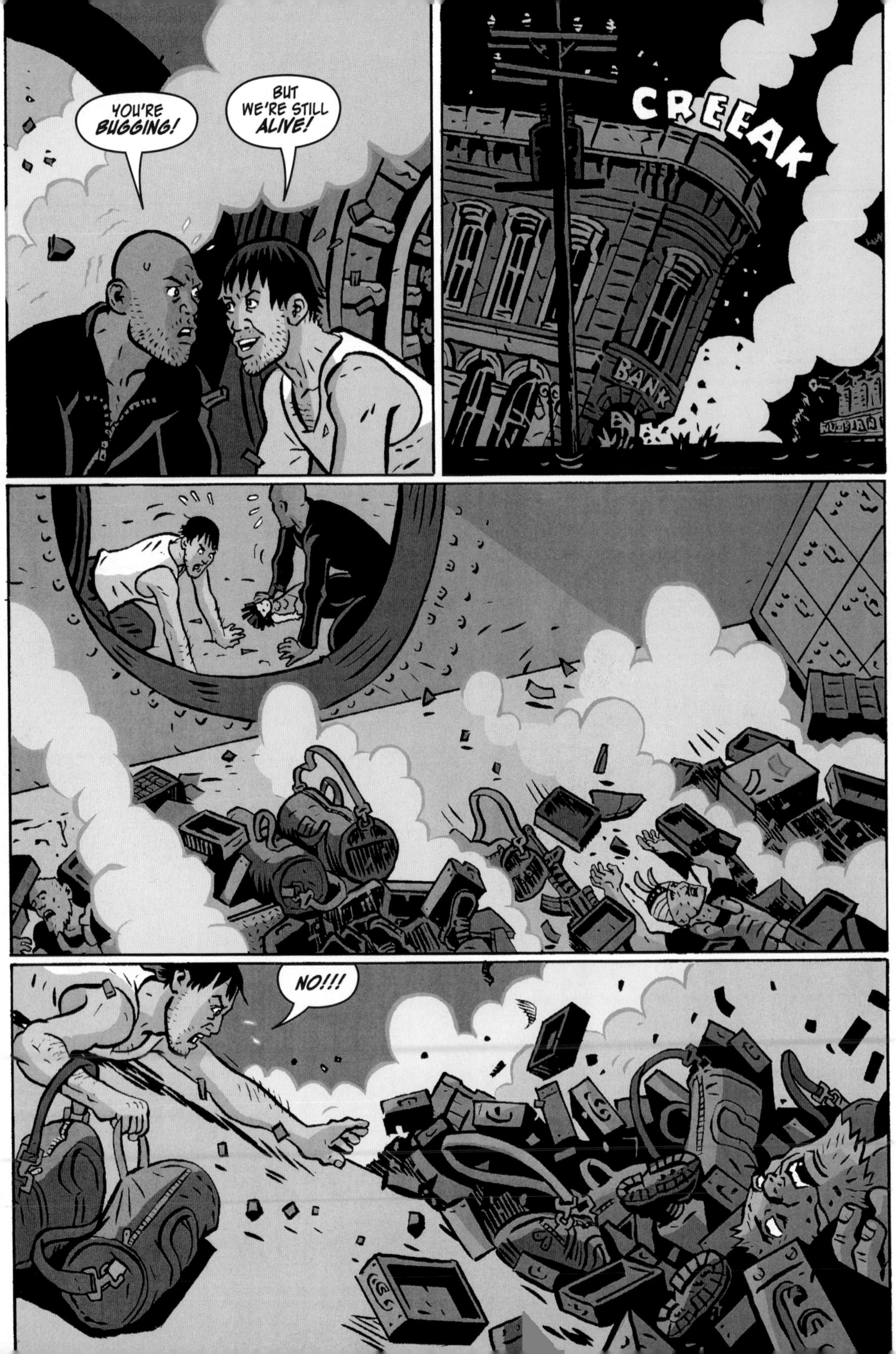
YOU'RE BUGGING!
BUT WE'RE STILL ALIVE!
CREEAK
BANK
NO!!!

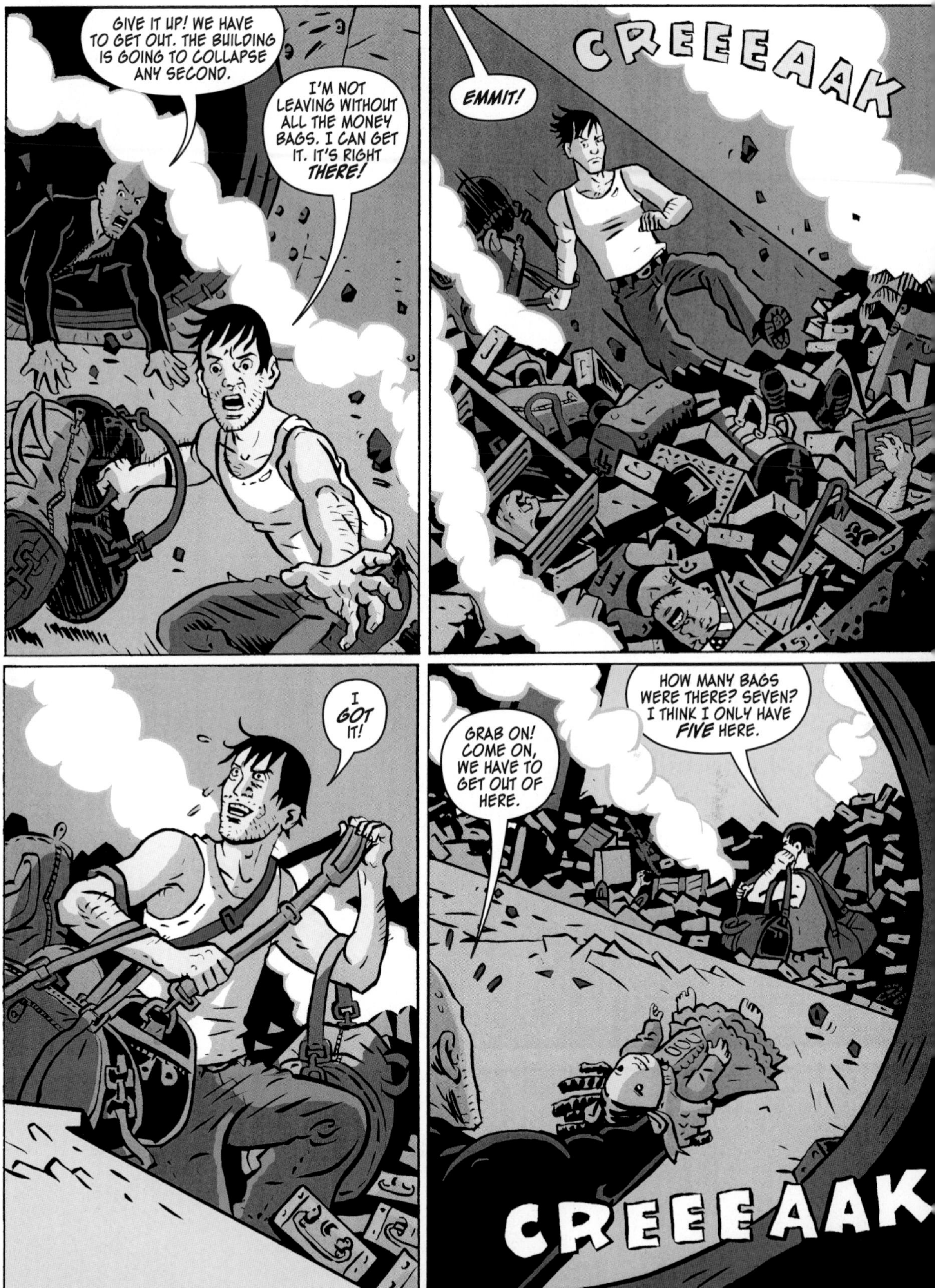
GIVE IT UP! WE HAVE TO GET OUT. THE BUILDING IS GOING TO COLLAPSE ANY SECOND.
I'M NOT LEAVING WITHOUT ALL THE MONEY BAGS. I CAN GET IT. IT'S RIGHT *THERE!*
EMMIT!
CREEEAAK
I *GOT* IT!
HOW MANY BAGS WERE THERE? SEVEN? I THINK I ONLY HAVE *FIVE* HERE.
GRAB ON! COME ON, WE HAVE TO GET OUT OF HERE.
CREEEAAK

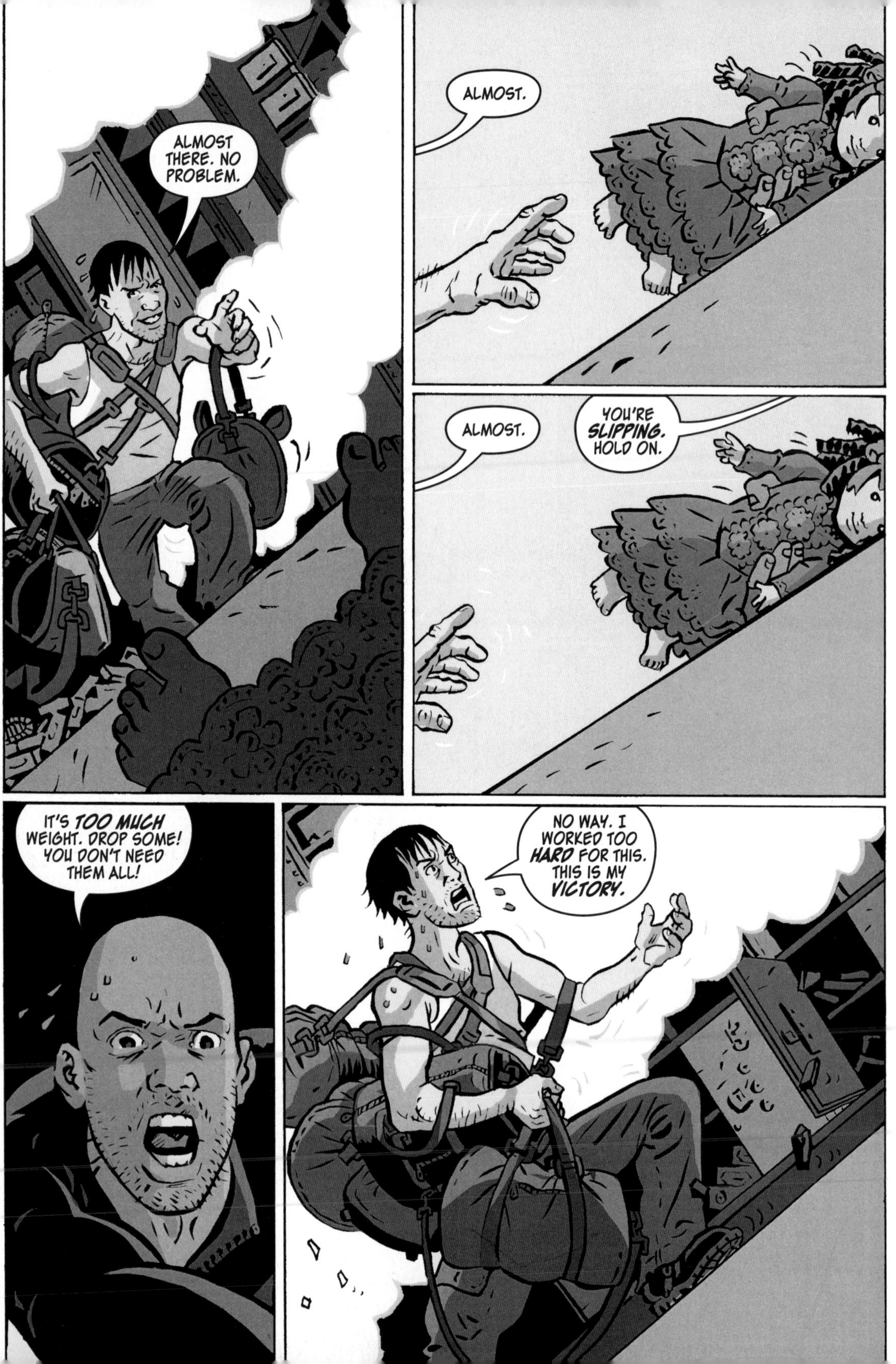
ALMOST THERE. NO PROBLEM.
ALMOST.
ALMOST.
YOU'RE SLIPPING. HOLD ON.
IT'S TOO MUCH WEIGHT. DROP SOME! YOU DON'T NEED THEM ALL!
NO WAY. I WORKED TOO HARD FOR THIS. THIS IS MY VICTORY.

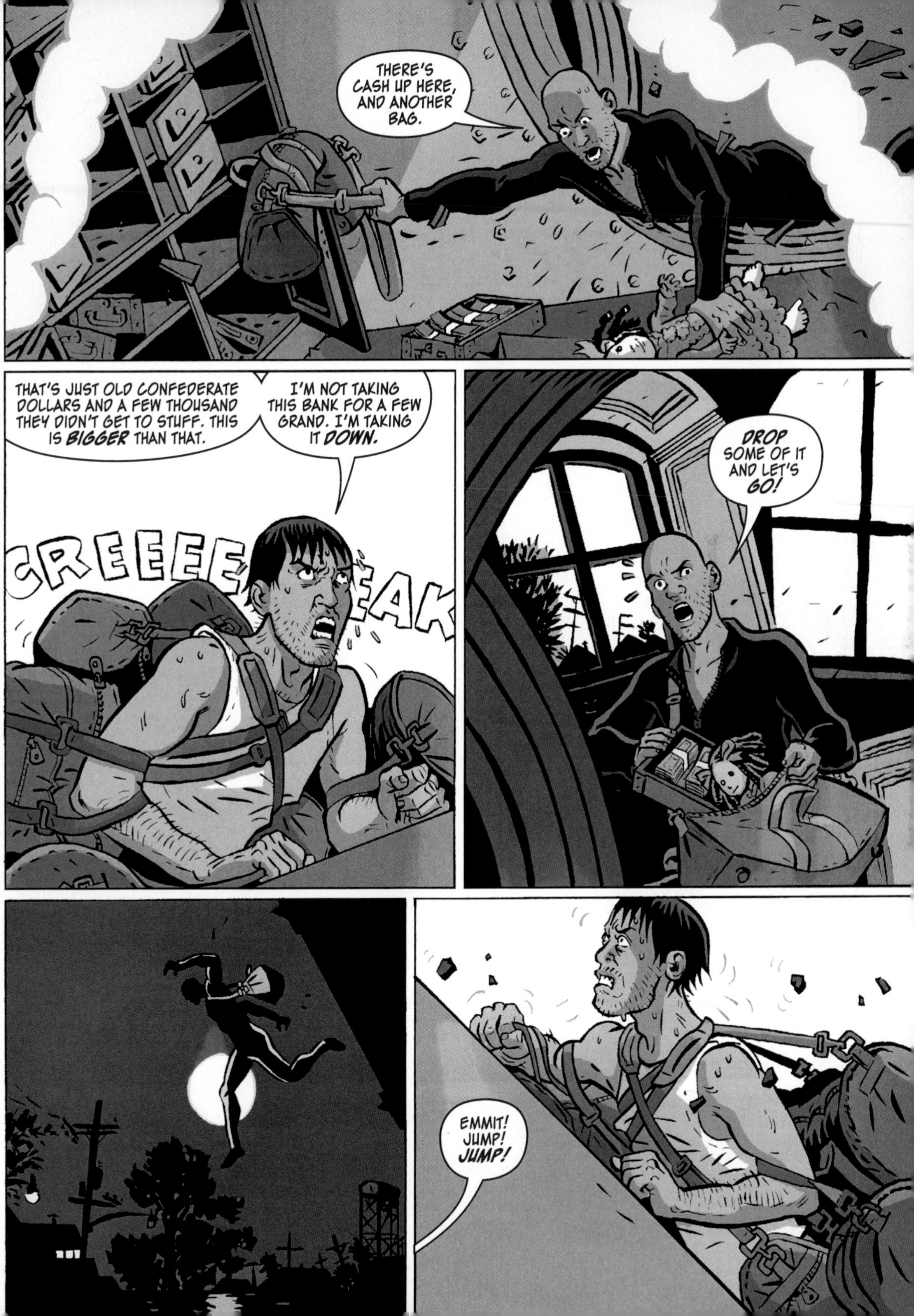
THERE'S CASH UP HERE, AND ANOTHER BAG.
THAT'S JUST OLD CONFEDERATE DOLLARS AND A FEW THOUSAND THEY DIDN'T GET TO STUFF. THIS IS BIGGER THAN THAT.
I'M NOT TAKING THIS BANK FOR A FEW GRAND. I'M TAKING IT DOWN.
CREEEEEAK
DROP SOME OF IT AND LET'S GO!
EMMIT! JUMP! JUMP!

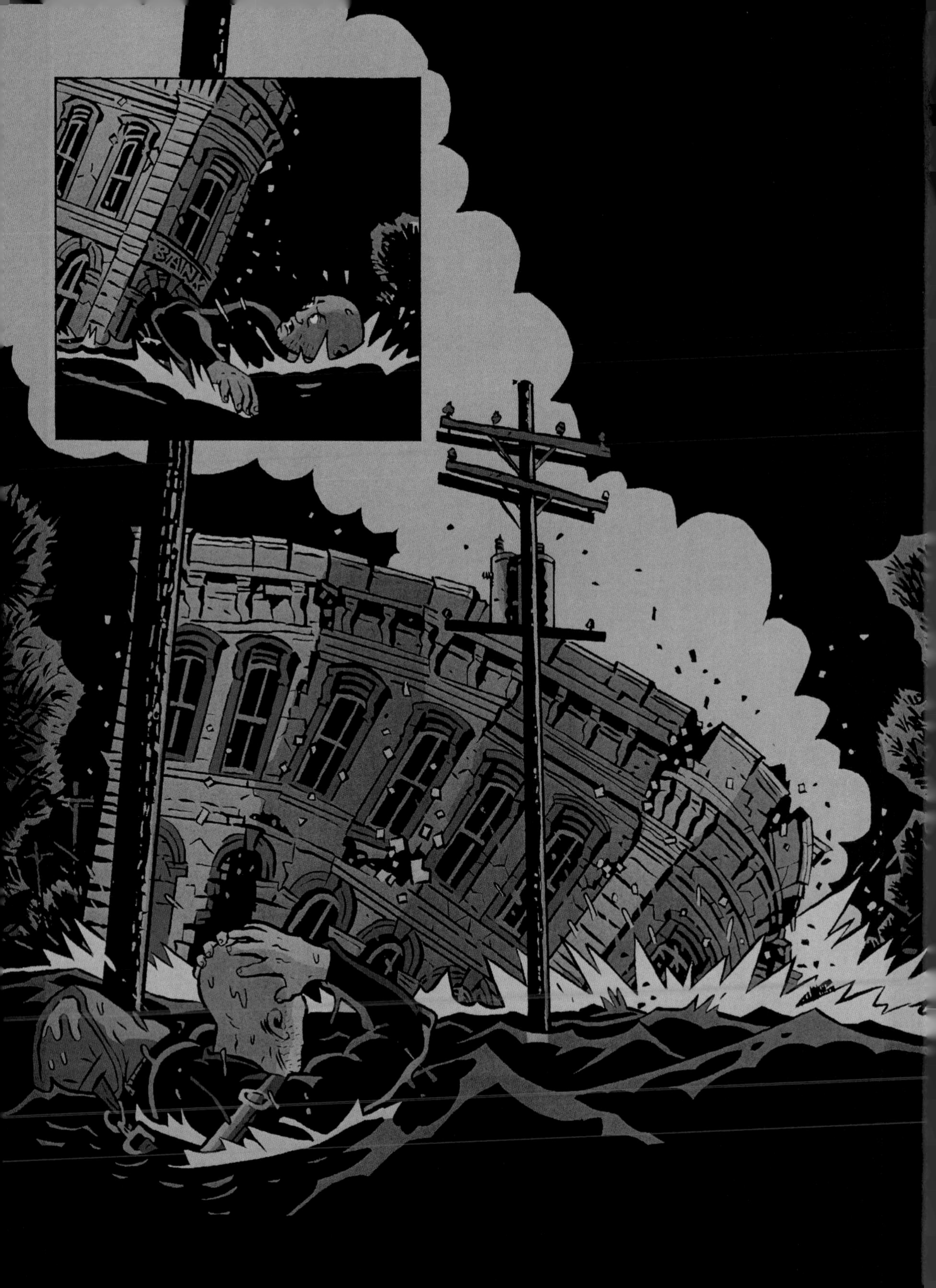
BANK

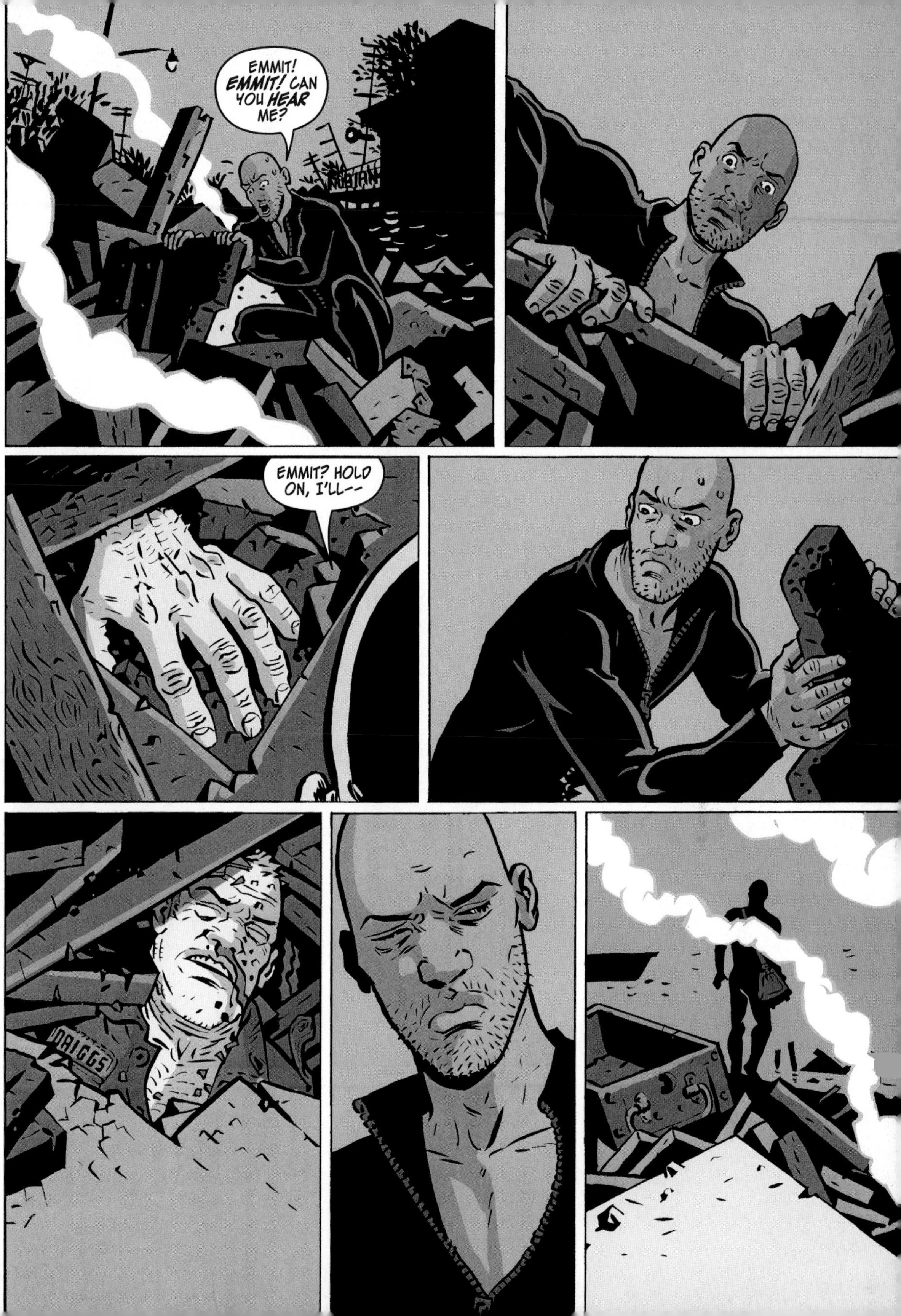
EMMIT! EMMIT! CAN YOU HEAR ME?
EMMIT? HOLD ON, I'LL--
DRIGGS

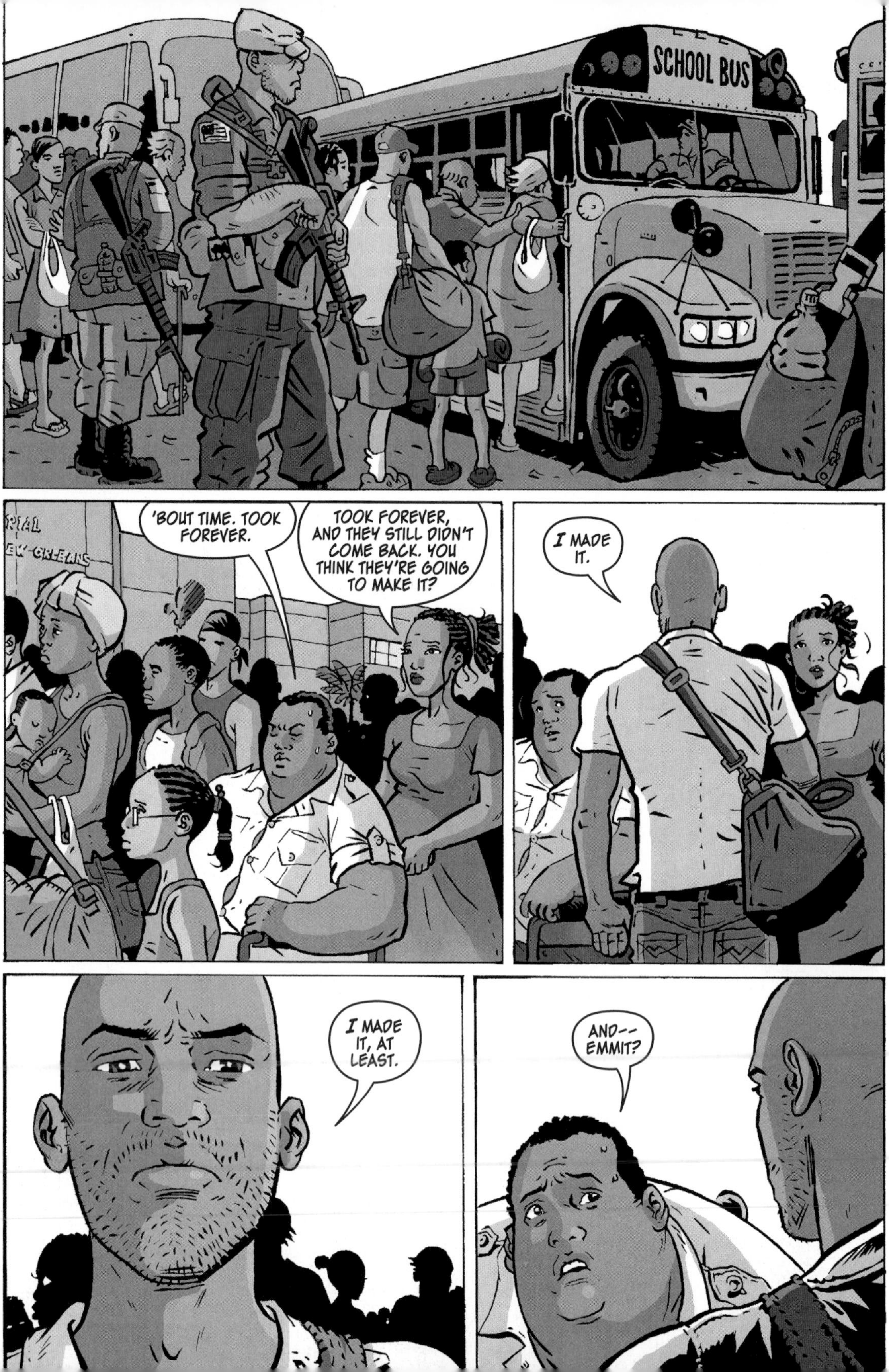
SCHOOL BUS
'BOUT TIME. TOOK FOREVER.
TOOK FOREVER, AND THEY STILL DIDN'T COME BACK. YOU THINK THEY'RE GOING TO MAKE IT?
I MADE IT.
I MADE IT, AT LEAST.
AND-- EMMIT?

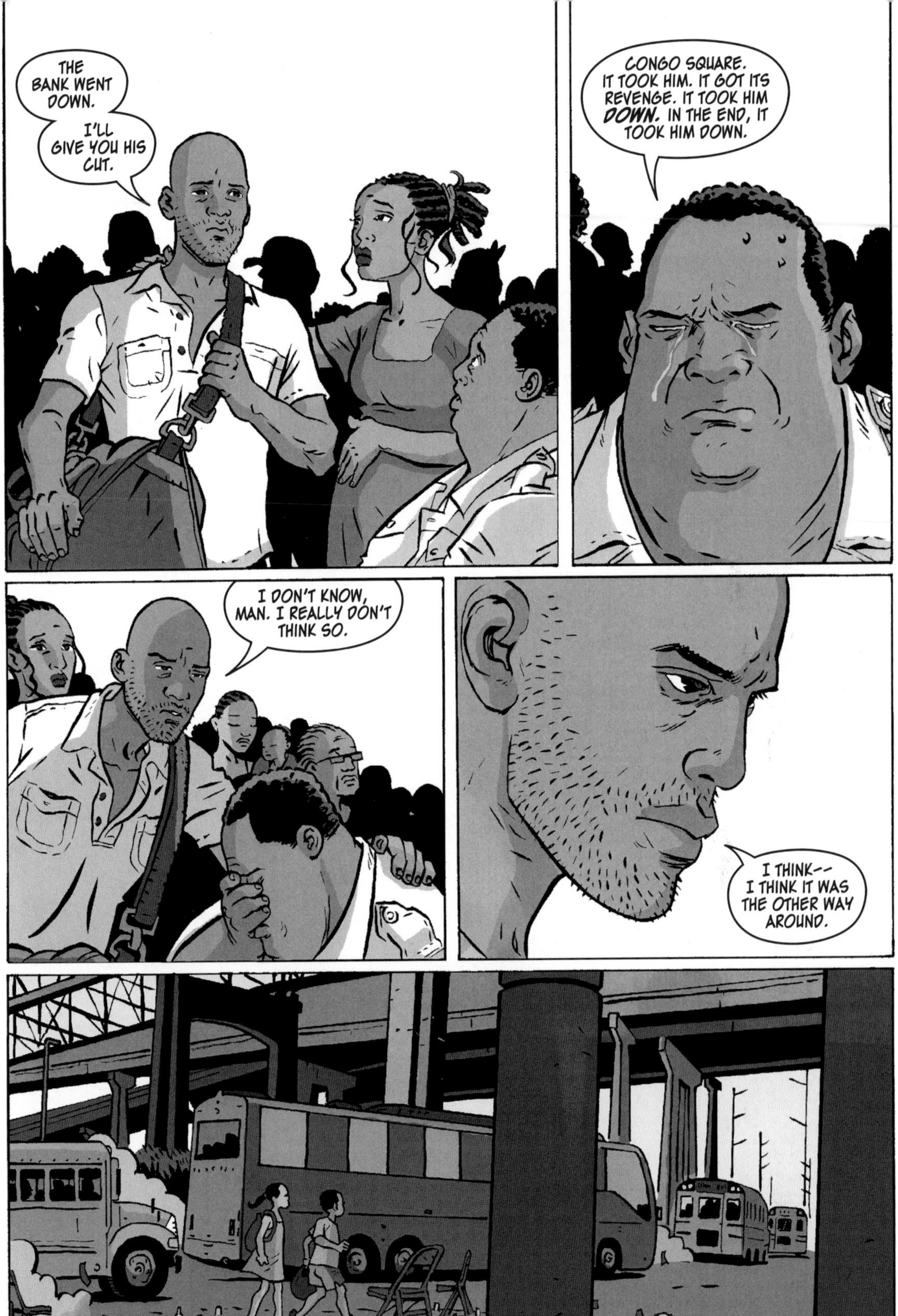
THE BANK WENT DOWN.
I'LL GIVE YOU HIS CUT.
CONGO SQUARE. IT TOOK HIM. IT GOT ITS REVENGE. IT TOOK HIM DOWN. IN THE END, IT TOOK HIM DOWN.
I DON'T KNOW, MAN. I REALLY DON'T THINK SO.
I THINK-- I THINK IT WAS THE OTHER WAY AROUND.

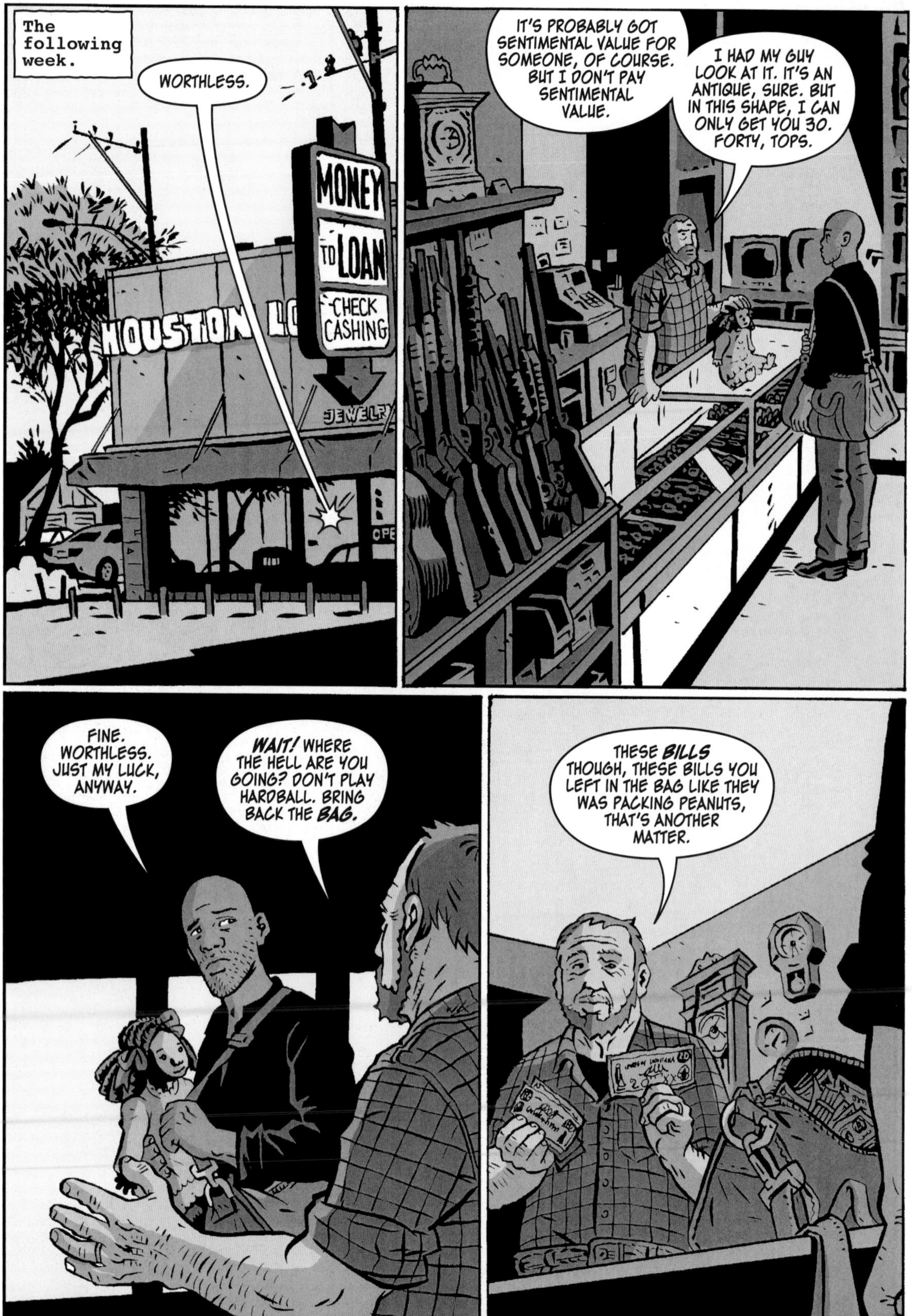
The following week.
WORTHLESS.
MONEY TO LOAN
CHECK CASHING
HOUSTON LO
JEWELRY
IT'S PROBABLY GOT SENTIMENTAL VALUE FOR SOMEONE, OF COURSE. BUT I DON'T PAY SENTIMENTAL VALUE.
I HAD MY GUY LOOK AT IT. IT'S AN ANTIQUE, SURE. BUT IN THIS SHAPE, I CAN ONLY GET YOU 30. FORTY, TOPS.
FINE. WORTHLESS. JUST MY LUCK, ANYWAY.
WAIT! WHERE THE HELL ARE YOU GOING? DON'T PLAY HARDBALL. BRING BACK THE BAG.
THESE BILLS THOUGH, THESE BILLS YOU LEFT IN THE BAG LIKE THEY WAS PACKING PEANUTS, THAT'S ANOTHER MATTER.

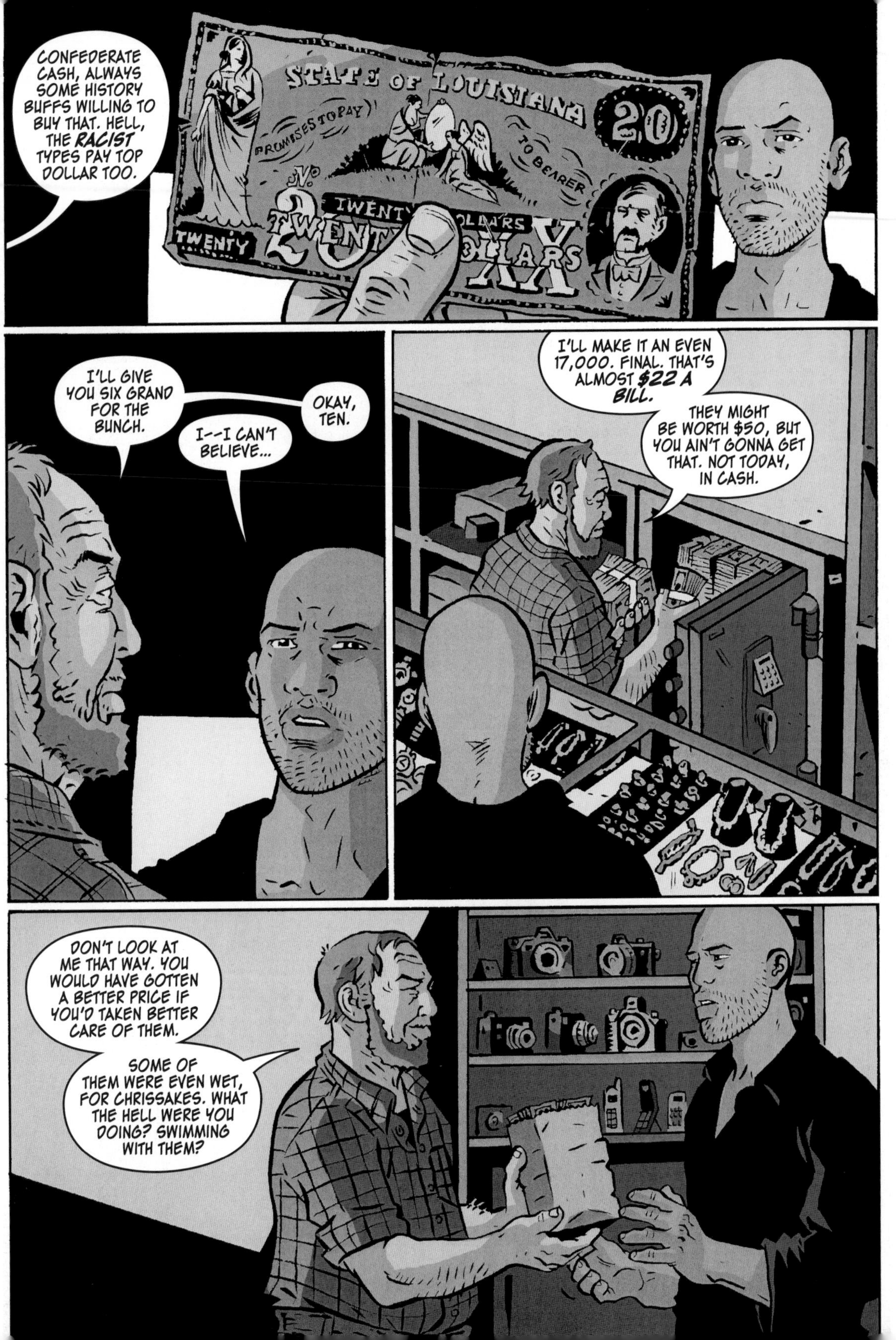
CONFEDERATE CASH, ALWAYS SOME HISTORY BUFFS WILLING TO BUY THAT. HELL, THE *RACIST* TYPES PAY TOP DOLLAR TOO.
STATE OF LOUISIANA
PROMISES TO PAY
TO BEARER
TWENTY DOLLARS
I'LL GIVE YOU SIX GRAND FOR THE BUNCH.
I--I CAN'T BELIEVE...
OKAY, TEN.
I'LL MAKE IT AN EVEN 17,000. FINAL. THAT'S ALMOST ***$22 A BILL.***
THEY MIGHT BE WORTH $50, BUT YOU AIN'T GONNA GET THAT. NOT TODAY, IN CASH.
DON'T LOOK AT ME THAT WAY. YOU WOULD HAVE GOTTEN A BETTER PRICE IF YOU'D TAKEN BETTER CARE OF THEM.
SOME OF THEM WERE EVEN WET, FOR CHRISSAKES. WHAT THE HELL WERE YOU DOING? SWIMMING WITH THEM?

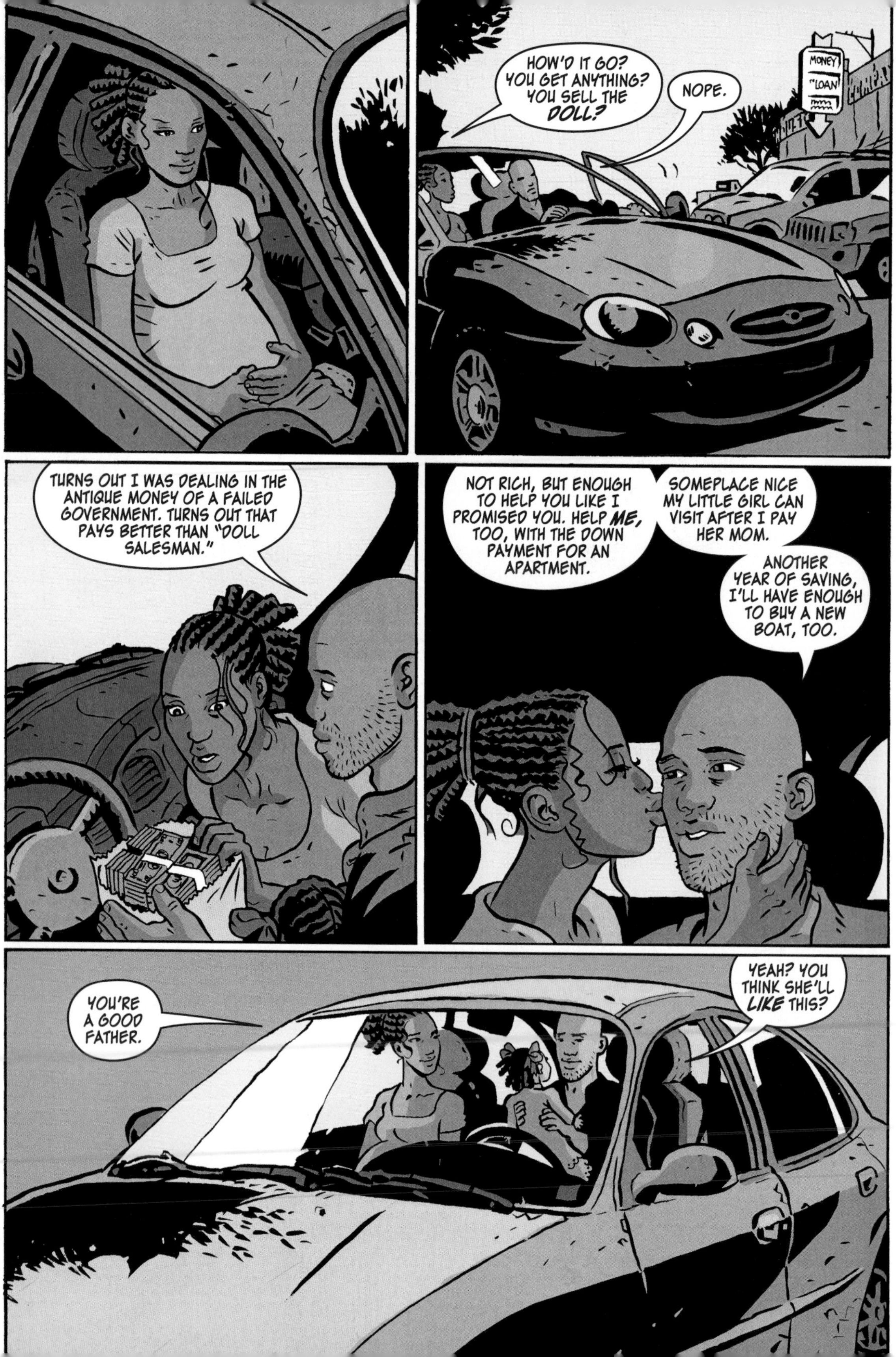
HOW'D IT GO? YOU GET ANYTHING? YOU SELL THE DOLL?
NOPE.
MONEY
LOAN
TURNS OUT I WAS DEALING IN THE ANTIQUE MONEY OF A FAILED GOVERNMENT. TURNS OUT THAT PAYS BETTER THAN "DOLL SALESMAN."
NOT RICH, BUT ENOUGH TO HELP YOU LIKE I PROMISED YOU. HELP ME, TOO, WITH THE DOWN PAYMENT FOR AN APARTMENT.
SOMEPLACE NICE MY LITTLE GIRL CAN VISIT AFTER I PAY HER MOM.
ANOTHER YEAR OF SAVING, I'LL HAVE ENOUGH TO BUY A NEW BOAT, TOO.
YOU'RE A GOOD FATHER.
YEAH? YOU THINK SHE'LL LIKE THIS?

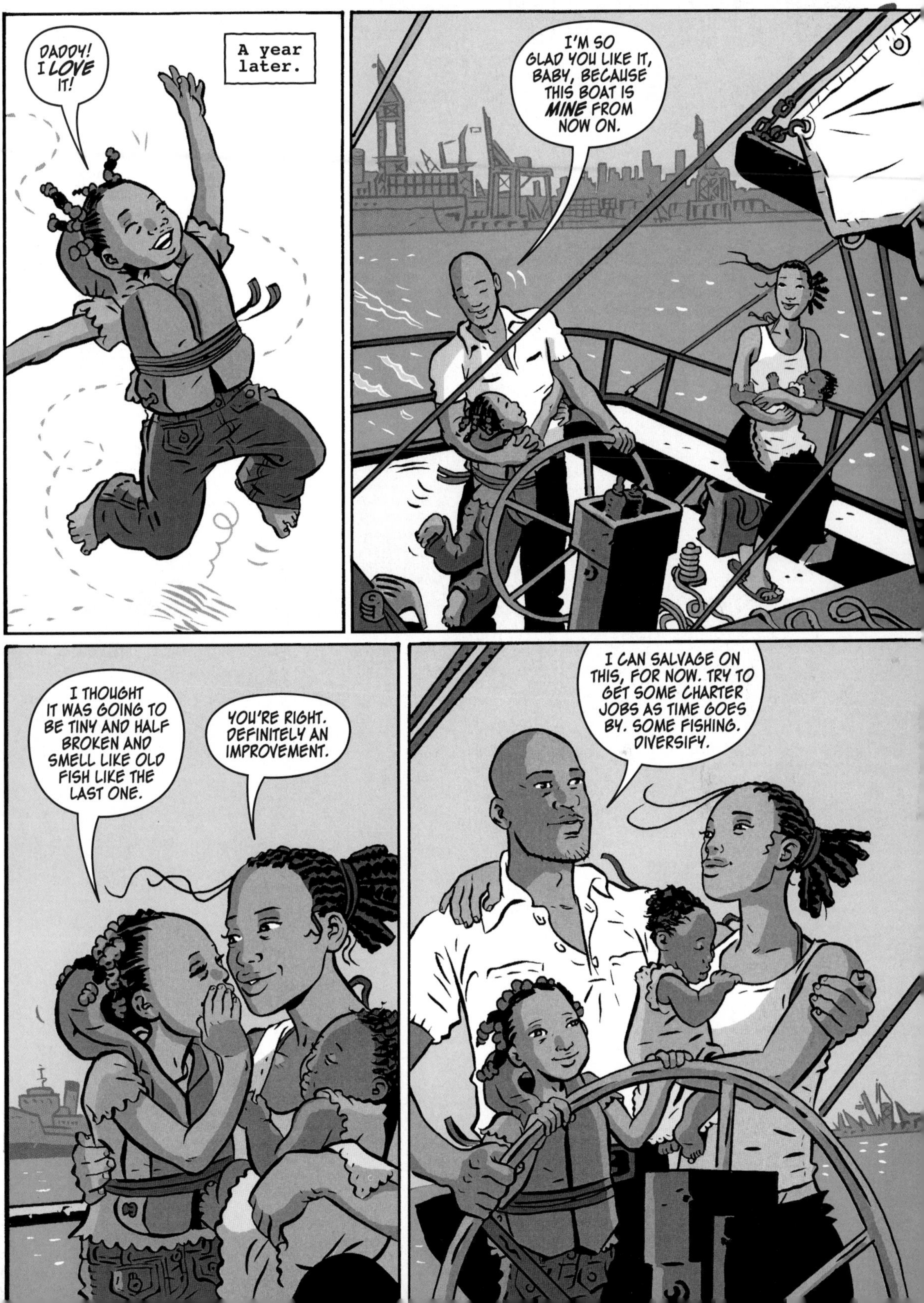
A year later.
DADDY! I LOVE IT!
I'M SO GLAD YOU LIKE IT, BABY, BECAUSE THIS BOAT IS MINE FROM NOW ON.
I THOUGHT IT WAS GOING TO BE TINY AND HALF BROKEN AND SMELL LIKE OLD FISH LIKE THE LAST ONE.
YOU'RE RIGHT. DEFINITELY AN IMPROVEMENT.
I CAN SALVAGE ON THIS, FOR NOW. TRY TO GET SOME CHARTER JOBS AS TIME GOES BY. SOME FISHING. DIVERSIFY.

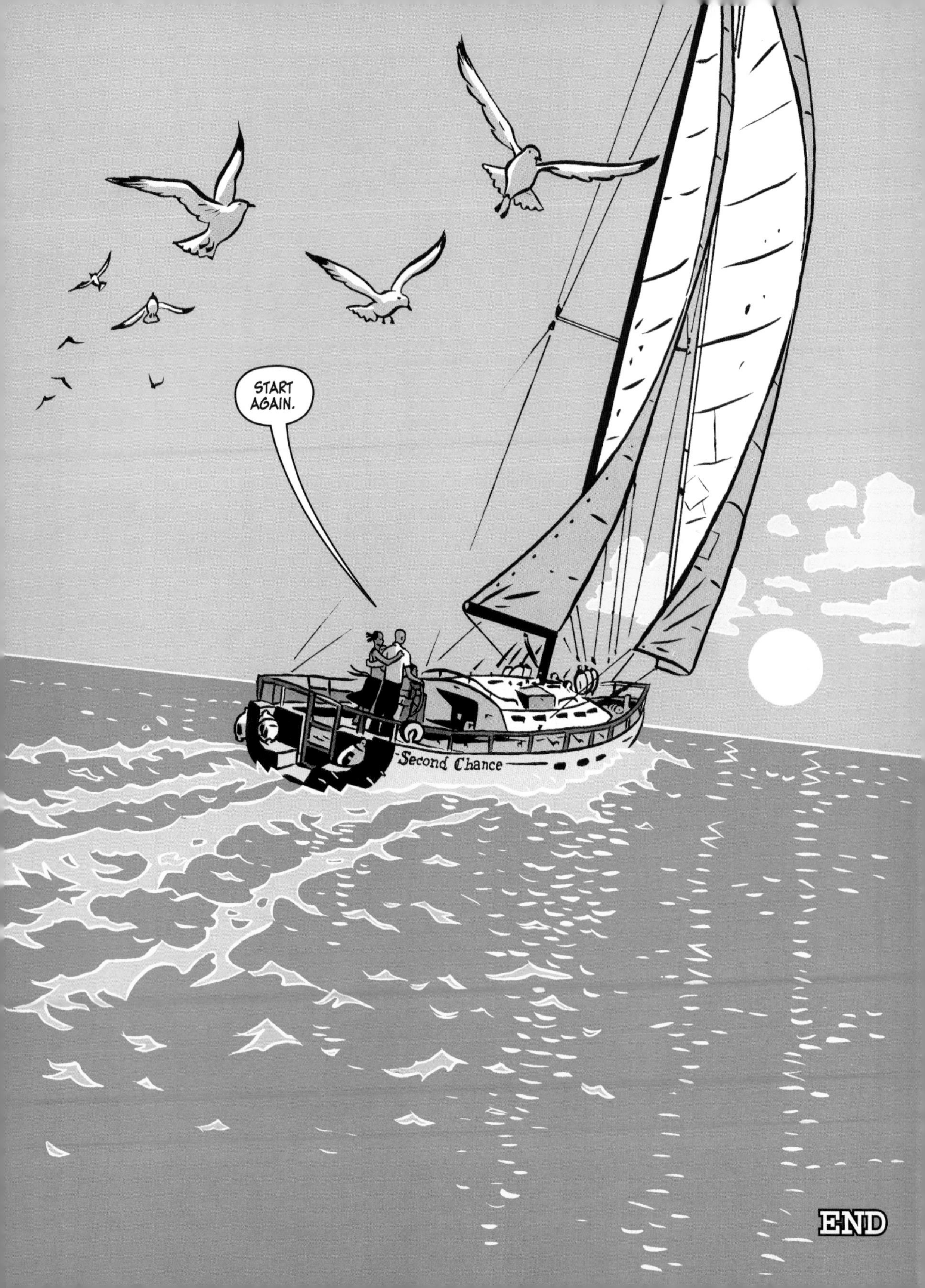
START AGAIN.
Second Chance
END

Mat Johnson is the award-winning author of the novels *Drop* and *Hunting in Harlem* as well as the Vertigo graphic novels *Incognegro* and *Hellblazer: Papa Midnite*. He has also written a nonfiction book, *The Great Negro Plot*. Mat is the recipient of the Hurston-Wright Legacy Award for fiction and the USA James Baldwin Fellowship for Literature. He is a writing professor at the University of Houston's Creative Writing Program and lives in the loop of Houston, Texas with his family.

Cartoonist and illustrator Simon Gane lives and works in Bath, England. His first published comics appeared in punk fanzines in the early 1990s, and recent projects include the DC/Vertigo series *The Vinyl Underground*, the graphic novel *Paris*, and the *Gym Shorts* series of children's books.